The Biopolitics of Race

The Biopolitics of Race

State Racism and U.S. Immigration

Sokthan Yeng

LEXINGTON BOOKS
Lanham • Boulder • New York • Toronto • Plymouth, UK

Published by Lexington Books
A wholly owned subsidiary of Rowman & Littlefield
4501 Forbes Boulevard, Suite 200, Lanham, Maryland 20706
www.rowman.com

10 Thornbury Road, Plymouth PL6 7PP, United Kingdom

British Library Cataloguing in Publication Information Available

Library of Congress Cataloging-in-Publication Data
Yeng, Sokthan, 1976–
The biopolitics of race : state racism and American immigration / Sokthan Yeng.
pages cm.
Includes bibliographical references.
ISBN 978-0-7391-8223-9 (cloth : alk. paper)— ISBN 978-0-7391-8224-6 (ebook)
1. United States—Emigration and immigration—Government policy. 2. United States—Emigration
and immigration—Social aspects. 3. Racism—United States. 4. Biopolitics—United States. I. Title.
JV6483.Y46 2014
325.73—dc23
2013031564

ISBN 978-1-4985-2099-7 (pbk : alk, paper)

∞™ The paper used in this publication meets the minimum requirements of American
National Standard for Information Sciences Permanence of Paper for Printed Library
Materials, ANSI/NISO Z39.48-1992.

Printed in the United States of America

Contents

Introduction: The Dynamics of Race   1

1   Immigration and the Modern Political State   21
2   The Problem of Immigration in the United States   43
3   State Racism and Neoliberal Immigration Policies   61
4   Biologizing the Race of Terror   83
5   The Race of Sexual Degenerates   103
6   Racing Gender   125

Conclusion: Immigrants as Indicators of Race   149
Bibliography   169
Index   177
About the Author   181

Introduction

The Dynamics of Race

The impetus for examining how race becomes intertwined with immigration debates is both plain and philosophical. Even a casual observer recognizes that race and racism often enter into the discussion about U.S. immigration policies. Untangling the connections between race and immigration can also be helpful for understanding contemporary philosophical conceptions of modern society. Philosophers such as Hannah Arendt, Michel Foucault, and Giorgio Agamben argue that modern politics is biopolitics because it operates by connecting the life of the nation to the life of the individual. This political structure, they add, inevitably leads to state racism. Individuals will ultimately be judged and classified by their perceived impact—good or bad—on the nation's prosperity. As Foucault notes, such forms of racism have become entangled with the neoliberal language of costs and benefits.

I attempt to draw out the way economic discourse has become embedded within present immigration regulations because I want to shift the debate away from illegal immigration. Although a discussion can be had about the ways illegal immigrants affect the economy, looking at immigration through the lens of economics enables us to consider the ways the United States has crafted immigration laws to benefit the country. This does not mean, however, that there are not other ways in which a cost/benefit analysis is at play within immigration controls. I do not focus on illegal immigration, in part, because there are many other works that explore that topic in depth. By concentrating on the process of legal immigration, I hope to show that immigration policies can criminalize even those immigrants who attempt to gain entrance into the United States within the bounds of the law. Viewing immigration primarily through the lens of law breaking can obscure places where the state defines ideas the unfit, deviant, and abnormal within immigration laws. In other words, immigration laws sanction favoritism towards those who are seen as beneficial to the state and discrimination against those who are seen as detrimental to it. We can better understand state racism, as Foucault understood it, by examining the legal parameters of immigration policies. Yet state racism is not wholly disconnected from previous incarnations of racism. Because Western mythology and history show that immigrants are easy and frequent targets of racism, a philosophical analysis of the

1

intersection between race and immigration could elucidate how ancient forms of racism become transformed into state racism.

Why does the topic of race always seem to enter into the debate over U.S. immigration? I suggest that this is the case because constructions of race and immigration policies are linked through a shared philosophy. Racial discourses, immigration regulations, are created through philosophically malleable themes of otherness and belonging. On the one hand, conceptions of race frequently turn on confrontations with the strange. It is no accident that the stranger, the foreigner, and the immigrant have become stand-ins for the raced other. In this way and in many others, of course, Ancient Greek thought is still with us. Various Greek tales convey the idea that being born or living in a foreign country was enough to signify that that person was of another race. These qualities, it should be noted, still play a role in present conceptions of race. On the other hand, an examination of historical formations of race will show that race is not a stable category. Not only has the meaning of race undergone crucial transformations but the divisions of race are also continually re-worked. Efforts by Westerners to establish a racial taxonomy include differences stemming from geographical location, mental capacities, genetic deficiencies, etc. Westerners may no longer look to Greek mythology for truth or an understanding of the proper world order but the myth of the suspicion-worthy immigrant remains. The immigrant, in both ancient and modern times, signals the entrance of foreign ideals that could disrupt the state.

The fear of the dissolution of modern societies expresses itself in the yearning for the restoration of a lost community and the attempts to find the fiber that can create a cohesive social fabric among the increasing divisions between the people. Jean-Luc Nancy suggests that Westerners retain the image of and long for the Athenian city, Roman republic, or first Christian community because they represent a harmonious state with sturdy bonds.[1] Within Benedict Anderson's "imagined community" and Charles Taylor's "social imaginary," community members cultivate solidarity by conjuring up ideas that provoke a sense of social unity.[2] Though the strands that lead to fellowship across the social imaginary may seem difficult to isolate because they are not tangible but rather exist in the minds of the people, Nira Yuval-Davis suggests that "people seek assurances in definitions of identities and cultures which are fixed and immutable, an inherent characteristic of people who belong to a specific community of origin."[3] Thus, the desire for community and the fear of disunion often manifests through mythologies that speak to the purported exceptional qualities of the people and the establishment of seemingly more concrete standards meant to keep the foreboding other out. The immigrant, therefore, is often cast as a treacherous character and is inevitably intertwined with themes of race and racism. Yet the specific threat that the immigrant or raced other poses varies. Following Foucault, I will chart how the immigrant threat changes to match what is considered to be problematic for society at that time. It should be no surprise, then, that attitudes concerning the immigrant make use of particular language that fits with the prevailing racial discourse. The reverse, I suggest, can also be said. Language surrounding immigration debates can provide insight about present formulations of race. I will argue that anxiety about other races and/or immigrants has expressed itself through myths, scientific theories, and currently through the economic discourse of neoliberalism.

GREEK AND AMERICAN MYTHOLOGY

The mythology surrounding the formation of the country suggests that Americans[4] do long for the Athenian community. Yet connections between Ancient Greek and American mythology are complicated by the place of the immigrant within these myths. Whereas Ancient Greek myths consistently conveyed a hostile attitude towards foreigners, part of American mythology depends upon the idea that this nation welcomed everyone: your tired, poor, weak, etc. The Ancient Greeks prided themselves on their autochthonous history. Many of their myths are widely regarded as vehicles that relay how the Greek people are special because they are born from the land. That is to say, outsiders do not influence them. Scholars such as Wm. Blake Tyrrell, Julia Kristeva, and Michel Foucault have noted that this theme is so important that myths will weave whatever tales necessary in order to maintain the exclusive control over Greek politics. Tyrrell shows that Greeks, in order to maintain their autochthonous nature, go so far as to claim that citizens grew like plants from seeds sown by the virgin Athena.[5] Foucault, likewise, analyzes how Euripides' *Ion* is a tale meant to reassure the Greeks that one of their most influential leaders did indeed have Greek heritage. Although Ion's Greek lineage is hidden by a series of regrettable acts, his Greek genealogy is finally revealed.[6] The purpose of the myth is clear. They allow Greeks to hold onto the myth of their autochthonous nature. Their stories are woven in such as way to show that they have had some connection to the land all along. In short, Greek myths work to reinforce the myth of a pure race. Immigrants who are accepted into Greek culture and society must be converted, in the psyche and lore of the people, into natives.

American mythology has worked to tell an opposite story. Despite the recent popularity of the new nativism movement,[7] America is generally considered as a land of immigrants. America is distinct from most other countries because its citizens, by and large, are not indigenous people. The tale of America has been spun in a positive manner. The United States of America has often been set apart from other nations—past and present—because of its history of open immigration. It claims a rich tradi-

tion of multiculturalism that others do not. While this legacy of hospital-
ity is complicated and not as rosy as many would like to believe, it is true
that the American identity was not built around an assertion of autochthony. The founders of America were not natives but immigrants. Unlike
in Greek mythology, the immigrant was the custodian of American civilization. Immigrants, rather than the indigenous peoples, have been
placed in a privileged place in American folklore. They were the ones
credited with bringing prosperity and order to a wild land and a burgeoning nation. The honored position of the immigrant also allows
Americans to develop dual stories about how their ancestors have come
to this land. These sometimes converging and sometimes conflicting storylines help Americans imagine themselves to be beacons on the hill for
all other peoples and nations. The purpose of these American myths, at
least in part, is to do away with the most unsavory portions of U.S.
history—particularly that which points to violence and racism against
non-whites. But this still means that American myths, like Greek myths,
have become enmeshed with racial discourse. The Ancient Greeks emphasized the issue of race in order to establish their superiority and purity. Conversely, Americans need to erase the legacy of racism through
their own myth-making in order to maintain the belief in their goodness
and strength of character.

While American mythology often contrasts the American immigrant
with his European brethren, the story of the American immigrant must
also be thought in relation to the "non-white" other.[8] The lives of
American settlers can be linked to their Anglo-European counterparts
without doing much harm to the favorable narrative of America. Such a
comparison, if anything, helps to build the reputation of Americans as a
fine and noble people. Europeans discriminated against those who fell
outside their class and/or religious circle. The European émigré turned
American was the victim of intolerance, prejudice, and ill treatment.
Once the American immigrant, however, is thought in connection with
those who inhabited the land before him or those who helped him live on
his adopted homeland, cracks begin to emerge in the story that
Americans tell about themselves and their upright ancestors. The latter
can be read as a means to conceal the American enslavement of Africans.
The former version of America glosses over the legacy of colonialism and
the massacre of Native Americans. The American immigrant is no longer
the only one who is subject to discrimination and abuse. Seen in this light,
American settlers were guilty, too, of prejudice and maltreatment of others.

Although American folklore privileges the immigrant, these myths
fulfill the same function as Ancient Greek myths. Americans—like their
predecessors—used myths to reinforce the idea that their community
was the epicenter of "goodness." The goodness of the people could only
be established in contrast with an inferior people. Each culture, therefore,

uses myth to define characteristics of its race and those of others. It is more evident that race plays a part in Ancient Greek than American mythology because of their insistence that Greeks are an autochthonous and, hence, pure people. The Greek community — as the story goes — has never been corrupted by outsiders of any kind. Americans cannot claim an innate connection to the land but race and geography are, nonetheless, important in the narratives they tell about themselves. They, too, believe that they inherit exceptional qualities from their homeland, which come into greater relief when compared with the inferior other. Pieces of the story may be reinterpreted but Westerners continue to create myths and discourse that tell of the superiority and specialness of their race. If we examine American mythology closely, we can still see many remnants of Greek mythology.

GEOGRAPHY AND RACE

While American-ness does not depend as much upon a direct connection to the land as does Greek-ness, American identity is shaped in a similar fashion to Greek identity — in relation to geography and land. Only certain races, coming from particular lands, are considered civilized. Americans, however, reconfigure the ancient relationship between race and land. Greek mythologies indicate that their understanding of race was constructed through birthright and an unyielding connection to the land. Many myths convey the need for a person to be born of a Greek citizen and be born on Greek soil to be considered part of the Greek race. These two requirements, of course, are strikingly similar to present qualifications for American citizenship. To be certain, there are differences between the rules for Greek and American citizenship. One must satisfy both requirements before laying claim to Greek citizenship whereas Americans only need — for the time being — to fulfill one of the categories.[10] In any case, the connection I want to draw between American and Greek identity has less to do with the fulfillment of these stipulations as it does with the way certain peoples become equated with the civilized race. Belonging to Western communities is supposed to signify that a person is civilized. It is general knowledge that Ancient Greeks really only conceived of two races. There was the Greek — civilized — race and all others — a barbarian race. If someone were born outside of Greece and to foreign parents, that person would be considered a barbarian and uncivilized.

Birth and land also work together — albeit to create a new narrative — to support the belief that Americans, the immigrants, are the civilized race. Because Americans are not an autochthonous people, they cannot construct racial supremacy in the same manner as the Greeks. The civility of Americans cannot depend on a physical connection with their land of birth. Americans, like other colonials, needed to believe that they could export their culture and civilization. Philosophers such as John Locke, Immanuel Kant, and G. W. F. Hegel provided just such accounts. These Modern philosophers argued that the particular environment and landscape of Europe created and bred an industrious people. It is this industriousness—earned and inherited through generational struggles with the land—that allowed Europeans to develop civilization. And there would be no fear that Europeans, no matter where they went, would lose these prized qualities because they have been strengthened over time. Land and geography, therefore, were just as important for breeding the modern civilized race.

Modern Westerners built on the ancient idea that civilization and the civilized race grew from a particular land. American mythology, however, needed to emphasize the transportability of civilization. This discourse about the Euro-American culture also solved a problem that the autochthonous Greek did not have. Americans would and should have rights to the land because they—not the Native Americans—have the ability to bring progress to the continent. Their industriousness and productivity—precisely the qualities that Native Americans and Africans lack—allow them to cultivate the land and, therefore, declare it as their own.[11] The Earth could not be left to the various uncivilized peoples such as the Native Americans and Africans. If the European colonials did not step in, these modern barbarians and large parts of the world would languish in a state of infancy—unable to move into the modern world. The privileged relationship between the civilized race and the land, for Americans, depended upon an ability to cultivate the land. With this purported ability to develop the wild continent, Americans claimed to be civilizing agents who would bring progress to an otherwise unproductive land. Colonialism, in American mythology, then, was made into the positive act of spreading civilization.

THE METAPHYSICS OF RACE

Since the mythology of America propagated the belief that the "good," civilized race need not be bound to its land of birth, the idea that geography separated races has waned. This move should not be altogether surprising because geography never operated alone as a way to distinguish races. National borders once seemed to be a sufficiently fixed boundary but even these differences in locale were laden with deeper meaning. Modern philosophers proposed that the land imparted varying physical and psychical qualities within the people who inhabited it. Even when geographical difference worked as the primary way to distinguish between races, these regional distinctions always brought with them invisible characteristics. The move away from a geographical understanding of race led to an emphasis on the unseen qualities of race. This narrative makes it so that obvious markers of difference were not the important aspects of race. Where people lived or, even, what people looked like was less important for distinguishing between the good and bad races. There were still, to be sure, easily recognizable indications of a person's race. The most important distinctions among races, however, were the ones that could not be seen.

This invisibility of race, I suggest, continues to play itself out in stories that Americans tell about their nation and themselves. Although prominent thinkers clearly believed that the nonphysical aspects of race pointed to greater disparities between races than physical characteristics, this philosophy which emphasized the invisible qualities of race eventually mutated into the convenient notion that race and racism play no part in Western, civilized life. The invisibility of race turned into the nonexistence of race and racism. These ideas are, of course, not the same thing but American mythologies have worked to elide the differences. The earliest American settlers lived in a time when it was common to think that the European mind and spirit were intrinsically superior to all others, which is how colonialism justified itself. Although Modern thinkers would probably not have seen these metaphysical theories as part of a Eurocentric attitude, contemporary thinkers (Paul Gilroy, Edward Said, and Linda Martin Alcoff— just to name a few) now widely consider these theories as an outgrowth of a racist perspective. The American public, conversely, conveniently misrecognizes and reshapes the attitudes and philosophies that were held by their ancestors. This transformation of America's complicated past, I suggest, is aided by the sleight of hand that turns the invisibility of race into a lack of racism. It is true that Locke, Kant, Hegel, and their contemporaries worked to stress the spiritual or mental superiority of Europeans but these theories are just as integral to racist discourse as those that deem others inferior because of their physical appearance or speech. It is not the case that Modern Euro-Americans did not see race. Even the most "enlightened" European thinkers worked to distinguish between races. The exploration of metaphysical qualities was not detached from physical ones.[12] Philosophers who searched for metaphysical differences between races served to strengthen the belief that Europeans were superior to people of color. This means that the physical was still in play and was a form of shorthand that pointed to white European supremacy.

SCIENCE AND RACE

The myth of a nonracist American society continues to be built on the idea that physical differences amount to very little. Those who argue that race is a meaningless and now defunct concept often turn to science to confirm their views but science cannot be totally disconnected from racist discourse. It should be remembered that science, too, was used to justify racist policies. In the not so distant past, some U.S. legislators wanted to limit the number of immigrants who did not hail from Northwestern European countries. Quotas were an option but they were immediately deemed racist by opposing policy makers.[13] The use of medical science, however, could achieve the same result while not attracting the same negative attention. Medical exams could be used to target specific immigrant bodies and reduce the influx of those thought to fall outside the white race. In other words, medical science helped to carry out racist policy. Although the task is made more difficult due to a less than cooperative scientific community, policy makers still try to lean on scientific discourse to obscure racism even today.

Now that scientists have shown that there is no genetic variance between people, there has been a push to do away with the concept of race. It is clear, though, that race remains socially significant and cannot be so easily erased from the cultural vocabulary or immigration debates. The move to dismiss any discussions about race and racism does not make the problem go away. Science may tell us that physical attributes cannot point to racial differences but this is nothing terribly new. Modern philosophy already shifted the focus elsewhere by seeking to establish a racial hierarchy through metaphysical differences. Modern metaphysics has made race invisible and science has proclaimed its nonexistence. Yet none of this has alleviated social tensions around race. Race continues to be a problem; it is just no longer couched in scientific terms. The language of scientific race may have gone out of fashion but this may say more about science than it does about race.

While it is now widely accepted in academic circles that there is no scientific, physiological, or genetic evidence to support the distinction between races, this does not mean that race—and by extension, racism—no longer exists. Part of the reason racism continues to function in Western culture is because it can be coded and hidden in a variety of ways. Science can still be used to discriminate against a "race" of people, even if there is no scientific data to support genetic variances between races. This was the case with past and present immigrants. It is well known that immigrants had to undergo a medical examination before entrance into the country was granted. These regulations may not seem out of the ordinary. Indeed, they are still part of the immigration process. What is hidden is that medical science was not used to determine the worthiness of all immigrants alike. A closer look at the administration of these medical exams shows that the use of these physical tests coincided with the rise of immigration from particular countries. To this day, regulations for entering the United States vary depending upon the individual's place of origin.[14] Science, medicine, physical exams did and do not target everyone equally. They are aimed at specific bodies that are deemed suspect.

While American mythology says that America welcomed everyone—including the sick, this is not the case. Past immigration regulations included medical exams that strategically targeted Irish, Italian, Polish, and other non-white immigrants. In other words, science allowed socially undesirable immigrants to be rejected. Medical science and results of physical exams were given as the reasons why Eastern and Southern Europeans, for instance, were turned away. These people were sick and threatened the health of the nation. Physical examinations allowed policy makers to claim that medical science, not racism, led them to deny entrance of certain immigrants into the United States.

Just because there is no scientific evidence that race exists does not mean that race ceases to be a problem for Western cultures. History shows that scientific discourse was just one among many that worked in concert with racist rhetoric. As in times past, there was a need to match the invisible strangeness of the other with something more concrete. Scientific testing and medical exams seemed to be able to deliver on this promise by finding disease in the already unwanted immigrant and foreigner.[15] It turns out that science cannot locate the invisible qualities that speak to a race's superiority. Erasing the invisible, however, is not such an easy task. The basic belief that there are meaningful differences between people does not disappear just because science cannot find genes that distinguish between races. The absence of scientific support emphasizes how difficult race can be to locate and how readily racial discourse can transition into a new language. This does not mean that we should stop trying to understand how race continues to operate through other discourses. Westerners may be hoping to avoid the trouble and tension that accompanies racial discourse by declaring that the search has turned up nothing. There is nothing to see and we should look no further. As Linda Martin Alcoff asserts, "Race dogs our steps; let us not run from it lest we cause it to increase its determination."[16] If the strength of racism is its invisibility, racism is bound to proliferate even more if it is not discussed and analyzed. At the very least, we can say that the problem of race has not subsided.

Part of the problem is that Americans are willing to concede that the nation was born with a birth defect of racism;[17] it is much more difficult for Americans to see or admit that racism continues to operate in the present. Race has always been a slippery category and discomfiting topic for discussion. It is, at once, obvious and mysterious. Classifications of race are seen as both automatic and arbitrary. On the one hand, many take it for granted that race exists. The recognition of differences among people and cultures translates into the belief in a wide array of races. On the other hand, there is greater awareness that racial categories have shifted over time. The "white" race, as can be seen through American immigration history, has grown to include different ethnicities and nationalities over time. If racial categories are dynamic and unstable, how, then, can race have any true meaning or reference? Considering the terrible events that can be traced back to racism, it would be convenient for Americans to believe that race is no longer a societal problem because race does not actually exist. If science cannot deliver racial difference, this may simply be an indication that the concept of race has once again taken a different form. We cannot look for race and racism to be found only in the past and easily recognizable characteristics (geography, skin color, genetic make-up, etc.). I do not mean to suggest that former conceptions of race do not still operate in present society. Rather, I want to follow Foucault and show that the problem of race will most likely express itself through the language and terminology that resonates with present society.

STATE RACISM

The racism of today, state racism, is neither completely separated from nor identical to past forms of racism. State racism is certainly used to discriminate against the same groups that are generally understood as being historically raced targets (foreigners, immigrants, non-white Others, etc.). However, classifications of race are expanding because state racism emphasizes the need to reject or problematize any group, which threatens the health of the nation. Since race can be seen as a meaningless and empty category, any grouping of people can fill it as long as they are deemed to be a danger to the state. Modern societies have translated the ancient split between the civilized and barbaric race into those who work towards or against the prosperity of the nation. This line of thinking allows disparate individuals to be organized into races through a wide variety of identifying markers such as their religious affiliation, sexual orientation, or gender. Although these profiles do not fit easily with present conceptions about race, Western mythology and history show that there was time when non-Christians, homosexuals, and women were thought to belong to a different and dangerous race. In other words, state racism is more pervasive and pernicious than prior forms of racism because it builds on ancient prejudices while coding it in the prevailing language of the day.

That discourse, as Foucault points out, is neoliberalism. Because neoliberalism couches benefits and costs to the nation in economic terms, state racism becomes more difficult to detect or easier to ignore. Despite its surreptitious nature, I suggest that state racism is on full display in present debates over immigration. Neoliberal language obscures ancient prejudices by embedding them in what is considered the most neutral discourse of the day—economics. Policy makers can say that they work to prohibit certain groups from entering the country simply because they would waste the nation's valuable resources and contribute nothing.

When Representative Joseph Wilson interrupted President Obama's 2009 Congressional health care speech by accusing him of lying, he gave the public a glimpse of the logic behind state racism. He later apologized for his breach of decorum but maintained his dissatisfaction over the access illegal immigrants have to American health care. Since the bill under consideration does not extend health insurance to illegal immigrants, Wilson's objection seems aimed at other health services. That target is the emergency room—where most illegal immigrants receive medical attention.[18] This means that Wilson wants to withhold from illegal immigrants medical services that cannot be legally denied to any person. The neoliberal justification behind this discrimination is that illegal immigrants use this loophole to take advantage of American resources. A less generous reading of these sentiments reveals the attempt to deprive human rights—a typical move within racist ideology—in the name of protecting the political state.

This shows that the language of immigration debates is beginning to line up with the way contemporary political philosophers describe modern racism. State racism is fast becoming the politician's favorite and most effective discourse against immigrants—illegal or otherwise. As the United States becomes less tied to its identity as a land of immigrants and less tolerant of overt racism, a new political riddle emerges. How is it possible to reject immigrants while not appearing hostile to those from different backgrounds? In other words, how is it possible to push through racist policies without actually appearing racist? The answer to this political question, as demonstrated by Wilson, is to depict undesirable immigrants as threats to the nation's overall health and prosperity. Once certain individuals are viewed as dangers to the nation's welfare, there is political cover to ignore even their most basic human concerns. Rationalizing the mistreatment and dehumanization of vulnerable individuals is an unfailing goal of racism and racist ideology. These hostilities against immigrants are aided by what Paul Gilroy believes is the nostalgia for the strength previously associated with Western nation-states. He states, "the new immigrants may be unwanted and abused precisely because they are the unwitting stimulus for the pain produced by memories of the vanished imperial and colonial past."[19] The arrival of immigrants signifies the loss of a strong community either because the nation now needs others for its survival or because the state cannot find a means to keep them out. What is novel about the state racism that grows from neoliberalism is that it justifies maltreatment of immigrants by evoking the need to protect the nation's welfare while concealing how these immigrants are an integral part of America's prosperity.[20] This neoliberal argument is only now becoming more publicly prevalent but it is based in a deeper philosophical tradition.

In light of this, what is needed is a philosophical analysis of immigration that can give cohesion and clarity to the role race plays in these

debates. Despite public suspicion that race factors into immigration policies, a traditional understanding of race that largely refers to phenotype
cannot sufficiently account for the movement against immigration. Not
only do immigration regulations extend beyond non-whites but the rationale for opposing non-white immigrants also cleverly steers clear of familiar racist rhetoric. A common theme, nonetheless, exists. I believe immigration restrictions levied against non-whites, homosexuals, and wom-
en point to an underlying philosophical shift in conceptions of race. The
claim that these chronically needy individuals would take up more than
their fair share of medical, social, and financial services allows state racism to build on the old imagery of degenerates. It, however, innovative-
ly opposes these inherently unhealthy figures to the healthy state. While
this most modern form of racism is increasingly making its way into
public debate over immigration through neoliberal discourse, a philosophical analysis can aid in understanding this transformation of race
and its implications for American society.

CONVENTIONAL CONCEPTIONS OF RACE AND STATE RACISM

In the following chapters, I will take a look at how the discourse of state
racism has overtaken the familiar rhetoric of racism. I think it is fair to say
that two groups draw the most attention when it concerns immigration
policies: those from the Middle East and Mexico. Before, the resistance to
these two groups could have easily been couched in the refusal of the
non-white other but today's political landscape has changed. Instead,
politicians and citizens alike seek to publicly distance themselves from
xenophobic language. I suggest that debates over immigrants from the
Middle East show how the philosophy of state racism has become the
preferred discourse. Although historical conflicts abound between the
West and the Middle East, there seems to be a concerted effort to reframe
the relationship between them. U.S. immigration debates concerning
those from the Middle East do not reference a dislike of the ethnic or
cultural other. The events of September 11, 2001 have allowed the public
debate to take a different shape. This movement is effective because it
substitutes the language and logic of traditional racism for that of state
racism. Americans can and should restrict the influx of Middle Eastern
immigrants not because they belong to another race but because they
threaten national welfare. Those from the Middle East should not be
allowed to enter the United States because they can literally destroy the
country through acts of terrorism.

Anti-immigration sentiment is bolstered by the hope of protecting not
only the health but also the cultural life of the country. While opponents
to immigrants from the Middle East deny that their rationale is tainted by
racism, they have not been successful in divorcing the two. It is still the

case, as we will see in a later chapter, that those from the Middle East represent a religiously racialized other. Even though few politicians are brazen enough to discriminate openly against immigrants because of their religion, policies are crafted just for these purposes. Religion may always be a reason for the extra scrutiny of those with ties to the Middle East. There are, however, attempts to downplay faith-based discrimination. A strange mix of biological science and concerns over public safety serve as the rationale for targeting those from the Middle East. These others are not heavily regulated so much for their religious practices. They are seen as a danger because the Islamic religion is understood to be a way to pass down an anti-Western germ from generation to generation. In other words, it is not the practice of Islam but the genetics encoded within this religious order that spells danger for the American population. If allowed to enter the country, these foreigners with a particularly destructive constitution could destroy America.

Politicians and the general public have shied away from using traditional racist rhetoric but this does not mean that another language of race and racism has not taken its place. On the one hand, the formulation of their opposition shows that familiar racist discourse is no longer tolerated in the public forum. On the other, racism does not disappear because easily identifiable racist tropes fade. It seems more the case that racist rhetoric has become more complex as it synchronizes with and borrows ideas from other disciplines and fields. Uncovering racism is further complicated by the fact that more conventional racist logic is couched in more politically acceptable language and rationale. Muslims are not simply targeted because of the fear of a religious other. They are problematic because their religion is a manifestation of an anti-Western biological code. State racism can be seen in the establishment of the visceral opposition to those from the Middle East. This new formulation of anti-Muslim racism is created through the modern political structure that allows the life of the individual to be connected to the life of the community. The (biological) anti-American germ within Muslims is understood to be the seed of terrorism that would destroy the country from without and within, if those from the Middle East were not heavily controlled.

THE PROLIFERATION OF STATE RACISM

Regulations targeting Middle Eastern immigrants reveal the prominence of state racism, but debates over Mexican immigrants reveal its proliferation. A philosophical analysis of Mexican immigration elucidates how the principles of state racism can be so productive and how they continue to be produced. Debates connecting Mexican immigration to national health, like that of Middle Eastern immigrants, point to the privileged position of state racism in the public arena. The case of Mexican immigration, however, can also relay why the philosophy of state racism is so abundant. It is beyond reproach, and it is versatile. State racism is the discourse of choice because it effectively plays on the neoliberal philosophy, which emphasizes continued national prosperity, especially economically. Many politicians and ordinary citizens alike center their arguments around the interest of state health because this motive is largely unassailable. What could possibly be wrong with wanting to protect the country? This sentiment leads to broad interpretations of national health that help justify arguments from all sides. Representative Joseph Wilson claimed that Mexicans would destroy the United States by draining its resources. His logic is as follows: Mexicans harm America's health when they seek medical attention to treat their physical problems. Their illnesses drain America's health and medical resources. Proponents of Mexican immigration, coincidentally, often use another strand of state racism to make their case. The most popular rationale for Mexican immigration is that Mexican immigrants will help the nation's fiscal health by providing much needed, affordable low-skilled labor. These interpretations of health show how valuable the philosophy of state racism is in determining the worth of individuals or groups.

Although state racism can cover over conventional discourses of race, state racism has further reach than conventional forms of racism. Opposition to those from the Middle East and Mexico could be seen as old-fashioned racism dressed up in more neutral language. I, however, want to suggest something more. I argue that state racism points to a shift in the public conception of race. The language of state racism becomes transposed onto groups that are not ordinarily organized as races. Following Foucault's lead, I argue immigration regulations apply the language of state racism to homosexuals and women. He explains that state racism portrays homosexuals and women as unhealthy figures; they have the potential to jeopardize the nation. It may not be surprising that homosexuals and the sexually abnormal have a more difficult time with the immigration process. Despite increased tolerance and acceptance of homosexuality, many Americans continue to view them as undesirable and dangerous.

What is telling is the way in which this dislike and suspicion of homosexuals gets translated into immigration policies. Arguments against homosexuals have a similar structure as arguments against those from the Middle Eastern and Mexico. They all revolve around the idea that the United States needs to be protected from individuals that threaten the national welfare. Regulations, therefore, reflect the perception that homosexuals are threats to the health of the nation because they are seen as literally and figuratively diseased bodies. The fear is that they are carriers of diseases such as AIDS and could threaten the fabric of America. The intersection of individual and public health also allows homosexuals to be viewed as a different race. It must be remembered that demarcations of species and race, as Charles Darwin explained, has a great deal to do with sexual reproduction.[21] They do not reproduce through "normal" heterosexual means but by converting heterosexuals into homosexuals. In other words, they infect others. Homosexuals are prevented from immigrating on the grounds that they belong to an inherently unhealthy race that could potentially spread their disease to healthy Americans. Because the health of the nation is at stake, "health" and "race" can come to have a variety of forms and meanings.

Foucault believed state racism to be the most dangerous form of racism because of its insidious and malleable nature. Its logic often remains hidden behind seemingly admirable goals and it can be used to target any subsection of the population—no matter how disparate. The racing of women perhaps best makes this case. Analyzing how women could be considered a race challenges us to examine the instability within race construction and stratification. Despite proclamations that Americans have moved beyond racism, there is still an understanding that those from the Middle East and Mexico represent distinct races. I suggested that thinking about homosexuals as a different race is also not so far-fetched. Some might even believe that they belong to another species, considering their inability to breed like "normal" humans. A philosophical analysis concerning the immigration of women, however, may go the furthest in challenging our understanding of race. Although there are no clearly delineated policies towards the restriction of women, immigration scholars such as Eithne Luibheid conclude that there is a bias against women. Examining this data within the philosophical framework of state racism could give us an explanation that allows for continuity. Women face restrictions for similar principles as those from the Middle East, Mexicans, and homosexuals. They represent a threat to the nation's welfare. For this reason, the state can effectively treat them like any other race that jeopardizes the health and prosperity of the nation. The idea of women as a race may strike us as odd, but it is not at all out of step with Western philosophy or mythology, which brings the story of Western racism full circle. Myths about Amazons, for example, have philosophical and cultural implications. The mythology surrounding this tribe of warrior women highlights the belief that this other is a threat to civilized (read patriarchal) society. I suggest that this view of women remains embedded within American immigration policy. An analysis of American immigration practices through the lens of state racism will help clarify this bias against women by contextualizing it within the conceptual history of race.

THE IMMIGRANT AS PHILOSOPHICAL AND ETHICAL FIGURE

What, then, do these shifts in thought and discourse about race mean for the immigrant as a philosophical figure? My hope is that this investigation leads to an understanding of the immigrant as philosophical persona and to an analysis of how state racism connects with broader anti-immigration sentiments. I argue that immigrants differ from concentration camp victims and refugees—figures privileged by Arendt and Agamben—because they represent the potential point of contact between races and cultures. Refugees exist in a distant and desperate sphere of existence. Because immigrants are physically closer than the refugee, they have the ability to change or destroy the landscape and fabric of America. I also want to make the case that American immigration more effectively relays the philosophy behind state racism than the examples provided by the contemporary philosophers who have thought so deeply about modern politics.[22] Arendt, Agamben, and Foucault aimed to expose how everyone's worth is connected to their perceived contribution to or hindrance of state prosperity. The ideal human is the one who helps the nation grow and prosper. They argue that Enlightenment or Modern philosophy naturally leads to this connection between the individual and the political state. I argue, however, that the prime examples of each obscure part of the philosophy behind state racism.

By analyzing the Holocaust, Arendt and Agamben demonstrate that states can unite disparate subsections of the population under the umbrella of political threat. This example makes clear the state's ability to devalue human beings and eventually exterminate them simply by depicting them as cancers to the state. What is not clear is that everyone is evaluated along the lines of state racism, even when they are not expelled or murdered. Foucault's reading of state racism through sexuality creates the inverse problem. He successfully elucidated that sexual norms are used to identify not only the sick but also the healthy individual. Sexual norms help place *everyone* along a spectrum of health and, ultimately, worth. Yet he himself complained that readers ignored how his treatise on sexuality connected to his larger thesis on state racism.[23] Lost was Foucault's idea that states privileged and encouraged particular sexual practices so as to cultivate a population of individuals who best served national interests.

Through examples provided by Arendt, Agamben, and Foucault, we see that wide interpretations of "health" create the most flexible and pernicious form of racism yet. They argue that the state can determine and re-determine the worth of anyone and everyone through categories of health. In effect, modern society works toward identifying two races—the healthy and the unhealthy. A closer look at the history of U.S. immigration shows the progression of this modern racism into the public arena. It should be no surprise that the Modern racism of Locke and Kant would express itself in the country that is the self-anointed leader of Western civilization. America inherited the ideals of European Enlightenment and deftly deployed them against immigrants. Federal regulations during waves of significant immigration into America matched philosophical shifts in racial discourse. There was a correlation between Modern conceptions and determinations of race and concrete immigration policies. This stretched from Kant's racial-geographical taxonomy to the Modern philosophical underpinnings of the science of race and into today. Because intolerance towards foreigners was more publicly accepted and tolerated in America's infancy, we tend to interpret past immigration regulations solely through this lens. I, however, want to explore how concerns about economic benefit and health continue to pervade racial discourses and immigration policies. The philosophy of state racism may not have been as prominent as Greek xenophobia but it was always there. I suggest that the rhetoric of state racism is more apparent now because the political climate requires racism to be couched in language of state health. The present disavowal of straightforward intolerance will only lead to the multiplication of these discourses. State racism will further multiply and continue to encompass more and more groups. The immigrant remains a constantly problematic figure and, for this reason, is invaluable for understanding how racism takes its many forms—including state racism.

Because the immigrant seems always to be identified with problems, the immigrant could be particularly helpful for understanding Foucault's theories about modern politics. As Alan Milchman and Alan Rosenberg explain, Foucault had two strands of focus in the last eight years of his life (1976–1984). He wanted to explore how certain matters had become a problem within society—when they had not been previously—or how the problem had been transformed. This is the origin of Foucault's neologism "problematization" and the foundation for his work on biopower. He also thought deeply about how modern power worked to incorporate all aspects of life, which is how he arrives at the term "biopower."[24] His famous studies on "problems" such as madness, criminality, and sexuality were part of an effort to understand how particular lives and bodies became a problem for the nation and the state. Foucault argued that the problem, in whatever form it took, needed to be understood in relation to political concerns. How did the life of the individual fit in with the desired trajectory of the nation? Biopolitical problems could be found where the life of the individual was seen to affect the life of the nation.[25] Foucault did not explore the discourse that joins together race and immigration in an in-depth manner but immigration seems to meet his criteria for biopolitical problems. Attitudes towards the immigrant have always pointed to various underlying problems within Western culture. And because immigrants seem to underscore the connection between the life of the individual and that of the nation, they are depicted as those who can destroy both.

While their weaponry of destruction is as diverse as they are, immigrants are seen as sharing a common tool. The immigrant figure is imagined to possess an ability to stir up discussion about race, even if there are greater attempts to cover over racist discourse. Jacques Rancière asserts that "racists . . . say less and less that Negroes are dirty or lazy; they explain more and more that there are economic constraints and thresholds of tolerance, and that, in the end, foreigners must be driven off, because if they are not, there is a risk of creating racism."[26] Any socially suspect group can be further stigmatized as the source of national problems. Racism need not use the language of yesteryear when there are so many other ways to describe how they are a detriment to the country. Immigrants cannot be tolerated because they could lead to the destruction of the country. The nation cannot withstand the economic demands they pose or other public safety concerns they bring. And if that argument does not sufficiently lead others away from the underlying racist rhetoric, racists can claim that the presence of foreigners causes race to become a problem that could tear the nation apart.

Supporters of anti-immigration movements like Proposition 187 believe immigrants, at the very least, cause a setback in the American evolution towards a color-blind society.[27] Race is seen as a barrier to a higher form of civilization and immigrants are the embodiment of this roadblock to a better America. Immigrants hinder the growth of the United States by drawing the nation backward toward a primitive mindset and/ or creating divisions among Americans through volatile debates over race. It is as if race was a plague of the undeveloped mind and immigrants are catalysts or carriers of that disease. Thus immigrants should be blocked to help ensure that this sickness of the mind does not inhibit America's growth or reignite debate that can potentially tear the nation apart. In other words, the logic of state racism can target specific groups of immigrants and immigrants in general. State racism helps us understand what the immigrant has come to symbolize and how this rationale plays into broader anti-immigration sentiment, which go hand-in-hand with fears of national disunity. Moreover, the logic of state racism works to label those who do and do not belong through circular reasoning. Immigration policies reinforce current race discourse by revealing who is or is not welcome. As long as the theme of national health remains central to modern politics, state racism will continue to increase. By analyzing the discourse surrounding who is granted or denied entrance into the U.S. through legal immigration, we gain a more complete picture of state racism and the desired subject. While these distinctions of human worth are made clear through the immigration process, they are also likely yardsticks for the entire U.S. population. Therefore, immigration policies and debates require further examination in the context of state racism. This means paying closer attention to regulations meant to control legal immigration.

NOTES

1. Jean-Luc Nancy, *The Inoperative Community*, trans. Christopher Fynsk (Minneapolis: University of Minnesota Press, 1991), 9.

2. While Anderson believes that the feeling of community relies upon images, he also pinpoints the circulation of language in print form as enabling a sense of community to arise. Even though many people would likely never meet or come into contact with each other, there was an understanding that others shared the same language, thoughts, and culture. See Benedict Anderson, *Imagined Communities: Reflections on the Origin and Spread of Nationalism* (London: Verso,1983) . See also: Charles Taylor, "Modern Social Imaginaries," *Public Culture* 14 (2004): 91–123.

3. Nira Yuval-Davis, "The 'Multi-Layered Citizen': Citizenship in the Age of 'Glocalization," *International Feminist Journal of Politics* 1 (1999): 130.

4. I use the term "Americans" here to refer to those who identify themselves with the United States of America, as it is commonly used, but I also recognize that this term is laden with many problems. Who is considered an American cannot be easily reduced to those with U.S. citizenship. The term is complicated even further because of geographical nomenclature. Canadians and Mexicans, for instance, could also be considered Americans because they also inhabit North America. South Americans, too, could lay claim to the title Americans. Despite all of these problems with the term, it seems like the least awkward term available.

5. Wm. Blake Tyrell, *Amazons: A Study in Athenian Mythmaking* (Baltimore: Johns Hopkins University Press, 1986), 117.

6. Michel Foucault, *The Government of Self and Others: Lectures at the Collège de France 1982–1983*, trans. Graham Burchell (New York: Palgrave Macmillan, 2010), 78.

7. See Robin Dale Jacobson, *New Nativism: Proposition 187 and the Debate over Immigration* (Minneapolis: The University of Minnesota Press, 2008).

8. Early Americans are cast as those who were cast out of Europe and other hostile lands. Through this story, race becomes a non-issue. It is religious discrimination rather than racial discrimination that led to the birth of the nation.

9. In addition to Euripides's *Ion*—as I mentioned previously, this sentiment can also be seen in Aeschylus' *The Suppliant Maidens*, trans. S. G. Benardete (Chicago: University of Chicago Press, 1991).

10. Prominent lawmakers such as Senator Lindsey Graham want to end birthright citizenship. If the *jus soli* is rescinded, then being born on American soil alone would no longer guarantee American citizenship. See Ezra Klein, "When Did Lindsey Graham Change His Mind on Immigration?," *The Washington Post*, July 30, 2010, accessed June 10, 2013, http://voices.washingtonpost.com/ezra-klein/2010/07/when_did_lindsey_graham_change.html.

11. John Locke, *Two Treatises of Government* (Cambridge: Cambridge University Press, 1988), sec. 25–51.

12. G. W. F. Hegel, *Philosophy of Mind*, trans. A.V. Miller (London: Oxford University Press, 1971), sec. 393.

13. Henry Pratt Fairchild, "The Immigration Law of 1924," *The Quarterly Journal of Economics* 38 (1924): 659–60.

14. Amy L. Fairchild and Eileen A. Tynan, "Policies of Containment: Immigration in the Era of AIDS," *American Journal of Public Health* 84 (1994): 2011.

15. Michael Omi suggests that scientific discourse is once again being invoked to substantiate racism. See Michael Omi, "'Slippin' into Darkness': The (Re)Biologization of Race," *Journal of Asian American Studies* 13 (2010): 349.

16. Linda Martin Alcoff, *Visible Identities: Race, Gender, and the Self* (New York: Oxford University Press, 2006), 246.

17. Former Secretary of State Condoleezza Rice, in an interview with the *Washington Times* in 2008, challenged both the mythology of America and the present reading of racism. She stated that there was a connection between the enslavement of Africans and the lack of opportunity within the African-American community today. Most

Americans cannot deny the history of slavery. It is with the latter part of her statement that Americans take issue because there is a resistance to thinking that racism still exists in the present. It is that particular birth defect—slavery—that makes it difficult for Americans to confront and discuss racism and its continuing relevance. See Nicholas Kraley, "Race Hits U.S. 'Birth Defect'; Secretary Sees Legacy of Race in Effect Today," *Newsmakers Interviews*, March 28, 2008, A01.

18. David M. Herszenhorn, "How Illegal Immigrants Fare," *The New York Times*, September 12, 2009, 10A.

19. Paul Gilroy, "From a Colonial Past to a New Multiculturalism," *Chronicle of Higher Education* 51, January 7, 2005, B7-B10.

20. Gail Russell Chaddock, "US Crackdown on Illegals Irks Business Community," *ChristianScience Monitor*, August 14, 2007, 3.

21. Charles Darwin, *The Descent of Man and the Selection in Relation to Sex* (New York: D. Appleton and Company, 1871), 240.

22. Girogio Agamben, *Homo Sacer: Sovereign Power and Bare Life*, trans. Daniel Heller-Roazen (Stanford: Stanford University Press, 1998), 120.

23. Arnold Davidson also notes that Foucault once remarked to him that he thought sex was boring. (Arnold Davidson, "Ethics as Ascetics: Foucault, the History of Ethics, and Ancient Thought," in *Cambridge Companion to Foucault*, ed. Gary Gutting (Cambridge: Cambridge University Press, 1994), 115.

24. Alan Milchman and Alan Rosenberg, "Michel Foucault: Crises and Problematizations," *The Review of Politics* 67 (2005): 335–36.

25. One can also see evidence of these tandem foci in the work that was put forth in the eight years prior to his death. They included, just to name a few, the published series on the *History of Sexuality* volumes and his College de France lectures on governmentality such as *Society Must Be Defended* and *Security, Territory, and Population*.

26. Jacques Rancière, *Chronicles of Consensual Times*, trans. Steven Corcoran (New York: Continuum, 2010), 13–14.

27. Jacobson, *New Nativism*, 26.

ONE

Immigration and the Modern Political State

Although illegal immigration draws a great deal of attention, connecting immigration policies to state racism requires an analysis of debates surrounding legal channels for entering the country and who can take them. Such examinations show that race discourse plays a large part in crafting legal immigration policies. Plenty of politicians, pundits, and media personalities have profited from fomenting anti-immigration sentiments.[1] The most successful among them push for greater injunctions while remaining indignant to the idea that their views have anything whatsoever to do with race or racism. There are those, for example, who tie their immigration opposition to the need to protect U.S. sovereignty from terrorists and a generation of "terror babies." This anti-immigration rationale is not as popular as ones that focus on economic concerns.[2] Yet these positions do have something in common. They all speak to the need to protect the health and well-being of the nation by properly allocating resources. I suggest, however, that the latter response is more pervasive and effective because it can more easily obfuscate the role of race in politics than the former. The American public is more sensitized to the notion that "terrorist" is too often code for Arab, Muslim, or someone from the Middle East.[3] Neoliberal discourse, which focuses on the management of the population through economics, is more successful in making race seem like a non-issue. The idea that politics should be and is indifferent to race is frequently evoked in present discussions over immigration. It is a belief that is also grounded in the Western philosophical tradition. Even Michel Foucault, who anchors his reading of biopolitics in an analysis of neoliberalism, relegates the issue of race to the margins of modern politics.[4] His understanding of how life and politics have become intertwined, nevertheless, provides insights into the ways econom-

21

ic discourse seemingly pervades all corners of modern society. Despite connections between race, politics, and economics in Western philosophy, Foucault treads the same path as many philosophers before him and many politicians before us. He largely ignores the topic of race. Contemporary thinkers such as Foucault, therefore, are similar to present-day politicians in that they tend to skirt the issue of race. I, however, seek to expose the intersection of race, politics, and economics that exist in the Western philosophical tradition. A closer examination of their tangled history could provide a backdrop for fruitful discussion about the place of race in the present political landscape.

WHAT IS BIOPOLITICS?

The idea that politics belongs to a different order of life than basic human functions is a foundation of Western thought. Foucault may have coined the term "biopolitics" but he was not the first to suggest that life and politics have now come to be joined together, when they were once separated. Hannah Arendt, too, believed that modern life represents a shift from the politics of Antiquity to that of contemporary times. Both philosophers trace a structural change that occurs from Greco-Roman times to modern society and use that transformation as a springboard for their philosophical critique of biopolitics. Giorgio Agamben theorizes biopolitics, in contrast, as a continuation of the *ancien régime* and focuses on the problematic philosophical construction of sovereignty. Despite Agamben's disagreements with Arendt, he seems to arrive at the same conclusion. They both want to disentangle life from politics. While biopolitics posits a connection between individual life and state policies, the critiques of Arendt and Agamben primarily attack the structure of the state and political sovereign. Because he connects biopolitics to neoliberalism, Foucault's analysis of modern society is more in tune with the present political landscape. Foucault picks up on the dominant discourse in modern politics. He, too, is interested in how power becomes invested in the individual subject rather than the governing body. A closer examination of Arendt and Agamben's reading of modern society will provide a contrast with the way Foucault's analysis of biopolitics focuses on the individual.

It is widely known that Arendt uses the Ancient Greek political system to reveal the failings of modern conceptions of politics. She praised the Ancient Greeks because they maintained a separation between the private and public realms. The Greeks, according to Arendt, understood that the integrity of the public or political sphere depended upon the exclusion of private or animal concerns.[5] Arendt's political philosophy is grounded in the Aristotelian notion that true human life is political life. In other words, humans are no different than animals in their pursuit of sheer survival. Politics is beyond animal nature. Everything related to the basic necessities of life and concerns of the body are relegated to the private realm. Arendt characterizes the public or political realm, in contrast, as one of ideas and action. Whereas private life is marked by unequal relationships between husband and wife or master and slave, politicians find themselves among equals in the political sphere. Arendt argues that this equality is possible because politicians do not have to worry about their sheer survival. Politics can be driven by vigorous debate about ideas rather than a desire to protect private interests. This agonal relationship among equals is also what allows humans to create a world of their own design rather than let nature or biology dictate life. For this reason, Arendt believed that the public and private needed to remain wholly separate if humanity were to rise above animal nature. She, therefore, calls for a restoration of the political realm.

While Agamben credits Arendt as one of the two philosophers who has thought the most deeply about modern society,[6] he believes she— like many others—misreads the ancient foundation of Western politics. He writes in "Absolute Immanence," "This inquiry, we may already state, will demonstrate that 'life' is not a medical and scientific notion but a philosophical, political, and theological concept, and that many of the categories of our philosophical tradition must therefore be rethought accordingly."[7] Agamben, in contrast to Arendt, seeks to expose the connection between life and politics. His analysis of biopolitics begins with a challenge to the Greek notion that politics excludes sheer life. Agamben wants to disrupt the traditional politico-philosophical discourse that *bios*, political life, and *zoe*, animal life, ever occupied two distinct realms. He criticizes the Ancients—and Arendt by extension—by pointing to this misreading of the foundation of Western politics.

Agamben suggests that much of Western politics rests on the purported distance between biological life and politics. Agamben strives to dislodge the myth of separation by exposing the secret bond between *bios* and *zoe*. He calls attention to the role of the discourse that calls for the separation of animal life and political life. On the one hand, Arendt paints a favorable picture of Greek politicians as those who have moved beyond the state of nature and are free from the prejudices of the body. Agamben, on the other, suggests that this tableau of nature is constructed precisely in order to justify political power. Because politics necessitates an excising of what is merely biological, *zoe* occupies an odd and often hidden space within the Western political system. If politics depends upon the exclusion of natural life, is it really excluded from the political realm? Agamben's answer is a resounding "no." Animal life operates, instead, as the inclusive exclusion. Natural or animal life becomes included within the political realm because politics cannot function unless biological life is excluded. Since political life necessitates the exclusion of biological life, it is actually included within politics. The move to exclude animal life from political life is precisely what melds them together in Western politics. Political life is not indifferent to sheer life. Because politics needs to exclude biological in order to function, Agamben questions the relationship or supposed non-relationship between political and natural life. In other words, Western political power is defined in relation to that which it excludes—biological life. What Agamben suggests is that the bond between the two is often overlooked or conveniently forgotten but strong nonetheless. His critique of Arendt and the Western conception of politics is an effort to think how animal life is simultaneously and necessarily included within and excluded from the political realm. In other words, this exclusion of natural life does not constitute a true separation of sheer life from political life. The political framework of the West, according to Agamben, is not a break but a continuation of the Ancient Greek system, which grounds political power in the seeming exclusion of natural life.

Because Agamben believes that wresting the public from the private will not undo biopolitics, he suggests another focus. He argues that a greater understanding of biopolitics entails a deeper analysis of the tandem figures of the sovereign and *homo sacer*. He states, "*It can be said that the biopolitical body is the original activity of sovereign power.*" [8] His analysis of biopolitics does not pivot on the distinction between political and animal life. Because the public and the private are actually joined, he believes understanding biopolitics means making sense of how the sovereign and the figure of *homo sacer* appear as approximate and even indistinguishable versions of each other.[9] The once hidden bond between *bios* and *zoe* is what produces both sovereign power and *homo sacer* or the phenomena of "bare life." Through his conception of *homo sacer*, Agamben pushes to transcend the long-held divide between politics and nature in the West. Agamben's reading of biopolitics highlights the emergence of bare life, which cannot be classified as natural or political life. The appearance of bare life reinforces the problem of this supposed dichotomy by calling into question our conceptualization of the public and private and civilization and nature. Agamben defines bare life not only as the life driven by basic bodily needs—what Arendt would categorize as natural—but also as the exposure of mere bodies. As is well-known, Agamben describes *homo sacer* as the one who cannot be sacrificed but can be killed with impunity. *Homo sacer* is not natural life in the sense that it corresponds to basic human needs because it is not considered human. Bare life is stripped of all meaning because what is considered sacred is that which falls outside of both the divine and human order. Part of what it means to be sacred is to be possessed by the gods of the underworld.[10] Such figures cannot be killed because they are already, in a sense, dead. They are the walking dead; shells of beings, which no longer belong to, but happen to appear in the world. Human law does not protect them because they fall outside its jurisdiction. Bare life is excluded from the law of the land, as an extension of policy and politics, but this does not make it, by default, natural life.[11]

He argues that the Western construction of sovereignty is directly related to the increasing production of bare life. The person of the sovereign and *homo sacer*'s life are mirror images of each other. The former is often described as sacred and inviolable while the latter represents that which can be killed by anyone but still does not constitute homicide.[12] This symmetry of being shows how important the state of exception is to the foundation of Western politics. Both the sovereign and *homo sacer* fall outside human and divine law. The sovereign is the being who can put the state of exception into place. Agamben states *"The sovereign sphere is the sphere in which it is permitted to kill without committing homicide and without celebrating a sacrifice, and sacred life — that is, life that may be killed but not sacrificed — is the life that has been captured in this sphere."*[13] Sovereign power is recognized as that which can suspend law by killing without appealing to a greater order. He has the ability to kill someone without justification or threat of punishment. When the sovereign takes the life of another, he does not need to do so within the context of divine ritual or sacrifice. Human law does not bind the sovereign either. He does not have to defend himself against the law because he supersedes it. And the evidence of this is that he can kill someone and not be guilty of murder. In other words, sovereignty is tied up with the ability to kill without recourse. Agamben's analysis shows that sovereignty depends upon the production of bare life. Sovereignty is recognized and strengthened through the identification and creation of *homo sacer*. Bare life serves to prove that sovereign power exists. Put otherwise, the sovereign needs *homo sacer* to substantiate and reinforce his power. The sovereign, therefore, emerges as a parallel figure to *homo sacer* in the state of exception that is increasingly becoming the norm in democratic governments.[14]

If Agamben believes that understanding biopolitcs means that we must break free from the paradigm that separates between the political and natural realm, Foucault believes that a more accurate analysis of biopolitics depends upon understanding a model that de-centers the sovereign and exclusive power. Foucault strives to do just that through his examination of the pervasiveness of neoliberal discourse — which differs from both Agamben and Arendt. Because Foucault believes that neoliberal ideology renders the sovereign largely irrelevant, his analysis provides a contrast with that of Agamben. And while Agamben's analysis is separate from Arendt's, they are similar in that they focus on the theme of exclusion. Foucault goes against this grain by analyzing how modern society operates through powers of addition. This is not to say that he does not believe that power operated through exclusion. He recognizes, as Arendt did, that former systems of power operated through exclusion. He even grants that negative power still operates within biopolitics. Yet his analysis, unlike Arendt, is not aimed at restoring a model of exclusion; it works towards articulating a model of power that proliferates and multiplies. The power to negate and exclude, according to Foucault, is no longer primary. It has been displaced by a conception of power that can elicit certain acts.

Foucault recognizes that Western politics has traditionally been understood through the sovereign and the power that accompanies him but he does not believe that biopolitics rests on the power of the king or head of state. To elucidate his point, he distinguishes between the right of death and the power over life. Foucault, not unlike Agamben, believed that the right of death was emblematic of sovereign power. The "power over life and death" was evidenced by the sovereign's ability to exercise the right to kill—without committing murder, of course—or his decision to refrain from killing.[15] Simply put, sovereign power revolved around death. Power over life and death could be seen in the taking or sparing of life. The allusion to the right of death is present even when the sovereign lets someone live. *Letting* someone live implies that the sovereign can always exercise but chooses not to act on the right to take life.

The highest function of the power over life is not found in the ability to kill but rather in the cultivation of life. Foucault suggests that "[t]he old power of death that symbolized sovereign power was now carefully supplanted by the administration of bodies and the calculation of life."[16] In place of a sovereign who is invested with the power to decide who lives or dies, life itself is invested with power. Because modern power structures center on the potential of life without the interference of a sovereign, Foucault sees the emergence of neoliberalism as the birth of biopolitics. Yet this move towards neoliberalism was not just a response to the modern individual's desire to see herself as a self-sufficient subject. Although neoliberal philosophy builds upon the idea that the individual is free because she is no longer under the thumb of the sovereign, neoliberalism also builds upon the popularity of naturalness. Instead of separating the natural from the political—as Arendt would have liked, neoliberalism grew in popularity because it came to represent a more natural form of governance.

In *The Birth of Biopolitics*—his 1978–1979 lecture series at the Collège de France, Foucault focused on the appeal of "natural" styles of governing. He shows that Marxists and neoliberals, alike, believed that modern society has moved away from the natural form of governance. They saw the problem of bourgeois and capitalist state as that which created a society that is far from a natural community. A familiar Marxist argument is that capitalism does not allow individuals to understand or communicate with each other because people are isolated from each other. Capitalism produces anonymous relationships between masses instead of direct communication between individuals, which represent the natural form of interaction.[17] Neoliberals, on the other hand, had to confront the role of "naïve naturalism" as it pertained to competition. While the driving theory behind liberalism is the idea that market competition will ensure the greatest amount of freedom within society, German neoliberals—and or-doliberals, in particular—began to realize that natural competition within society was not so natural.

If competition were not natural, then the idea of natural governments or political states would also have to be revisited. Foucault credits ordo-liberals for understanding that competition is not natural but rather a result of the technicization of the state.[18] This does not mean that natural-ness has lost its caché in modern society. Neoliberals, instead, want to manage and organize the state in such a way as to mimic the rationality of nature. Foucault believes the present project of neoliberalism is to understand ". . . how the overall exercise of political power can be mod-eled on the principles of market economy."[19] In other words, neoliberals recognize that competition is not natural but they suggest that there can be an art of governing that operates more or less naturally. This more natural art of governance depends upon the reduced prominence of the sovereign and the formation of the competitive individual. The neoliberal subject and individual life, therefore, is governed by the market econo-my, not the sovereign.

Thus Foucault's reading of biopolitics requires a deeper examination of the entrepreneurial self rather than the man of rights. A political sys-tem built upon the latter enumerates the right of man and simultaneously limits sovereign power. The man of rights, like Agamben's *homo sacer*—the man of no rights, is forever entangled with the sovereign. The entre-preneurial self or *homo oeconomicus*, on the other hand, is created in and through a political system that challenges the need for sovereign power. Neoliberalism springs from the logic that the individual can be most productive through self-government. The governing structures of the sovereign would only get in the way. Foucault states "the subject of right is integrated into the system of other subjects of right by a dialectic of the renunciation of his own rights or their transfer to someone else, while *homo oeconomicus* is integrated into the system of which he is a part, into the economic domain, not by a transfer, subtraction, or dialectic of renun-ciation, but by a dialectic of spontaneous multiplication."[20] Foucault contrasts these two systems to show that the problem between the indi-vidual and society has shifted. The rise of neoliberalism, which corre-sponds with the birth of biopolitics, does not focus on which rights man and citizen can claim and which they concede to the sovereign in the efforts to form a civil society.[21] Neoliberal ideology elucidates how the reproduction of power depends upon self-interest and the investment in the self.

Life and politics become joined through the idea that the self-govern-ing individual can and will create the most interest for herself and soci-ety. But as Foucault pointed out, this push towards self-improvement does not happen without a multiplication of state powers.[22] Governmen-

tal agencies and programs dealing with education, health, and wellness
are all necessary to the project of improving and investing in the self.
Growth and empowerment of the self is tied to the increase of the state
and the multiplication of its powers. State powers have greater reach into
individual lives because of the proliferation of agencies and institutions
that promote self-improvement. Because discourse remains focused on
the individual, governmental powers can grow with little notice.

BIOPOLITICS IN PRESENT DEBATES ON IMMIGRATION

While Arendt and Agamben use the Holocaust and Foucault uses sexuality as prime examples of the way in which biopolitics works in modern
society, I believe that these different theories of biopolitics also play
themselves out within immigration debates in America. Public discourse
about this increasingly controversial topic reflects the insights of each
philosopher. But it is also telling that the most popular and politically
viable—one probably because of the other—arguments against immigration trade on neoliberal philosophy. Concerns about U.S. sovereignty and
protection of wages and income, to be sure, are a part of the resistance
against incoming immigrants. Anti-immigrant positions that emphasize
the prosperity of "Americans"[23] and America, however, are the most
common and appeal to the widest audience. This suggests that Foucault's
reading of modern society and biopolitics could be particularly insightful
because of his focus on neoliberalism and a logic that privileges individual growth and self-improvement. Applying Foucault's analysis to U.S.
immigration debates will show that neoliberal ideology channels power
to affect public policy.

A Foucauldian reading of biopolitics does not mean that sovereign
power is no longer an issue in modern society. He claims, nonetheless,
that neoliberal themes that focus on individual growth and prosperity
displace concerns about sovereign power. This is evidenced in the myriad controversies surrounding U.S. immigration. The clamor over the re-
peal of the 14th Amendment or the *jus soli*, for instance, relays how the
issue of sovereignty still appeals to part of the public. But if the goal is to
use "outsiders" as a channel for anger and frustration around—which I
think it is, it seems that arguments which directly connect to neoliberal
ideology are more successful in doing so.

There are those who want to abolish birthright citizenship because
they believe it threatens U.S. sovereignty.[24] Senator John Kyl (Arizona)
echoes Senator Lindsey Graham (South Carolina) in his push to revisit
the 14th Amendment. Both Graham and Kyl believe that leaving birthright citizenship untouched leads to an increased lawlessness that will
destroy the United States, figuratively and literally. Graham argues that
the law encourages foreigners to break laws and cheapens the status of

U.S. citizenship for which others died.[25] Kyl claims that this law has led to increased violence by and against illegal immigrants. It is also telling that the destruction of goods is cited as a black mark against an open immigration policy. Greater violence leads, to among other things, a destruction of property.[26] If children of foreigners are granted citizenship simply because they were born on U.S. soil, it can lead to the destruction of what Americans hold most dear. Property and goods that signify economic status fall, of course, into that category.

Neoliberalism also encompasses concerns over national security and prosperity. This fear of "foreign" violence inflicted by homegrown terrorists and immigrants has further escalated. Representative Louie Gohmert[27] believes that Americans can save themselves from physical violence by repealing the 14th Amendment. He sees birthright citizenship as counterproductive to the efforts to keep the fight off U.S. soil. If the 14th Amendment is allowed to stand, then anti-American foreigners will use the cover of this law to breed "terror babies." These children will be raised to terrorize and destroy the United States from within. Furthermore, they will no longer have to apply for visas or undergo background checks before entering the country. They are already here. Gohmert and his sympathizers suggest that babies will be bred to hate the United States and are simply biding their time until they can stage another major terrorist attack on home soil.[28]

This same rationale for preventing violence on American turf is the basis of Arizona's controversial immigration law. Arizona lawmakers contend that their law will not only rein in bloodshed and criminal activity but also restore order in the streets. The law dictates that police, in the course of enforcing other laws, have the duty to ask for documents proving legal status of anyone they find suspicious.[29] This decree has caused a firestorm and even caused many to liken it to laws of Nazi Germany.[30] Agamben, who outlines the connection between sovereign rule and the state of exception, could give philosophical support to this comparison. He suggests that martial law is becoming more and more common. This phenomena, effectively, closes the gap between democracies and totalitarian states because the sovereign can declare a state of exception where his rule supersedes all others. On the one hand, Agamben is alarmed by the creation of laws that suspend other laws.[31] Arizona's controversial immigration law, for instance, allows the police to disregard the law that protects against police harassment, for instance, that many of us who live in the United States take for granted. On the other hand, he cannot be surprised by it because his philosophical analysis shows that the state of exception is the foundation of the Western concept of sovereignty. Because sovereign power is recognized and reinforced through the suspension of law or the creation of the state of exception, there will be a larger and larger number of *homo sacer* (the mirror image of the sovereign) within American borders.

Agamben outlines this modern tragedy but he is not the only one who makes note and is suspicious of it. Many in the United States have also protested the treatment of both legal and illegal immigrants who seem to be caught in a gray zone between law and violence. Anti-immigration campaigns that make use of neoliberal principles, in contrast, are met with less resistance and are, therefore, more effective. Those who use neoliberal arguments, I argue, target immigrants just as much as their counterparts who evoke concerns over sovereignty. Attacks on health services for immigrants, made famous by Representative Joseph Wilson, criminalize foreigners and their children but they receive much less critical press. The claim that these foreign children and their parents rob "true" Americans of resources appeals to a wider audience.

Wilson's outburst (You lie!) during President Obama's 2009 Congressional health care speech worked as a call to arms against immigrant "others" who would drain U.S. resources. His reasoning follows the familiar refrain that illegal immigrants do not deserve care because they contribute nothing to the system. Immigrants who need health services are depicted as incapable of self-improvement and a hindrance to the prosperity of the United States. Wilson later apologized for his breach of decorum but maintained his dissatisfaction over the access illegal immigrants have to American health care.[32] Since the bill under consideration does not extend health insurance to illegal immigrants, Wilson's objection seems aimed at other health services. That target is the emergency room—where most illegal immigrants receive medical attention. This means that Wilson wants to withhold from illegal immigrants medical services that cannot be legally denied to anyone. The justification behind this discrimination is that illegal immigrants use this loophole to take advantage of the system. A less charitable reading of these sentiments reveals the attempt to mistreat vulnerable groups in the name of protecting the political state.

While this argument is framed as a defense of the state, it is not a defense of a sovereign figure. If anything, it is just as much an assault on the national head of politics—President Obama—as it is of illegal immigrants. This line of attack against immigrants, however, elucidates the tension Foucault sees within neoliberal philosophy. The fight for individual freedom, growth, and prosperity goes hand-in-hand with the proliferation of governmental agencies and foundations. Those who oppose immigration on neoliberal grounds do not necessarily oppose federal aid in the form of money or institutions. Their objection comes from the notion that governmental resources are funneled to the immigrant when they should really be used to foster the prosperity of ordinary Americans. Wilson and his allies claim that illegal immigrants, with the help of the president, are fleecing the people of America.[33] This particular case focuses on medical services but it fits with the greater narrative about immigrants.

Both legal and illegal immigrants are seen as an impediment to American greatness because they need and use more than their fair share of medical, social, and financial resources. Those who believe and support American ideals, the theory goes, are deprived of these very benefits. Real Americans who are invested in the nation cannot better themselves. And as advocates of neoliberalism suggest, the nation as a whole will not prosper unless common citizens are given the opportunity to improve and invest in themselves. In short, the decline of the United States is sure to come if immigrants are prioritized over true Americans. The fact that more and more politicians are able to garner support by employing similar rhetoric about resources shows the power of neoliberal philosophy within modern society.

BIOPOLITICS AND RACE

While anti-immigration politicians and pundits want to focus on neoliberal arguments, they also want to deflect any accusations of racism. I suggest that public figures, in part, use neoliberalism to oppose immigration because it seems to provide a path to sidestep questions about race and racism. The ability to blunt charges of racism contributes to the popularity and pervasiveness of neoliberal theories. By evoking neoliberal principles of national prosperity and self-improvement, opponents of immigration can shield themselves from allegations of racism. They insist that their positions have nothing to do with race but are, instead, motivated by economic concerns. The implication is that economics is not connected to race.

Arendt, of course, would disagree because she warned about the mixing of politics and economics. She believed that racism would necessarily appear on the political stage once the *oikos*—Greek for "household" and root of "economics"—become conflated with dealings of the state. Arendt argues that we, moderns, could learn something from the Ancient Greeks. We could prevent the integration of racism into politics, if we maintained the separation between public and private spheres. Foucault's historical analysis of neoliberalism and the birth of biopolitics move towards an opposite conclusion of the one proposed by Arendt. While Arendt believes that the Ancient Greeks excluded all matters of the body—such as race—from the political realm, Foucault's reading of Euripides' *Ion* shows that race was a factor in the politics of Antiquity. And while Arendt argues that race is now unfortunately entangled with modern politics, Foucault suggests that race is not currently a major political issue. He briefly mentions how the idea of an "entrepreneurial gene" operates within neoliberalism but he does not fully develop this connection. Despite his interest in Immanuel Kant's anthropological project and his knowledge of Kant's *Of the Different Human Races*,[34] he does not see that the entrepreneurial self implicates race.

I will argue that neoliberal philosophy cannot be so neatly extricated from the Western history of racism. The creative, autonomous self is not only the neoliberal subject par excellence but also the one who sits, not coincidentally, atop the Western race hierarchy. Foucault, therefore, follows Arendt and many other philosophers who came before them by trying to undo the ties between race and politics. Arendt believes that race has become political but wants to remove it from the political forum. Foucault, in contrast, believes that race is largely a non-issue for a politics driven by neoliberal concerns. Politicians and philosophers may attempt to ignore race or brush it to the side but the controversy over immigration shows that race is a recurring theme in politics. Thus, immigration debates in America not only reflect theories of biopolitics but also the tendency to dismiss political discussions of race.

In order to show that race did not suddenly appear in contemporary Western politics, I want to return briefly to Arendt's understanding of the Greek *polis* in order to contrast it with Foucault's reading of Greek culture. Arendt believed that the Ancient Greeks did not conflate life with politics and were, therefore, able to keep race from entering the public sphere. Her defense of the Greeks works as an argument against the impoverishment of the modern public sphere through—among other things—the infection of racism into politics. But her reading also ignores the ancient connection between politics and race. Arendt applauded Ancient Greek politicians who valued vigorous public debate about ideas. Of course, not everyone was deemed capable and worthy of discussing the good of the city-state. Foreigners—along with women, merchants, slaves, etc.—were among those excluded from politics. Foucault's retelling of Euripides' *Ion* suggests something quite to the contrary. Ion's status as a foreigner not only marks him as a different race from the Athenians but also strips him of the ability to speak appropriately about politics. The tale about Ion shows that race was a factor in Ancient Greek politics. Public and private concerns intermingled even then.

Arendt describes modern society as "... the form in which the fact of mutual dependence for the sake of life and nothing else assumes public significance and where the activities connected with sheer survival are permitted to appear in public."[35] Modern politics has become entangled with base human needs and represents a break with the Ancient Greek political tradition. Whereas the Greeks managed to keep concerns about the body within the private realm, we have not been able to do so. The conflation of the private and public, in her opinion, is what allows racism to enter into politics. She argues that the more animal life becomes equated with political life, the more the political sphere would resemble the private realm. On the one hand, the Greeks determined the course of political action on the merit and strength of ideas. On the other hand, they also allowed for physical differences and violence to determine the order of things in the private sphere. If state policy becomes consumed with basic human concerns, then politics will also inevitably reflect prejudices that had previously remained within the confines of the home.

Arendt's analysis suggests that racism is natural and, therefore, belongs in the private realm that deals with all other concerns of natural life. She concedes that discrimination and racism will never be eradicated in the population as a whole. The goal, then, should be to make sure that race discrimination is relegated to the private sphere. Arendt's insistence that private resorts have a right to enforce segregation policies shows that her critique is not aimed at racism as such.[36] She, instead, targets state racism: the legal enforcement of racism. Her solution to the problem of state racism, of course, is to separate the political from the private—as the Greeks did. But as Agamben argued, bare life was never truly excluded from the political realm. The belief in this separation was grounded in illusion. Agamben's argument that bare life was always a part of politics suggests that race could have also been a factor even in the Ancient Greek political system that Arendt admired. The legacy of Ion, as examined by Foucault, further reveals that the body and politics were not so easy to separate in Ancient times. And race as an extension of the body, by Arendt's own account, also entered in the Greek *polis*.

While Foucault situates his reading of Euripides' *Ion* around the idea of *parresia*—the ability to speak the truth, it works, nonetheless, to show that race was important race in Ancient Greek politics. The meaning behind the myth of Ion, as Foucault sees it, is that parresia is grounded in the land. Without this inheritance from the land, he would not be able to enter politics. Only if Ion was Athenian by birth—which he was eventually found to be, could he then engage in truth-speaking. Foucault's rehashing of Ion's story shows that the ability to engage in public debate, which Arendt highlighted, was directly tied to one's race.

By Euripides' account, Ion was not an immigrant. He was born from an encounter between an Athenian woman and Apollo. Because the Athenians distinguished themselves from other Greeks by asserting that they were an autochthonous people, it was of utmost importance that Ion did not come from a foreign land. Only if he was of authentic Athenian stock could he enter politics. Foucault cites a passage in *Ion* where the protagonist laments that he will never be able to enter Athenian politics, much less achieve greatness, because he is not accepted as one of them. "It is said that the autochthonous and glorious people of Athens is free of any foreign mixture. Now this is where I fall down, afflicted by the double misfortune of being both the son of a foreigner and a bastard. Branded as such, if I do not have power, I will remain, as the saying goes, a *Nobody, son of Nobody*."[37] Ion is tormented by the fact that Athenian prejudices will condemn him to a life without distinction. He would be a bastard and a foreigner—which is to say a nobody. This is further sup-

ported by the character's awareness that foreigners could never hope to
equal true Athenians in speech or politics, no matter what his talents.
Foucault cites from Euripides' *Ion*: "If a stranger enters a town where the
race is without stain, the law may make him a citizen, but his tongue will
remain servile."[38] For someone as ambitious as Ion, the call to racial
purity is problematic because it will not allow his speech to be recognized
as parresia.

Even if he did have the gift of parresia, his words would be questioned by a variety of native Athenians. Ion knows that his attempt to
enter politics will be challenged by citizens of all stripes and merit. There
are the inferior who will resent him for his talent, the wise who will scoff
at his desire to become involved with politics, and those with power and
position who will attack him as a rival.[39] Ion and his revolutionary ideas
would have been banned from the public forum of Ancient Greece that
Arendt lauded. Euripides' *Ion* shows that politicians needed to meet certain criteria before they could engage in public speaking or political
speech. Race, it appears, was one such bodily precondition.

Ion's Athenian birthright, Foucault notes, was a great subject of interest for many Ancient writers because of his legacy as a great reformer of
the Athenian constitution. Because the mythology of Athens is connected
to Ion's legacy, it is not only Ion's reputation that is at stake. The greatness of the land as home of truth-seekers and truth-speakers is also on the
line. Euripides gives Ion Athenian lineage in order to establish Ion's racial purity but also to reinforce Athens' superiority over all other Greek
city-states. Athenians believe themselves special not only because they
are an autochthonous people but also because they are a race of truth-
speakers.[40]

Foucault's examination of parresia opens up a connection between
Ancient politics and race via the land, even if it is not his primary concern. But he takes a stronger stance on the importance of race in his
analysis of modern politics. Foucault dismisses the idea that race is an
important political issue.[41] He thinks that understanding modern politics
hinges on an analysis of the neoliberal subject but he does not recognize
how the entrepreneurial self is also raced. I argue that the characteristic of
enterprise is very much a part of the traditional Western construct of
race. Kant used a scale of industriousness to create his human taxonomy.
Furthermore, he argued that the land of origin shaped each race. Land
determined the particular level of enterprise and diligence for each race.
If race is implicated in the neoliberal subject and the neoliberal subject is
the focus of modern politics, then race—even if Foucault largely ignores
it—is an important political issue.

The controversy over immigration into the U.S. is further evidence
that race is an important political issue. As much as some politicians
would like to remove race from the discussion on immigration, they find
themselves having to address the issue of race. Because politicians often

use neoliberal philosophy to skirt the issue of race, I believe an analysis of race within neoliberalism is necessary to address how race functions in politics and philosophy. Despite the cliché that philosophers live in a world of their own and that their ideas have no bearing on the "real' world, the issue of immigration shows that philosophy is reflected in the world. There is a tendency in both politics and philosophy to dismiss the political importance of race.

On the one hand, Foucault recognizes that there is a racist element within the discourse of neoliberalism and the rise of the entrepreneurial self. On the other hand, he does not believe that it is worth pursuing how "traditional" racism and capitalism intertwine. Foucault states:

> What I mean is that if the problem of genetics currently provokes such anxiety, I do not think it is either useful or interesting to translate this anxiety into the traditional terms of racism. . . . So, the political problem of the use of genetics arises in terms of the formation, growth, accumulation, and improvement of human capital. What we might call the racist effects of genetics is certainly something to be feared, and they are far from being eradicated, but this does not seem to me to be major political issue at the moment. [42]

He believes that the specter of racism is important insofar as it elucidates how certain individuals are privileged because they can acquire, accumulate, and sustain capital. Yet Foucault refuses to understand that the theme of enterprise has been a part of the traditional rubric of racism. More to the point, he does not believe that racism—in general—is central to modern society and biopolitics.

I suggest that the idea that some possess the entrepreneur gene while others lack it is very much a part of traditional constructions of race and major political issues of the moment. While conventional racism often uses skin color as markers of different races, Western racism and philosophy has a history of reading plenty into skin color. Early classifications of race used skin color as a means to bundle hereditary traits that appeared in different peoples around the globe. And a description of something like the entrepreneur gene was not uncommon. In Kant's *Of the Different Human Races*, he describes how the laziness of African peoples is due to climate, environment, and land. A combination of fertile earth and plentiful sun has provided everything that Africans could want. [43] The same sun that made them dark also made it easy for them to procure food. Vegetation flourished and animals were abundant in the African climate. Paradoxically, the only beings that did not thrive according to Kant were the people. Without the need to invent or take initiative, the people remained stagnant and tied to the most animal of life forms, only fulfilling their most basic needs.

Kant claims that particular races are more industrious than others and are, therefore, superior to those he deemed lazy. His description of

African nations worked to highlight, unsurprisingly, the ideal and entrepreneurial spirit of the Europeans. If the Africans were given everything
by the copious amounts of sun that drenched their land, the Europeans
had to fight against the harsh elements. This meant that they had to be
inventive in order just to survive. While Africans inherited indolence,
Europeans passed down a strong work ethic. This instilled sense of enterprise is what allowed them to conquer not only their indigenous sur-
roundings but also foreign lands.[44] In short, Europeans possessed the
entrepreneurial gene and African races—among others—lacked it. Europeans were the epitome of the creative, autonomous self.

 This logic also helped justify the colonization of other nations. Instead
of seeing colonization as an act of aggression, it was read as an extension
of this entrepreneurial spirit. Yet it is precisely the equation of movement
and migration with the enterprise of the "good" race that makes race an
important political topic or at least an issue that requires more investigation. Migration, once positive, is now considered something negative and
an activity of the inferior. Why should this be the case and what role does
race play in the converse interpretation of migration? Foucault's reading
of neoliberalism, however, allows the act of migration to be seen again in
a positive light.

> Migration is an investment; the migrant is an investor. . . . The mobility
> of a population and its ability to make choices of mobility as invest-
> ment choices for improving income enable the phenomena of migra-
> tion to be brought back into economic analysis, not as pure and simple
> effects of economic mechanisms which extend beyond individuals and
> which, as it were, bind them to an immense machine which they do not
> control, but as behavior in terms individual enterprise of oneself with
> investments and incomes.[45]

While Kant's taxonomy of races was an exposition on why Northern
Europeans—in particular—were superior to other peoples, the neoliberal
interpretation of migrating peoples does not necessarily conflict with
Kant's reading. For both Kant and neoliberal theorists, migrants refuse to
be limited by that which seems to be out of their control. They are not
restricted by the opportunities of their homeland. And as Foucault explains it, migrants epitomize the entrepreneurial subject. The basis of the
neoliberal reading of migration begins with the investment of oneself.
Migrants of today often travel from one land to another for greater economic gain, stability, and improved quality of life for future generations.[46] When faced with insufficient opportunity to live, work, or thrive,
the migrant chooses to leave. Yet this movement across lands is not without cost. It cannot be done without some money and this money represents an investment in oneself.[47] The money spent to migrate is also the
money risked in the hopes of a better, more financially stable life.

Movement around the globe is no longer limited to Europeans. But the plethora of neoliberal philosophy within present-day politics has not sufficiently disrupted this notion that only European migrants are blessed with entrepreneurial genes. Now that migration is largely associated with non-Europeans, migration is no longer seen as a source of enterprise. Neoliberal discourse, it seems, has undergone a reversal. Those who are migrating are not investors in their adopted lands or in themselves. Immigrants, instead, are a burden to their host country. They drain valuable resources and depress wages. It is not uncommon for opponents to immigration to bemoan the costs of immigrants. While there are benefits from cheap immigrant labor, the theory is that the American economy does not really benefit from this influx of migrants.[48] And to make matters worse, they drain resources by taking advantage of governmental services ranging from free schooling for their children to emergency room attention. Likewise, migration is not seen as an investment in oneself—despite the fact that migrating still requires a substantial amount of money. The desire for greater economic stability no longer signals an investment in the life of the migrant. Quite to the contrary, anti-immigration discourse paints a picture of the immigrant as a willfully ignorant person who refuses to learn the English language or do anything to assimilate to the American way of life.[49] The migrant of today is not an investor but a leech. Considering the reversal in interpretation of the migrant, it seems difficult to make the case that race is not a factor and not at the center of immigration debates. Neoliberalism cuts both ways in terms of attracting cheap labor and unwanted immigrants.

CONCLUSION

Even though I have focused on the anti-immigration movement in America, this wave is not limited to the United States. Issues over the treatment of immigrants are appearing all over the globe. These controversies, whether in the United States or various Western countries, follow a similar pattern. One visible contingent represents those who assert that the mistreatment of immigrants is motivated by race and racism. Another represents those who respond with indignation to this suggestion and claim, instead, that their positions are rooted in self-improvement—monetarily or otherwise. I have tried to show that, with or without the discourse of economics, race has been a part of Western politics. The figure of the immigrant in ancient and present times allows us to see this connection between race and politics. At the moment, neoliberal ideology is prominent in the efforts to obfuscate the role race plays in politics. There is no doubt that the modern political forum is difficult to navigate and that the topic of race is fraught with ambiguities. However, the answer to the riddle of race and politics is not—as leading public and philosophical figures are apt to do—to pretend that race and politics should not or do not intersect.

If we were to take a cynical view about politicians, then it would make sense to believe that they would go to great lengths to avoid openly joining politics and race. Very few people win or keep public offices by employing this strategy. The most successful tactic is to make race a marginal—at most—player in politics. Politicians correctly read the political landscape. The public does not have a great appetite for discussing race.[50] But I do not think that dismissing the importance of race helps Foucault's appraisal of modern politics. While Foucault's analysis of biopolitics is different than that of Arendt or Agamben in that he tries to give a descriptive rather than prescriptive reading of biopolitics, he, nonetheless, works to problematize neoliberal philosophy. I suggest that a further examination of how race functions in economic discourse is important for disrupting neoliberalism and for understanding tensions surrounding immigration. Foucault could have used his analysis of biopolitics to illuminate the encoding of race in the language of resourcefulness and enterprise. His examination of the contradiction that emerges from neoliberal philosophy could also shed light on the immigration issue.

The political firestorm around immigration elucidates the neoliberal friction between the attainment of freedoms and the growth of state powers. Opponents of immigration in the U.S. seem willing to accept some of the incongruity within neoliberalism. On the one hand, supporters of Arizona's immigration regulations believe that increased police presence and incursion will result in greater freedom. On the other hand, the public seems unwilling to make the connection between the free market that the state is supposed to ensure and the influx of immigration into the country. The governmental powers that support neoliberal economics also lead to increases in immigration. Foucault's analysis of biopolitics could be used to fill in the gap in logic between neoliberal philosophy and the politicization of race. There is a contradiction that eludes many opponents to immigration. Opponents of immigration want to support neoliberal policies but they do not want to be confronted by the raced other. American business leaders seem to recognize that there cannot be one without the other. This could help explain why American businesses—which tend to side with conservatives—are rather quiet on the issue of immigration.[51] Economics may seem to shield politicians, pundits, and philosophers from the discussion of race but race is actually intimately connected to an economics of enterprise. Dealing with the problem of race also requires reckoning with a central biopolitical idea that the life of the nation-state is connected to the life of the individual.

NOTES

1. There is speculation that moderate Republicans such as Senator Lindsey Graham try to gain greater favor with conservatives by pushing for stricter immigration regulations. See E.J. Dionne, "Is the GOP Shedding a Birthright?," *The Washington Post*, August 5, 2010, accessed June 10, 2013, http://www.washingtonpost.com/wpdyn/content/article/2010/08/04/AR2010080405453.html.

2. While talk of "terror babies" has attracted a certain amount of media attention, prominent politicians steer clear from this issue. Representative Louie Gohmert has voiced his fear of terror babies but his position is perhaps too easily mixed up with bigotry to be popular with other politicians who favor stricter immigration regulations. See Clarence Page, "Let's Keep Our Enemies Straight," *Buffalo News*, September 10, 2010, accessed July 3, 2012, http://www.highbeam.com/doc/1P2-25820902.html.

3. While these categories are not the same, they often become conflated in the public sphere. See Sarah Ahmed, "Affective Economies," *Social Text* 22 (2010): 131.

4. Foucault is not completely silent on the topic of race. Many scholars argue that he does not enough analysis on the issue of race, save for the few connections to Nazism. This is even more apparent after the lectures at the College de France were released. Certainly, his work on race are much more limited than his work on sexuality, madness, or criminality. See Chloe Taylor, "Race and Racism in the College de France Lectures," *Philosophy Compass* 6 (2011): 746–56.

5. Hannah Arendt, *The Human Condition* (Chicago: Chicago University Press, 1958), 28–32.

6. Michel Foucault is the other. See Giorgio Agamben, *Homo Sacer: Sovereign Power and Bare Life*, trans. D. Heller-Roazen (Stanford: Stanford University Press, 1995), 120.

7. Giorgio Agamben, "Absolute Immanence" in *Potentialities: Collected Essays in Philosophy*, ed. D. Heller-Roazen (Stanford: Stanford University Press, 2000), 239.

8. Agamben, *Homo Sacer*, 6. Italics are in the original.

9. Agamben, *Homo Sacer*, 94.

10. Agamben, *Homo Sacer*, 73.

11. Agamben's analysis of *homo sacer* should not be read as a return from *bios* to *zoe*. Bare life is not synonymous with *zoe*. It represents, rather, the dismantling of *bios* because it is a life stripped of all positive determinations. To equate bare life with natural life, à la Arendt, is to undermine Agamben's goal to transcend the ontopolitical tradition that rests on the opposition between nature and politics. See Sergei Prozorov, "The Appropriation of Abandonment: Giorgio Agamben on the State of Nature and the Political," *Continental Philosophy Review* 42 (2009): 341–42.

12. Agamben, *Homo Sacer*, 102.

13. Agamben, *Homo Sacer*, 83. Italics are in the original.

14. Giorgio Agamben, *State of Exception*, trans. Kevin Attell (Chicago: Chicago University Press, 2005), 7.

15. Michel Foucault, *The History of Sexuality: An Introduction*, trans. Robert Hurley (New York: Vintage Books, 1990), 136.

16. Foucault, *History of Sexuality*, 139–40.

17. Michel Foucault, *The Birth of Biopolitics: Lectures at the Collège de France 1978 – 1979*, trans. Graham Burchell (New York: Picador, 2008), 113.

18. Foucault, *Birth of Biopolitics*, 115–20.

19. Foucault, *Birth of Biopolitics*, 131.

20. Foucault, *Birth of Biopolitics*, 292.

21. Foucault, like Agamben, challenges the long-held notion that the political state put an end to the brutality of the state of nature. Concepts of the state of nature and civil society are created to validate and legitimize the state's existence. See Prozorov, "Appropriation of Abandonment," 333. This sentiment can also be found in *The Birth of Biopolitics* when Foucault writes, "Civil society is like madness and sexuality, what [Foucault calls] transactional realities." (Michel Foucault, *Birth of Biopolitics*, 296.)

22. The ambiguous relationship between control and the promotion of human rights and well-being remains a tension within the construct of biopower. It is at the heart of Foucault's conception of biopower and those who have followed him such as Giorgio Agamben, Jacques Rancière, and Antonio Negri. See Noël O'Sullivan, "The Concepts of the Public, the Private and the Political in Contemporary Western Political Theory," *Critical Review of International Social and Political Philosophy* 12 (2009): 150.

23. Who counts as true and certifiable Americans is up for debate. Part of the controversy over Arizona's immigration law has to do with this exact problem. Opponents of the bill point out that racial profiling is necessary to carry out the law. Those who "look" Mexican are targeted, even if they are U.S. citizens.

24. The issue of "anchor babies" can be linked to the proclaimed desire to protect U.S. sovereignty. Both feed the movement to challenge the 14th Amendment. See D.A. King, "Should U.S. Deny Citizenship to Children of Illegal Immigrants?," *The Atlanta Journal Constitution*, June 17, 2009, 11A.

25. Graham mentions specifically those who speed up the citizenship process through military service. See interview on Fox News, "On the Record," August 3, 2010.

26. "Kyl: Illegals' Kids Shouldn't Be U.S. Citizens," last modified August 1, 2010, http://www.cbsnews.com/8301-3460_162-6733905.html.

27. He is, admittedly, considered a more marginal and conservative figure than either Kyl or Graham. Kyl and Graham, as explained above, are not so different than Gohmert in that they all question the validity of the 14th Amendment.

28. Julia Nissen, "New Attacks on Birthright Citizenship: 'Anchor Babies' and the 14th Amendment," States News Service, 2010.

29. Nicholas Riccardi, "Arizona Passes Stricter Border Rule; Police Would Gain Broad Powers to Investigate Anyone They Suspect Is an Illegal Immigrant," *Los Angeles Times*, April 13, 2010, 1.

30. Ross Douthat, "The Borders We Deserve," *The New York Times*, May 2, 2010, 25.

31. Agamben, *State of Exception*, 4.

32. Carl Hulse, "In Lawmaker's Outburst, a Rare Breach of Protocol," *The New York Times*, September 9, 2009, 26.

33. Raul Reyes, "Immigration Issue Is a Red Herring," *USA Today*, September 25 2009, 9A.

34. In the *Introduction to Kant's Anthropology*, Foucault not only mentions Kant's *Of the Different Human Races* but he connects it to his larger anthropological project. See Foucault, *Introduction to Kant's Anthropology*, trans. Roberto Nigro and Kate Briggs (Los Angeles: Semiotext(e), 2008), 32.

35. Arendt, *Human Condition*, 46.

36. It would be unfair to claim that Arendt favored these policies but it is also clear that she believed discrimination was indicative of and, therefore, acceptable within the private sphere. In "Reflections on Little Rock," she stated: "Discrimination is to society what equality is to the body politic. The question is not how to abolish discrimination but how to keep it in the social sphere." Quoted in Katherine T. Gines, "Hannah Arendt, Liberalism, and Racism: Controversies Concerning Violence, Segregation, and Education," *The Southern Journal* 47 (2009): 63–64.

37. Michel Foucault, *The Government of Self and Others: Lectures at the Collège de France 1982-1983*, trans. Graham Burchell (New York: Palgrave Macmillan, 2010), 98.

38. Foucault, *Government of Self and Others*, 103.

39. Foucault, *Government of Self and Others*, 100.

40. Athens gave birth to both Ion, at least in Euripides' version, and to Socrates— another famous speaker of truth. Foucault goes on to explain how Socrates represents a different form (and historical phase to that of Ion) of parresia as opposition to sophistry and rhetoric but this does not negate the fact that Socrates, too, is native to Athens. Socrates is perhaps the most famous of all Athenian citizens. He is widely remembered as one who never wanted to travel to foreign lands for leisure or even as a means to save his own life. And if the second form of parresia contrasts philosophy

with sophistry, this can also be seen as a privilege of the natural-born Athenian citizen over the stranger. Sophistry, unlike philosophy, is not thought to be an Athenian practice or art. Likewise, the sophists that Socrates defeats are outsiders or non-Athenians. See Plato, *Gorgias*, trans. R. Waterfield (New York: Oxford World Classics, 2008), Cf. 3. I suggest that these exchanges between Socrates and sophists and rhetoricians also show the opposition between Athenian citizen and foreigner. An analysis of Socrates underscores the idea that Athenians have a particular claim to truth-speaking.

41. He notes that there could be interest in a biological study on the hereditary elements of human capital but believes this is a project, largely, for science-fiction and not reality. See Foucault, *Birth of Biopolitics*, 227-228.

42. See Foucault, *Birth of Biopolitics*, 228-229.

43. Immanuel Kant, "Of the Different Human Races" in *The Idea of Race*, eds., Robert Bernasconi and Tommy L. Lott (New York: Hackett, 2000), 17.

44. Kant, *Different Human Races*, 19-20.

45. Foucault, *Birth of Biopolitics*, 230.

46. Immigrants are seen as incapable of investing in both the host country and homeland. Immigration opponents believe immigrants are a symptom of a people that do not value education enough to invest in it. See Julie Whitaker, "Mexican Deaths in the Arizona Desert: The Culpability of Migrants, Humanitarian Workers, Governments, and Business," *Journal of Business Ethics* 88 (2009): 365–76.

47. The problem of immigration is, of course, not solved if immigration was viewed as a self-investment. The immigrant-investor should also make us think about how mobility is linked to privileges. The poor do not have the economic means to migrate. See Peter Higgins, "Open Borders and the Right to Immigration," *Human Rights Review* 9 (2008): 525–35.

48. Audrey Macklin, "Freeing Migration from the State: Michael Trebilcock on Migration Policy," *The University of Toronto Law Journal* 60 (2010): 326.

49. The discourse of assimilation is also connected to liberal ideology. Liberal discourse casts the immigrant as an autonomous subject who is free to assimilate or not. Assimilation, however, is often much more complicated and challenges long-held Western notions about subjectivity. See Mariana Ortega, "Multiplicity, Inbetweeness, and the Question of Assimilation," *The Southern Journal of Philosophy* 46 (2008): 65–80.

50. Linda Martin Alcoff, *Visible Identities: Race, Gender, and the Self* (New York: Oxford University Press, 2006), 13–14.

51. Julie Whitaker, "Mexican Deaths in the Arizona Desert: The Culpability of Migrants, Humanitarian Workers, Governments, and Business," *Journal of Business Ethics* 88 (2009): 371–72.

TWO

The Problem of Immigration in the United States

Using Foucault's work on biopolitics to shed light on immigration policies may seem to be a strange fit since he did not produce a study on
immigration. However, there are similarities between his studies on the
history of sexuality and the history of immigration in the United States. I
will focus here on problems surrounding U.S. immigration as they raise
similar philosophical and political issues as sexuality in three main ways.
1) His examination of sexuality helped him to trace the changing attitudes toward sexuality. Varying sexual norms within Western culture
revealed what was thought to be of particular danger to society. Attitudes towards immigration and particular immigrants, too, have
changed in the course of U.S. history. 2) Because they affect the population's constitution, immigration and sexuality arouse fears over racial
congruity. And anxieties about homogeneity, in both cases, manifest
themselves explicitly in policies. Yet, modern policy makers work to cover over such concerns. 3) Among the most acceptable motives to control
immigration or sexuality is the notion that society must be defended.
Foucault famously analyzed various ways the state used sexuality to regulate the health of individuals. Likewise, the discourse surrounding immigration increasingly focuses on the impact individual immigrants can
potentially have on the life and health of the state. 4) Discourse about
immigration takes many forms while maintaining a connection to the
nation's welfare. Concerns about immigration, as with sexuality, lead to
greater controls.

Like the problem of sexuality, the problem of immigration has
changed over the course of U.S. history. Foucault's historico-philosophi-
cal analysis of sexuality shows that sexuality has been a constant problem
for the West. The ways in which the problem of sexuality was articulated

throughout Western history, however, reveal points of tension within culture and society. In different eras, concerns surrounding sexuality were highlighted as dangers to the optimal functioning of society. He shows, for instance, that Ancient Greek readings of male-male sexual practices had nothing to do with homophobia.[1] These sexual practices were a problem because they were connected to the management of the nation-state. Sexuality, Foucault argued, was a forum for men with political power to cultivate virtue and temperance.[2] Foucault analyzes contemporary attitudes toward sexuality because they relay, in similar fashion, the ways power operates in modern states. Because sexual discourse helps to produce social conventions, it contributes to the greater conversation about how citizens can best aid the prosperity and growth of the nation. Regulating sexuality helps to reveal the creation of norms within modern society.

The problem surrounding immigration has also changed throughout the history of the Western society. What is now believed to be the predominant problem of immigration—too many immigrants—is the inverse of the problem of times past. Early Americans wanted more immigrants to come to the country. Yet there is a biopolitical thread that joins these problems of immigration throughout time. The problem of immigration is intimately connected with the survival and prosperity of the nation because the immigrant can affect the life of the nation. Furthermore, immigrants bring to the fore the pressing problems of American life. The problem of immigration is connected to the livelihood of individual Americans and the American way of life, which includes the promotion of tolerance and acceptance of others and the representation of Western freedom and democracy. For these reasons, discourse about immigration—like sexuality—continues to grow. Biopolitics runs throughout immigration debates because immigration touches upon both the life of the individual and the life of the nation.

If Foucault's goal in analyzing biopolitics was to point out how modern governments controlled and regulated their populations, this project cannot be fully understood without understanding the influx of outsiders. Such regulations are not aimed only at the already included members of society. Those who would like to be a part of the community are also subject to these controls. For these reasons, many scholars have explored the intersections between sexuality and immigration. Eithne Luibhéid, Siobhan Somerville, and Aihwa Ong have shown that analyses of immigration policies help to reinforce Foucault's theories. They show that immigration studies operate at the physical and figurative borders of inclusion and exclusion. Luibhéid and Somerville, in particular, focus on the ways sexual identity is used to identify those who should be denied entrance or admitted into the country.

Immigration scholars, in other words, show that immigration policies help shape sexual norms. Immigration regulations not only work to weed out undesirable sexuality but help support sexual codes. Because immigration controls contribute to the creation of normal sexuality, they reinforce Foucault's idea that modern power is not negative but positive power. This form of modern power, he argues, operates less through restriction and more through production. Increased discourse about particularly important problems (sexuality and immigration) is another sign of productive modern power. The growing number of debates surrounding immigration and the volatility of them only further prove Foucault's point about modern power and nation-states. Laws restricting immigration do not put an end to the problem of immigration. Quite to the contrary, these measures only produce greater discussion about immigration and its impact on the American way of life.

My aim is neither to address every argument concerning immigration nor is it to prove the merits of one argument above all others. I will, instead, briefly address a variety of cases for and against immigration to show how immigration, an issue that has historically been wrought with problems, has become even more problematic as it touches upon ever-increasing facets of life. I will highlight examples that make their claims by appealing to the concern for the life of the individual and the life of the state. I believe this will illustrate that immigration works similarly to sexuality as a mechanism of power as it incites discourse, draws everyone's attention, and, thereby, intensifies the forces of power. Immigration is gaining more attention because many individuals view immigration as a public matter that has a direct effect on America and Americans. That is, many Americans believe that federal immigration policies will have consequences for their lives.

THE CHANGING PROBLEM OF IMMIGRATION

Although some have argued that immigration is America's oldest problem, the immigration problem, as we know it today, was not recognized as a problem until roughly the early 1900s. The United States had an immigration problem seemingly since its inception. During colonial America, the problem was that the country did not attract enough immigrants. Too few people were willing to come to sufficiently subdue the wilderness and assure the foothold of the white man.[3] The Europeans who claimed to first settle America did not have any particular anxiety against immigration as such.[4] This is not to say, however, that they had no ill feelings towards foreigners; they did. Their concerns about foreigners manifested themselves within the Alien Acts but no moves to enact such laws pertaining to immigration had yet come to pass. The era between America's break with England until roughly 1830 was recognized as the Period of Free Immigration.[5] No attempts were made to block or regulate the influx of new people to America for the simple fact that

America needed them to help develop the country. Simply put, American colonists needed new bodies and more workers. It was not until 1882 that fundamental changes were made to immigration policy.[6] Yet from 1830 to 1882, concern grew that the American people were shouldering the burden of poor, sick, insane, and criminal immigrants.[7] Despite the change in mind-set toward the incoming people, there were no laws passed until 1882. When the immigration law passed in 1882, the main objective of the law was to weed out undesirables rather than to stop immigrants from entering altogether. Distinguishing the undesirable from the desirable often meant deciding who could assimilate and who could not.

Immigrants fit into the "old" and "new" group. Those of the older group were seen as more quickly assimilating and those of the newer group were suspected of not being able to integrate as quickly or at all. Because the question of assimilation was central to the attitudes towards immigration, it is not surprising that there would be a push to put in place measures to test how well one could assimilate. This regulation took shape in the form of the literacy test of 1917. The literacy test worked in two ways. It helped to limit the sheer number of immigrants to the U.S. Many immigrants who could have entered before found a new obstacle. Requiring a literacy test also helped to determine the quality of immigrants who would enter the country after 1917. Those with an education clearly had an advantage over those without proper schooling.[8] As the United States began to put immigration regulations in place, policies began to reflect yet another dimension: racial concerns.

IMMIGRATION AND RACE

Discussions surrounding immigration emphasized race and racial affiliations for the first time. Where assimilation took the form of the literacy test in 1917, assimilation was put into question in terms of race starting in 1924. The racial make-up of America would determine how many and which immigrants could enter the country. A quota system was developed to ensure racial homogeneity. The allowance of two percent of the number of one group of bona fide American citizens would be admitted into the United States.[9]

In order to gain a fuller picture of U.S. immigration laws, we must take into account the impact of the First World War. Because the European elite, the most desired immigrants, had not chosen to immigrate to the United States despite the new awareness that America was a much more peaceful and attractive place to live than many parts of war-ravaged Europe, U.S. immigration legislation seemed to be all the more necessary. Americans feared that the onslaught of new, non-Northern European immigrants who sought to leave behind European slums and ghettoes would affect the nation negatively. The United States could be over-run with the diseased, the decrepit, the mentally unstable, and hopelessly disabled that felt the brunt of war-ravaged Europe.

While Americans were desperate to find a way to restrict the flow of immigrants after this tumultuous time, European governments took advantage of the nascent immigration policy in America. Without firm immigration regulations, emigration of war-struck populations meant a lesser burden for European nations. America served as a logical place to send or dump the undesirables of Europe.[10] Although the United States was already moving towards regulations of foreigners, the war sped up the process. The war also helped to articulate a focus on welcoming immigrants who shared particular European heritage rather than restricting those from other lands.[11] Such recruitment efforts still worked to reduce the numbers of immigrants. Qualitative tests, in this case, lessened the quantity of immigrants. The addition of the literacy test to immigration regulations in 1917 also helped to ease the concern that those coming into the United States would not bring a burden to those who had emigrated earlier. Policy makers justified limiting undesirable immigrants because they could hinder the future prosperity of the nation. Crafting a more selective policy for legal immigration resulted in fewer immigrants.

POWERS OF REGULATIONS

The fact that Alien Acts were being legislated while there were no immigration laws until around 1830 spoke to the problem of immigration in the United States. This law shows that more attention should be paid to the parameters for legal immigration because they signal when immigration has become a sufficient problem for the state. Although illegal immigration garners greater attention from the general public and even academic circles, an analysis of the laws surrounding legal immigration can shed light on the ways state power mobilizes efforts to define who is worthy, productive, and desirable.

Mary M. Kritz argues that the best illustration of how policy shapes our understanding of migrants is illegal immigrants. If movement of populations was not recognized and tracked through governmental regulations, she argues that there would be no distinction between international and internal migration. Both would be seen as simply moving populations. Moreover, the concept of illegal immigration would not exist.[12] She believes that determining the parameters for certain categories of population movement is key for understanding the identification of illegal immigrants.

Kritz points to the connection between tracking illegal immigrants and the advent of policies that track the restrictions around population movement. Although the state attempts to identify all who are within the country (resident, naturalized citizen, visitor, etc.), she argues that it is the illegal immigrant who garners the most attention. The name already suggests a transgression of the law. The increasingly suspicious and negative attitude towards the illegal immigrant is triggered by the definition. By this logic, rules and regulations better define the illegal immigrant who disobeys them. Because immigration laws work to identify illegal immigrants, the creation of such laws also produces a greater number of illegal immigrants.[13] As governments attempt to restrict the level of foreigners allowed to enter their nations, policies tend to proliferate. Policies function as a way to refine understandings of the desirable or undesirable and permitted or prohibited. Once new categories of illegal statuses are created, there will be more people who will fit that category even if they had once had a different, more favorable position within the system. In other words, efforts to regulate and control immigrants do not rid the United States of immigration problems. In some cases, it can contribute to the creation of more problems. Immigration regulations beget even more governmental controls and designations. The state further shapes the identity and worth of the individual. As Milchman and Rosenberg show through their reading of Foucault, problematizations and crises are an intimately connected to mechanisms of bio-power. States will have greater reach into the life of the individual since the immigration problem and crisis has been identified.

An examination of the immigration laws has shown that there have been attempts to regulate and control immigration problems but this has not resolved any issues. This suggests that laws surrounding immigration are not really directed towards curbing illegal immigration or tempering anxieties about incoming immigrants. If anything, the discourse on immigration has increased and become even more heated. I suggest, instead, that immigration regulations work to set the parameters of what constitutes acceptable behavior and practices for legal immigrants and residents alike. The powers of regulations in modern society, according to Foucault, is not seen in its ability to restrict but rather to generate more attention and involve more individuals. This helps to assure that everybody will be touched by power. While immigration laws may explicitly address the behavior and condition of immigrants, they also send a message to those who enter the country legally and those already identified as citizens. If the justification of immigration laws stems from the desire to protect the state, any individual—legal or not—is implicated by such determinations of unproductive behavior or unhealthy constitutions. Heightening awareness of unacceptable behavior may, indeed, do more to reinforce norms for the greater population than to stem the tide of illegal immigrants.

PROTECTING THE AMERICAN WAY(S) OF LIFE

A surreptitious but sure way to establish codes of conduct is to grow the concern surrounding immigration by connecting it to a wider variety of issues. The more the people become aware of immigration problems, the more they will become aware of what standards the state finds acceptable for defining the good citizen. While one argument may not interest certain people, continued debate over immigration will likely spawn more and more debates that will eventually reach the interests of everyone.

Although some debates are more volatile than others, there is an overlap between the discussions about who and why someone should or should not be able to immigrate to the United States. I will illustrate that many of the discussions are effective in gaining public support because they frame immigration within the context of the either the nation's welfare or the well-being of the members of the state. While I will eventually turn to the more high-profile cases that include threats of terror, I will first examine the debate that addresses whether or not there is an obligation to accept outsiders. What I hope to show in this case is that despite the difference in opinion—if there is or is not an obligation to allow immigrants entrance into the country—the attempts to justify positions on immigration turn on the defense of the nation. Those who seek to defend against attacking forces and those seeking to defend American ideology both use this theme.

Despite concerns over immigration, there are certain reasons for immigrating that tend to draw more support and sympathy than others. One of them is the right to immigrate on the basis of family reunification.[14] Of course, some object to this stipulation because they believe that every person who joins the community dilutes the rights of those who are already citizens. Those who want to become permanent residents, according to detractors, weaken the American system. Particular opponents may focus solely on pecuniary matters[15] but I will explore, for the moment, arguments proposed by those like Stephen Kershnar. He suggests, "it would be strange for a person to be able to bind his fellow citizens by his family decision, action, or relation itself."[16] It seems that society is always at stake. Even though one citizen has made connections with someone outside the community, this does not require that all other citizens do the same. By allowing the immigrant to enter the country, he suggests that there is a concession that members of the community who have not chosen to associate with the individual in question are obliged to do so. This case, then, like many others highlights the dangers to the community when outsiders enter. He argues that:

> To the extent that immigration threatens to change the nature of these institutions without the consent of the current members, it would follow that such immigration threatens to harm the citizens of the country

> by changing the character of the institutions to which the current citi-
> zens have consented. And this threat of harm justifies, other things
> being equal, preventing other persons from occupying a position
> where they could change the institutions in question.[17]

Because immigrants have the potential to disrupt and, therefore, jeopardize the workings of the state, he believes that immigrants should be scrutinized despite any familial ties. The familial relations bind the non-citi-
zen to *a* citizen but not to all U.S. citizens.

Allowing someone to enter the country to reunite with a family mem-
ber could potentially affect negatively the entire community and not just
the citizen who considers him family. The idea is that the individual has
the ability to jeopardize the community but this argument is not altogether new. Kershnar's call to protect political institutions and the nation
from the influence of outsiders echoes those made by Walter F. George.
George, a Democratic senator from Georgia in 1952, also sought to defend the nation by urging Americans to keep control over their immigration policies and not become swayed by those who are not citizens. Although he stops short of saying that allowing people outside the nation to
determine immigration policies is un-American, he alludes to the idea of
the dissolution of the nation if Americans succumb to the pressure of
outsiders by consenting to a more lax immigration policy.[18] In this particular case, George defends the merits of the Immigration Act of 1924 by
stating that, "The real basic purpose of the immigration act which we
finally enacted in 1924 was to preserve something of homogeneity of the
American people. . . . "[19] For both Kershnar and George, they make their
case by evoking the need to protect the nation's identity and (racial)
cohesion.

Proponents of more open immigration policies, however, also believe
that they are guardians of American identity. For them, anti-immigration
policies are a sign of un-American-ness. They believe, in contrast to
George and Kershnar, that granting citizenship rights on the basis of
family ties is a means to protect the American community.[20] Those who
seek to justify family reunification appeal to the need to uphold
American institutions and values in much the same way as those who
seek to restrict immigration to America. Because Americans tout themselves as defenders of human rights, some argue that family reunification
is a part of civil liberties.[21] Indeed, this is the case made by Joseph H.
Carens. He makes the case that no one should have to choose between
home and family. Carens argues that family life is such an important
aspect to many people that forcing a choice between the two is unfair.[22] If
every American shall have the right to pursue happiness, both home and
family are necessary for happiness. Forcing someone to pick either home
or family would be a violation of that precept and, therefore, un-
American.

These discourses show not only the divergent paths of power available when the life of the individual is joined to the life of the state but also the possibility of unlikely allies joining forces to support particular immigration laws. It might seem obvious that those who are not in favor of family reunification also seem to be suspicious of more open immigration policies. Likewise, one might assume that those who believe that there should be family reunification rights are the same as those who are sympathetic to fewer restrictions for immigrants. But these are not the only sides of the debate; the discussion on immigration illustrates how those with seemingly distant motives can come to support similar positions.

Not everyone who objects to family reunification policies is against more open immigration policies. Some, who support immigration rights, argue that the family reunification formula for obtaining citizenship is biased against groups that do not have a long-standing history with America. Although they fight for less restrictive immigration policies, they do not promote the use of the right to family reunification.

> Supporters of a first-come, first-served application process believe family reunification discriminates against immigrants from countries with few familial and historical connections to the United States. In its place, they suggest that the government process visa applications as they are received. Because family reunification relies on blood ties, argues Peter Salins, a senior fellow at the Manhattan Institute, it fails to "validate the concept of individual ambition" central to American society.[23]

Not only do the supporters of a "first-come, first-served" philosophy object to the policy on the grounds of tacit racism but they also believe it should be rejected because it does not fit within American ideology. They infer that family reunification discriminates against those who have demonstrated that they are willing to work for their aspirations; this is not the American way. These challengers charge that family reunification policies actually work to produce the same effect that Senator George had proposed. Family reunification ensures that immigrants of certain backgrounds and heritage will be privileged and furthers ethnic homogeneity. According to George, the purpose of the Immigration Act of 1924 is ". . . to preserve something of the homogeneity of the American people, something of the character of the men who loved self-government, who understood it, and who had some concept of it."[24] Salins, however, wants to preserve what he thinks is integral to American culture—self-determination and enterprise. These are, of course, characteristic of the autonomous and enterprising neoliberal subject, which is at the center of Foucault's biopolitics.

IMMIGRANTS AND ECONOMICS

Salins is only one of many like him who seeks to view immigration policies through the lens of a cost/benefit analysis for the nation. Those who
couch immigration in economic terms also work to connect their position
to the nation's health and prosperity. [25] There are those who oppose strict
immigration laws because they believe that immigrants deplete
American funds for other uses. In contrast, there are those who believe
that immigrants are a much needed labor force. They believe that strict
immigration policies would stunt the economy. Therefore, they do not
believe greater immigration controls would benefit the nation.

The first argument takes up the position that has continued to gain
social currency. Yet this is not a new way of understanding the immigration problem; this theory has existed since the first major federal regulations attempted to address the problem of foreigners. They claim that
allowing immigrants to partake in programs which they did not help
build socially or financially would be irresponsible to the current citizens
of the United States. Immigrants, therefore, must not be able to enter the
country too easily or it will be Americans who will eventually have to
pay the price through social programs and public aid. Stockwell notes
that "[t]he delinquent and defective strains thus introduced into the
country are believed to have been the genesis of that wonderful system of
public institutions which today require one-quarter of our total taxes—
direct and indirect—for their support." [26] While Stockwell draws a connection between immigrants and the creation of social services in an attempt to convince others that Americans have paid the price for incoming
immigrants, Kershnar, who is also in favor of limiting immigrants, does
not disparage the availability of social services to make his point. He
suggests that social services should only be available for those who deserve them—citizens. Kershnar, unlike Stockwell, believes that social services are valuable but immigrants should not be able to take advantage of
them. Kershnar, nonetheless, does echo Stockwell's sentiment.

> Immigration would result in a dilution of each citizen's portion of this
> public property. And if every poor U.S. has a legitimate claim to certain
> benefits, e.g. Medicaid, Supplemental Social Security, or educational
> support for her children, immigration of relatively poor persons will at
> least in the short term require a redistribution of the wealth of current
> U.S. citizens. [27]

Because immigrants at the very least put a strain on economic aid programs, they pose a strain on the system and on Americans.

George Borjas takes a bit more cautious approach in his interpretation
of the effect of immigration. He notes that countries that have had a large
influx of immigrants have yet to process the data and understand the
impact on their communities. However, he does believe it is reasonable to

conclude that immigrants may have played a part in the decline of earnings for low-skilled native workers.[28] Nonetheless, his argument is like the others because he seems most interested in the ways immigrants help or hinder the nation and its citizens. By pitting the welfare of immigrants against poor citizens in particular, he contributes to arguments that seek to protect limited national resources. Immigrants, simply put, take funds that could be used to support those already living in America. This feeds into the popular notion that allowing more immigrants to enter America will jeopardize the livelihood of Americans, especially those who do not have a high level of education. Thus, employing immigrants takes away from the ability of citizens to support themselves and their families.

Immigrants are, therefore, portrayed as a direct threat to the livelihood and indirectly to the lives of Americans. Despite the concession by some that immigrants want to live and work in America because there are little to no opportunities in that person's homeland, this does little to diminish anxieties that Americans, too, will suffer because of immigrants who are willing to work for poorer working conditions and compensation. Immigrants are a threat because they will take what little job opportunities remain in the United States. This argument bridges the gap between low levels of job employment and life. And the immigrant is positioned as the catalyst for poor job prospects and diminishing wages.

In response to this familiar position, there are those like Senator Herbert Lehman who argued that it is a "... myth that immigration is a burden on the national economy and that immigrants threaten the jobs and wage levels of American workers."[29] He claimed that this reaction to incoming immigrants is unfounded. Although he believes that there must be immigration restrictions, he thinks it would be a mistake to stop the flow of immigration especially on the grounds that it would improve the quality of living in America. Senator Lehman argued that the greatest periods of economic growth directly followed large tides of immigration. He adds that the U.S. economy has successfully absorbed the waves of immigrants who have arrived on its shores.[30] He seems to suggest that continued immigration not only helps the continued prosperity of the United States but also believes that if there were a moratorium on immigration, the American standard of living would decline. His conclusion seems clear. It would not only be unnecessary to place more severe restrictions on immigration policies but it would be a detriment to the United States.

Senator Lehman's position is not one of a bygone era. Michael Bloomberg, New York City mayor, has publicly stated that the national and New York City economies would collapse if the purported eleven million immigrants were forced to leave America.[31] In order for businesses, let alone the country, to function, there must be people who are willing to occupy certain posts and fill particular jobs. Not all of these jobs are glamorous or high paying. Most businesses and industries have positions that are seen as undesirable for one reason or another. While it may be difficult to entice those who are already established in America to take these jobs, it is much less difficult to find immigrants to do the work under less than favorable conditions.[32] Immigrants are a great pool of resources.[33] Like arguments for restricting immigration, arguments encouraging immigration on economic grounds are not altogether new. We can trace this philosophy all the way back to the first European settlers in America, who also wanted to encourage immigration when their growth depended upon it but felt differently when conditions changed. While this argument concentrates on the benefits that immigrants benefit the U.S. economy, those who endorse this position also seem to believe that immigrants profit from being able to enter the country. They argue that allowing immigrants to come to America is good for both the economy and the immigrants.

This leads to yet another interpretation of U.S. immigration laws that turn more on the conditions provided for immigrant workers. There are those who oppose immigration policies precisely because they believe present regulations exploit the immigrant in order to grow the economy. For them, the main goal of such immigration reform should be to ensure that immigrant laborers would be able to voice their demands. They focus on the welfare of the immigrant rather than the nation's economic life. Yet, this position is still grounded in the idea that immigration laws reflect the growth and decline of the economy. When there is a need for low-wage workers, immigration restrictions are relaxed. When these conditions are altered, efforts to stop the flow of immigration begin.[34] Through research done in conjunction with the Phillipine Women's Centre, G. Pratt notes that the United States has a long history of drawing labor from other parts of the world when it suits economic and social conditions. Americans recognized that they would not be able to do everything on their own; they needed more help from others.

The economic view of immigration, however, is sometimes at odds with the mythology of America as moral beacon for the world. Because Americans identify their way of life with fairness and the ability to succeed through hard work, they believe that the nation is in serious trouble if Americans continue to sacrifice their moral values for economic gain.[35] In order to protect the state, those defending this core American ideal need to protect against the maltreatment of immigrants. If they are not successful, the nation will lose its integrity and fall into decline. What is at stake for both, though their narrative diverges, is the life of the country.

IMMIGRATION AND TERRORISM

Concerns about the way immigrants can affect the life of the nation are perhaps most clearly expressed by those who desire to reduce the number of immigrants in the hopes of reducing terrorist acts. While there has always, to some extent, been a suspicious attitude towards immigrants, the question of immigration has intensified since the events of September 11, 2001.[36] In this particular case, there are those who believe that immigration should be severely restricted or completely halted, if possible, in order to prevent further attacks and loss of American life.

Many Americans believe that one of the surest ways to prevent another terrorist attack is to put strict regulations on who can come to America. This is the position of the executive director of the Center for Immigration Studies, Mark Krikorian. Protecting the nation means finding a way to prevent those who intend to do harm to the American people and the government. If no new immigrants were allowed into U.S. territory, then terrorists would have fewer chances to do harm and threaten American lives. Put in this context, immigration could be seen as a matter of life or death for the citizens. In order to protect the lives of Americans, stricter controls over immigrants need to be enacted and some even argue that immigration needs to halt completely.

Those who believe that immigration should be strongly curtailed often argue that it is a matter of national security. Since the terrorist attacks on September 11, 2001, immigration controls have been targeted as one of the primary ways to decrease the number of possible terrorists. The logic seems clear. Stricter immigration laws or the complete refusal of certain immigrants would result in fewer chances that terrorists have access to American soil. Because anti-immigrant sentiments are not exactly new phenomena, it may be easy to believe that many problems originate from immigrants and if America could limit or get rid of immigrants, the situation would become better.[37] If terrorists are not admitted into the nation, through loose immigration controls, then there is less danger to both national and individual security.

Of course, there are those who work to dismantle the connection between the immigrant and the terrorist. Despite the polarity of these arguments, they both make reference to American life. They argue that it is racism that spurs such anxieties and beliefs. Preserving the American way, for them, means upholding America's identity as a nation that has been accepting of immigrants. Unlike many European nations, the offshoots of those nations such as Canada, Australia, and the United States consider themselves countries of immigration.[38] James Ziglar, INS (Immigration and Naturalization Services) commissioner, warns against shutting out precisely those who have helped to make America great—immigrants.[39] To disallow immigrants the ability to enter the country would be to renounce a distinct part of American culture.

Cecilia Muñoz (National Council of La Raza) rejects the relationship between immigrants and terrorism by baldly connecting such fears to racism.[40] Those like Muñoz suggest that the culture of fear is such that it is tempting to blame all the problems facing the United States on those who have few resources to defend themselves. To combat the tendency to equate immigrants with terrorists, leaders of immigration rights organizations seek to publicize the ways immigrants positively impact American life. Muñoz believes that part of undoing the link that ties immigrants to terrorists in the minds of some Americans is to show that immigrants are an asset and are loyal to America.[41] If Americans could be convinced that immigrants are also concerned about the welfare of the nation, this would go a long way in combatting the association between immigrant and terrorist. In other words, if immigrants were portrayed as people who held that the preservation of life of the community was the highest good and worked toward that goal, then they would not face as much adversity or racism.

Although there are very few people who believe that U.S. immigration policies are satisfactory, some suggest that attempts to target terrorists through immigration regulations are misguided and ineffective. They claim that these policies do not work to exclude would-be terrorists but, rather, limit those who could contribute positively to American life. For instance, students are often the ones to suffer the consequences of stricter border regulations. Spencer Ante also cites the rejection of skilled workers as the wrong result of tighter controls.

>
> While no one doubts the need for more rigorous border controls now, there are critics who say the federal government is doing a poor job of distinguishing between potential terrorists and legitimate travelers. Students, for instance, are seeing their visa applications rejected in record numbers: The refusal rate hit 35 percent last year, up from the previous record of 34 percent in 2002 and the 20 percent rate in 1999. Plus, the immigrants with the most to offer the U.S. seem to be having the hardest time getting in: The number of workers with advanced degrees or exceptional skills who were admitted plummeted 65 percent last year, to 15,459. "We're slapping these people in the face," says National Academy of Engineering President William A. Wulf. "The long-term costs in goodwill will be enormous."[42]

Tying together two arguments concerning the life of the nation, he suggests that present immigration rules weed out those who could contribute to America's intellectual and economic growth. Far from harming the nation, these are exactly the people who should be admitted into the country because they can help the nation prosper.[43] It is not only the American economy that is at stake but also the identity of America. Past and present immigration laws seem to be working through a contradiction of sorts. Past policy makers tried to craft laws in order to attract skilled workers; present regulations work against this goal.

CONCLUSION

What is at stake is not only the life of the individual livelihood but of the social body. It is this connection between the individual and the larger community that expresses itself again and again in political discourse. Posing immigration within the context of biopolitics shows that the individual is poised, in myriad ways, to affect the life of the nation. In exploring these various opinions on immigration, I did not want to focus on what is the "right" or even better position but rather demonstrate that each opinion conveys how life and politics have become intermingled.

Still, the motivation and the discourses that are offered in support of or against continued immigration have a common theme. Each group claims to be working towards the best interest of the country and each group believes that the outcome of immigration policy greatly affects American lives. On the one hand, some believe that immigration has an impact on the broader economics of the United States. And, of course, many feel that if the general standard of living falls, this would affect the lives of the individual members of society. In this way, immigration connects the individual to the larger community. Immigration policy is so volatile precisely because it touches the ordinary American. Many, quite to the contrary, believe that such policies can have great influence on the functioning of their households. They endeavor to preserve the quality of their everyday lives. On the other hand, there are those who believe that a dramatic change in immigration policy would, in a sense, transform American identity and what America represents. They are fighting for the preservation of what American culture means to them. Some Americans still want to hold onto the mythology that Americans are an open and welcoming people. I also suggest that immigration allows for a greater sense of the connection between the life of the individual and the larger global community. Immigration exposes the relationship between one's life and the lives of not only those in one's immediate community but also of those in the international community. And with ever-increasing globalization, there is no sense that the problems surrounding immigration are going to disappear any time soon.

According to Foucault's theory of biopolitics, immigration will continue to be a problem for the nation as long as the life of the individual and the life of the society are intertwined. Foucault describes sexuality as ". . . becoming the theme of political operations, economic interventions (through incitements to or curbs on procreation), and ideological campaigns for raising standards of morality and responsibility: it was put forward as an index of a society's strength, revealing of both its political energy and its biological vigor."[44] I argued that immigration has shown that it has access to many of the same themes that have raised awareness around sexuality. Although I do not suggest that immigration will replace Westerners' preoccupation with sexuality, it does seem that the attention surrounding immigration problems rivals that of sexuality in modern society.

NOTES

1. David M. Halperin argues that Ancient Greek sexuality cannot be adequately understood through the heterosexual/homosexual divide. See Halperin, David. M., *One Hundred Years of Homosexuality: And Other Essays on Greek Love* (New York: Routledge, 1989).

2. See Michel Foucault, *History of Sexuality, Vol. 2: The Use of Pleasure*, trans. Robert Hurley (New York: Vintage Books, 1990).

3. Alcott W. Stockwell, "Our Oldest National Problem," *The American Journal of Sociology* 32 (1927): 743.

4. Of course, it must be noted that there were other peoples inhabiting the North American continent before the white settlers came.

5. Although Henry Pratt Fairchild argues that 1830 marks the beginning of another attitude towards immigration, others such as Alcott Stockwell, who worked for the United States Immigration Service in Boston, set the date at 1820. Fairchild is aware of the discrepancy of a decade but believes that the year 1820 was given prominence purely from a statistical point of view. He argues that it was until 1830 that there was pressure to put forth measures to control immigration. Indeed, Stockwell saw that there was significance in the fact that immigrants were first being counted in 1820. (Stockwell, "Our Oldest National Problem," 743) Both Stockwell and Fairchild agree, however, that there were two distinct attitudes towards immigration between 1776 and 1882. One lasted from the 1776 to 1820 or 1830; this was the time when immigration was only a problem insofar as America had need for more immigrants. The second era lasted between 1820 or 1830 to 1882. During this time period, more attention was starting to be paid to who entered the country. See Henry Pratt Fairchild, "The Immigration Law of 1924," *The Quarterly Journal of Economics* 38 (1924): 654.

6. Stockwell, "Our Oldest National Problem," 743.

7. Fairchild, "Immigration Law of 1924," 564.

8. Fairchild, "Immigration Law of 1924," 655–56.

9. Fairchild, "Immigration Law of 1924," 659-660.

10. Stockwell, "Our Oldest National Problem," 745.

11. Fairchild, "Immigration Law of 1924," 657.

12. Mary M. Kritz, "International Migration Policies: Conceptual Problems," *International Migration Review* 21 (1987): 957.

13. Kritz's own work draws from Denis Maillat. See Denis Maillat, *The Politics of Migration Policies* (New York: Center for Migration Studies, 1979).

14. The other example to which most Americans are sympathetic is that of refugees. But this is also a complicated issue and not without debate. Stepen Kershnar claims that it is only considered a right if the refugee is in such a state because the United States had caused her nation to be incapable of supporting citizens. See Stephen Kershnar, "There's No Moral Right to Immigrate to the United States," *Public Affairs Quarterly* 14 (2000): 155.

15. James Hudson claims that the acceptance of immigrants infringes upon property rights in collective property as well as draining communal wealth by causing a redistribution of wealth. See James Hudson, "The Ethics of Immigration Restriction," *Social Theory and Practice* 19 (1984): 219.

16. Kershnar, "No Moral Right," 154.

17. Kershnar, "No Moral Right," 143.

18. Walter F. George, "Should Basic Changes Be Made in U.S. Immigration Policy?," *Congressional Digest* 35 (1956): 13.

19. George, "Basic Changes," 14.

20. Joseph H. Carens notes that, even if one believes in the right of family reunification as he does, there are further problems that develop. In particular, he notes that the term "family" can also pose another problem for immigration policies. While some might consider only certain relationships as familial, others might have a different definition of what constitutes a family. Again, this shows that immigration is a topic that is similar and even collides with sexuality as it produces more and more discourse around emerging questions. As another note, I recognize that this is a good opportunity to discuss the correlation between immigration and sexuality. However, since I am concerned about relaying the ways family reunification, immigration restrictions, and the American way of life can be grouped to support various positions that crisscross and intermingle, I will not be able to address the intersection of sexuality and immigration here. See Joseph Carens, "Who Should Get in? The Ethics of Immigration Admissions," *Ethics and International Affairs* 17 (2003): 95–110.

21. See Julie Quiroz-Martinez, "Immigrants Hit the Road for Civil Rights," *The Nation*, October 9, 2003, 14.

22. Carens, "Who Should Get in?," 97.

23. Nick Gillespie, "Beyond the Family Way," *Reason* 26 (1994): 44.

24. George, "Basic Changes," 14.

25. Although I will turn my attention to the ways immigration and economics intertwine in the next chapter, I wanted to give a brief history of the ways economic arguments are used to support or oppose greater immigration. While I touch upon how some use economic analysis to argue for and against the need of Mexican immigrants here, I will go into further detail in chapter 3.

26. Stockwell, "Our Oldest National Problem," 746.

27. Kershnar, "No Moral Right," 145.

28. Although Borjas makes this claim, he also adds that there is only a weak correlation between the presence of immigrants and the earnings of the native worker. See George J. Borjas, "The Economics of Immigration," *Journal of Economic Literature* 32 (1994): 1713.

29. The New York Democrat gave this testimony in an effort to speak out against the McCarran-Walter Act. The act was an attempt to revise the National Origins Quota System. Though Lehman believed there were some improvements made in the McCarran-Walter Act, he believed it still made use of prejudices and was unwilling to support it. See Herbert Lehman, "Should Basic Changes Be Made?," *Congressional Digest* 35 (1956): 12.

30. George, "Basic Changes," 16.

31. David Seifman, "McCain Boosts Illegals," *New York Post*, July 25, 2006, 2.

32. Of course, there are many issues concerning low-wage jobs and that the pay is only one among many things that makes certain jobs unattractive.

33. Vicente Fox, former Mexican president, made remarks defending Mexican immigration to America on the basis that they fill positions that no one wants. See Vicente Fox, "Tough-But-Fair Rules for Tomorrow's Legal Immigrants," *Business Week*, July 18, 2005, 96.

34. Pratt was originally cited by Alison Mountz et al., "Lives in Limbo: Temporary Protected Status and Immigrant Identities," *Global Networks* 2 (2002): 304. See also Geraldine Pratt, "Inscribing Domestic Work on Filipina Bodies," in *Places through the Body*, eds. Heidi Nast and Steve Pile (London: Routledge, 1998), 304.

35. Robert Wunthrow, *Poor Richard's Principle: Recovering the American Dream through the Moral Dimension of Work, Business, and Money* (New Jersey: Princeton University Press, 1996).

36. I will return to the intersection of terror and immigration in chapter 4 but I will focus on the ways religion and science become factors for determining would-be terrorists.

37. Molly Ivins, "More Immigrant-Bashing on the Way," *The Buffalo News*, July 7, 2006, A7.

38. Carens, "Who Should Get in?," 96.

39. Mark Krikorian, "Get Tight," *National Review*, March 25, 2002, 40–41.

40. Krikorian, "Get Tight," 40–41.

41. She is quoted as challenging Pat Buchanan on CNN's *Crossfire* by asking him not to question the loyalty of immigrants. See "In the Media," *Hispanic* 11 (1998):14.

42. Spencer Ante, "Keeping Out the Wrong People," *Business Week*, October 4, 2004, 92.

43. Krikorian responds by stating that the cutback in student visas is necessary because this will help unburden the Immigration and Naturalization Services (INS) bureau. Since the INS has come under the umbrella of the Department of Homeland Security, the work of wading through the sea of applications is especially difficult. He argues that limiting student visas would alleviate part of the problem and help the Department of Homeland Security be able to ferret out the would-be terrorists more effectively. See Krikorian, "Get Tight," 40–41.

44. Michel Foucault, *The History of Sexuality: An Introduction*, trans. Alan Sheridan (New York: Vintage Books, 1990), 146.

THREE

State Racism and Neoliberal Immigration Policies

Anxieties about immigration, particularly those rooted in economics, are not new. That many politicians seem to use this line of attack as a way to divert the issue away from charges of racism shows a shift in tactic from previous legislators. Policies such as the quota system did little to hide concerns over racial cohesion. Politicians who couch their positions on immigration in economic language, however, are rarely so bold as to admit that they mean to block entry to people of color. They argue instead that immigrants pose too great a cost for the country. Yet their arguments do little to quell the notion that immigration policies are laced with racism. Is it possible, then, that hiding such racist undertones is not the real goal? Perhaps it is easy to connect the economics to issues of traditional racism because this link helps promote neoliberal policies. In this chapter, I will show the connection between neoliberalism and racism through the debate over Mexican[1] immigrants. I further suggest that traditional racist language can help support neoliberal policies by diverting attention away from modern forms of racism, which reaches beyond people of color.

Although proponents of neoliberalism insist that U.S. policies concerning Mexican immigration are not racist, critics might see that these regulations systematize discrimination against people of color. Perhaps even more damning, Foucauldian skeptics of neoliberal governance claim that this philosophy leads to a greater, more insidious form of racism. This modern form of racism encompasses more than people of color. Neoliberalism, as Foucault contends, leads to the birth of biopolitics because the pursuit of national security allows the state to treat larger and larger portions of the population as if they were disposable. Anyone who seeks or is in need of federal aid or services is seen as a threat to the

61

nation's life and future prosperity. Resources must be devoted to sustaining the life of the nation above all else.

That the state should make use of Mexican migrant labor and let them die if they require assistance—medical or otherwise—is apparently not so offensive to society at large. Indeed, many politicians campaign on a platform that paints migrant workers as leeches to the system.[2] Their handiest tool for deflecting attacks of racism is often neoliberal philosophy. Yet their attempts to cover over racist sentiments in their anti-immigration stances are sometimes so thinly veiled that it seems as if concealing a prejudice against people of color is hardly the goal at all.[3] Is it possible that these politicians and proponents of neoliberalism secretly acknowledge that they benefit if neoliberal policies are tied to discrimination against people of color? If more attention were drawn, à la Foucauldian critics of neoliberalism, to the ever-growing population that has become disposable in the face of shrinking public safety nets, there might be more public outrage from dominant society. Policies that seem to target the historically disadvantaged would likely meet less resistance, unfortunately, than ones that openly declare that anyone—regardless of color or relative privilege in society—can be deemed superfluous as resources are increasingly diverted towards securing the life of the nation. In order for neoliberal ideology to be accepted, proponents of this worldview would do well to conceal how the biopolitical version of racism works within their policies. Charges of conventional racism can act not as an attack against but as a shield for neoliberal policies. Allowing the debate to be framed around more traditional forms of racism could help hide the workings of modern racism within neoliberal governing strategies.

What needs to be blocked from entering the public consciousness is the idea that many "true" Americans will be in the same position as immigrants, and sooner than they think. Opponents of immigration often use neoliberal discourse, which highlights the necessity of securing the state against economic disruptions and imbalances, to argue for the regulation and/or restriction of immigration. The real trouble caused by immigrants, however, is that they serve as a constant reminder of what is in store for a large segment of the U.S. population. Emergency room visits by immigrants, and not necessarily their work within the country, are considered a problem for proponents of neoliberalism because they are reminders that the U.S. economy depends upon the exploitation of an increasing amount of people. What is problematic about the neediness of immigrants is that it points to the growing number of people, citizens or otherwise, that the U.S. economy will not be able to support. The more immigrants' needs are made visible, the more likely Americans will recognize that resources will not be available for them either. If, conversely, immigrants' needs are made invisible, there is a chance that "regular" Americans will not become aware of their passage from the desirable to disposable population. The underserved provide a window into the possible future of the vast majority of Americans who are themselves struggling to find health coverage and other support services. Embedding traditional racist sentiments within political rhetoric could work to focus attention away from the failings of the neoliberal system and the biopolitics of disposability.

NEOLIBERALIM AND BIOPOLITICS

To trace how neoliberalism gives birth to biopolitics,[4] Foucault contrasts German ordoliberalism with the laissez-faire theory of Adam Smith's classical liberalism. Unlike their predecessors, ordoliberals do not subscribe to a "naïve naturalism" of the markets. Liberals believe that the market should be supervised by the state while neoliberals propose that the market should supervise the state. According to classical liberalism, the market can function naturally and of its own accord. The role of the state is to supervise the market and interfere as little as possible so that the market can follow its natural ebb and flow. Since ordoliberals do not subscribe to "naïve naturalism," they believe that the government has a substantial role to play. Neoliberals believe it is not enough to limit the state from intervening in the market. They suggest that that which is good and right about the market (competition) does not come about naturally. Competition, instead, is produced when inequalities between individuals are properly balanced through the art of government. The governing strategy that can best regulate competition should be backed. Because the market is seen as the organizing principle of the state, government interventions on behalf of the market are justified. Once the people accept the idea that the state should be structured around the economy, they also accept—perhaps unwittingly—that everything that could hinder the economy from operating at its optimal level must be identified and controlled. Governmental functions and regulations, therefore, can stretch far and wide into the lives of individuals.

While neoliberal ideology has become synonymous with fewer governmental controls and greater individual freedom, neoliberalism—according to Foucault—allows for an increase in governmental controls.[5] Neoliberal economics is lauded in popular culture because it has become synonymous with the freedom of the individual, who is no longer under the thumb of sovereign powers. Common individuals are seen as the epicenter of the market and, therefore, have a greater sense of freedom through neoliberal economics. "Neoliberalism, as we have seen, is devoted to the regulation of the market, understood as free competition of enterprises and differences, of heterogeneities supported by the proliferation of the sense of freedom. . ."[6] The popularity of such an economic philosophy is propagated on the idea of greater freedom and minimal governmental intrusion. If neoliberal policies work for the market, why can't they work for other areas of social governance? A heightened focus on the economy makes the birth of biopolitics possible because all aspects of life can be manipulated in the efforts to ensure market growth.

Modern societies, as Foucault has shown, create policies and programs to regulate sexual deviants, control the mentally ill, and quarantine criminals so that they do not pose too great of a cost for society. These attitudes, in turn, make it so that everyone must pay attention to and guard against abnormalities and unhealthy behavior in their own lives. If the individual does not guard against such deviations, she, too, could contribute to an economic downturn and eventual downfall of the state.[7] The relationship between the individual and the economy, then, seems to be misunderstood or misrepresented. It is not the individual who decides the course of the market. Rather, it is the national economy that regulates the lives of individuals—and creates the economic subject along the way. Neoliberalism promises to provide greater freedom but its supporters often fail to mention the increases in regulations that accompany this system. This seemingly contradictory logic is often hidden by the singular focus on ensuring the economic stability of the nation. Although the population at large is unaware of the growth in governmental regulations, the state can enact myriad programs to aid the market. After all, the government can only deliver economic growth if the population is organized and used to serve the market. Biopolitical controls, therefore, become more and more abundant.

Since we, in the modern West, are conditioned to think that the quality of our lives is interwoven with the health of the national economy, we become less aware or lose sight of the ways that the government regulates the population for the express purpose of growing the economy. Because the neoliberal art of governing means that all other areas of life must be brought in line with economics, biopolitical intervention is needed to synchronize the life of the individual with the life of the nation—even if these interventions go unnoticed. Life does not mimic the market; it must be analyzed in relation to it in order to optimize both the life of the nation and its population. As Brett Levinson notes, "[i]t is through the prism of the market form that we *know* the past and the present, and also try to foresee the future."[8] The market is credited with the power to decode the past and present and predict the future because it is the lens in which Westerners see life. Economic readings ground modern understanding of life because it is chosen as the privileged perspective. Even if the market does not naturally influence and control other areas of life, the belief in neoliberalism justifies moves to subvert all else to the economic motive. Levinson, following Foucault, suggests that interventions are made so that all noneconomic sites are structured like a market.[9] No aspect of life is out of reach of governmental intervention as long as it can be connected to the economic lifeline of the nation. Therefore, neoliberalism is not simply an economic strategy. It is also a governmental project that works to regulate the population through the promise of greater economic freedoms.

Philip Kretsedemas adds:

> In the most basic of terms, neoliberalism can be equated with a free market agenda that is oriented toward the expansion of trade and minimal regulation of private corporations (this policy agenda is sometimes referred to as "neoconservativism" in U.S. policy discourse). According to many Foucauldian scholars, however, neoliberalism is not merely an economic platform that weakens government controls, but comprises an array of strategies and techniques that are used to actively create new kinds of political and economic subjects. This process does not merely "shrink the state"; it transforms the organizational form of the state, limiting its authority in some ways and radically expanding its authority in other ways. [10]

Neoliberal philosophy provides more than an economic platform that preaches deregulation of the market. It also transforms our conception of the modern subject. Because the successes and failures of the nation and modern society are supposedly recorded by market fluctuations, "good" citizens are those who can secure the economic future for themselves and the nation.

Conversely, those who are viewed as dependent are deemed disposable. Because economics has come to dominate the way we moderns understand the world, modern states and its citizens begin to see the population, at large, and individual subjects through the prism of economic worth. More than anything else, they are economic subjects. Under neoliberal philosophy, all those who can survive without aid are entrepreneurs who can thrive in modern times. Those who need services and support must be left behind so that the nation's economic future can be secured. Judging the population in terms of its economic value not only leads to a new way of thinking subjectivity but also a new form of racism.

RACE AND NEOLIBERAL RACISM

In particular, many readers of Foucault pick up on the idea that neoliberalism leads to state racism. [11] Since the life of the state is prioritized above all else, governmental regulations, which work to promote the continued growth of the economy, need to be put in place. The sustained fiscal prosperity of the nation goes hand-in-hand with the decrease in federal aid and services. Deciding who gets care and who is disposable is a function of state racism. While popular conceptions of racism that deal with skin color should not be forgotten and certainly contribute to the discourse about who does and does not deserve healthcare, neoliberal governments put in play another form of racism that transcends the color divide. This kind of racism, which hinges on broad interpretations of national health, helps to justify a shrinking safety net and the lack of care for greater and greater portions of the population.

State racism is, apparently, not without its seductions. The rationale of defending national health and welfare above all is seemingly beyond reproach. It is also versatile. State racism is the discourse of choice because it effectively plays on the desire to see the nation continue to prosper—particularly economically. Many politicians and ordinary citizens who oppose Mexican immigration, for instance, claim that they do so in the interest of national economy. They insist that they do not oppose immigration, as their critics charge, because they are racist. While these opponents of immigration believe that they have escaped the shadow of racism by appealing to economic rationale, they may have unwittingly marked the entrance of a modern form of racism into public discourse. The protection of the country's resources becomes the rationale for disposing of those who have contributed to the economy but now need services.

It is not surprising that debates about services for immigrants lead to discussions about race and racism. That this economic debate is cloaked in rhetoric of national health and security only reinforces Foucault's idea that neoliberalism gives rise to a modern form of racism, which shapes and privileges the entrepreneurial subject. Talk of the economy turns towards racism, and rightly so, when politicians wrangle over who deserves and can be afforded care. It is clear that a sizable amount of the U.S. population believes that immigrant workers should not be given access to health services.

Representative Joseph Wilson's "You lie!" shouted in the midst of President Obama's Congressional address concerning healthcare is just one example of how economics and racism collide.[12] On the one hand, Wilson's outburst can be seen as an expression of conventional color prejudice. Why should un-American, brown people be helped? On the other hand, the emphasis on economic factors reveals a manifestation of Foucauldian state racism. Wilson claimed that Mexicans would destroy America by draining its resources. His logic is as follows: Mexicans harm the nation's health when they seek medical attention to treat their physical problems. Their illnesses drain America's economic and medical resources.[13] They must not be allowed to deplete state's resources and jeopardize the country's economic future and life. This logic of state racism allows politicians like Wilson to stereotype those who seek services as disposable—to be used but not supported. As long as this philosophy is validated and maintained, discourses of health and state racism will continue to increase.

Yet politicians who support this position seem to want to distance themselves from racism. They proclaim that such resources should be withheld from migrant workers not because they are, generally, non-

white but because they are not completely within the system of regulations. If they are not properly regulated, they cannot pay taxes or contribute their fair share.[14] The real challenge for neoliberal states, however, is
to conceal how large segments of the population are no longer protected
and are, therefore, as disposable as the migrant worker who is labeled as
lazy and needy. As Charles T. Lee and Henry Giroux explain, certain
populations are necessarily rendered disposable in neoliberal states. This
form of racism can pose a greater threat to neoliberalism than the traditional form of racism because it disrupts the myth of a self-reliant and
prosperous America. Dominant society would rather give up the myth of
a color-blind America than question the myth of self-sufficient, white
America. The latter allows dominant culture to hold onto the central
figure within neoliberalism—the (white) entrepreneur—by blaming non-
whites for the decline of America that is evidenced in diminished support
services.

This logic shows that neoliberal expressions of state racism overlap
with conventional ones. The reason that the uncovering of neoliberal or,
as Foucault calls it, modern forms of racism can be more detrimental to
Western societies, however, is because it reveals the necessity to treat an
ever-growing mass of the population as disposable. It is, in some ways,
more beneficial for politicians to keep the conversation circling around
traditional forms of racism. The discussion about nondeserving non-
whites is not new and does not point to what dominant society would
consider a real flaw within neoliberal governments. When those cases of
racism start to become more aligned with a form of racism that determines who is disposable—regardless of color—it is recognized as an unbearable defect within the system because it implicates a larger portion of
the (white) population.[15] This revelation is also closer to Foucault's finding on neoliberal society. Racism within modern society is pernicious and
deadly because greater and greater portions of the population are becoming disposable. Everyone is subject to judgment regarding one's economic self-reliance.

MEXICAN MIGRANT WORKERS

Although migrant workers are judged to be bad economic subjects and
depicted as leeches to the system, they are actually indispensible to the
welfare of the state. The way in which policies work to control immigration is only further indication that immigrant labor is useful and desirable to the U.S. economy. While new governmental agencies have been
developed to respond to immigration, the eradication of immigration and
immigrant labor is not the goal of these agencies. Discussion about immigration enforcement agencies may employ forceful rhetoric but the elimi-
nation of immigrant labor is out of the question because it would under-

mine the economy. "[I]nstead of using get-tough enforcement to reduce immigration flows, . . . immigration reform [agendas tend] to support the expansion of immigration enforcement as a precondition for expanding the supply of noncitizen labor."[16] Efforts to patrol the border are not meant to stem the tide of immigration. The goal, as Kretsedemas explains, is quite the opposite. Border controls work to expand—while regulating—the immigrant labor force.

The absence of immigrant labor is just as unacceptable as the unregulated mass of immigrant workers. In order to keep the economy functioning, migrant workers must not only provide cheap labor but they must also be tracked and controlled. If immigrants are not properly regulated, there would be no way of measuring how much more foreign labor will be needed to keep the economy afloat or to further propel it. Neoliberal ideology does not, therefore, mandate border patrol for the sake of protecting the national economy from immigrant workers. Borders must be controlled, instead, to track and regulate immigrants so as to increase the influx of low-wage workers. The development of such agencies is a signal, ironically, of the growing acceptance of immigrants into the workforce. "Different sides of the same coin, these apparently contradictory directives have their operating logics in security, the governing rationale of neoliberalism."[17] These seemingly divergent goals—controlling the border and increasing migrant labor—show the flexibility within neoliberal discourse. Placing an emphasis on national security can allow contradictory policies to be pursued because the neoliberal emphasis on security can also allow policies to be framed in radically divergent ways. Depending on the audience, governmental regulations can be interpreted as pro- or anti-immigration. Critics might even argue that the focus on security within neoliberal rhetoric, especially concerning Mexican migrant workers, allows for one policy to be pursued while presented in an opposite manner.

All the bluster directed at keeping foreign workers out of the U.S. labor market may only be for show. However, when migrant workers seek services—medical or otherwise—this does cause a genuine problem for neoliberal governments. Although this problem is often cast in terms of the unworthy, illegal immigrant who drains the economy of scarce resources, the cracks in the system that these immigrants expose when they seek medical attention are the greater concern for neoliberals. The illegal migrant worker is a convenient scapegoat for a flailing economy. They can be depicted as unwanted and unneeded people who do nothing but take advantage of the nation's valuable assets.

This story does not, as Kretsedemas points out, hold up. Immigrants, for the most part, aid neoliberal governments by providing low-wage workers. Yet it is no coincidence that the debate around immigrants becomes more heated when the discussion turns to medical treatment. The entrance of immigrants into the labor market is not a problem, as long as their presence is contained within that sphere. Once immigrants enter into other areas of society, they become a problem. If migrant workers can simply provide their labor and ask for nothing in return, politicians and the public might be content to have them serve as an invisible engine for the economy. When migrant workers seek health services, they not only become visible reminders of America's dependence on outsiders but they also call attention to the underbelly of society. Even opponents of open immigration policies occasionally acknowledge that a direct connection cannot be made between the immigrant and the strained economy.[18] Migrant workers do, as representatives of those without any support system, make the stresses entailed with managing the national economy easier to see. They also bring into focus how the needy and poor are treated. The state of the economy and the lack of public resources dictate that certain segments of society will be underserved or neglected altogether.[19]

The case that migrant workers are and should exist outside society, and therefore not be eligible for support services, is perhaps easy to sell. Modern societies are accustomed to thinking that support services should be provided by one's nation of origin.[20] They are, in legal terms, foreigners who are not supposed to have the same rights and privileges as citizens. Their exclusion from the support system would be easier to justify except that, as Lee notes, "[m]igrant workers are not simply excluded: they are deliberately brought in, sought after, and tolerated by the capitalist regime to play a crucial part as the disposable and compliant labor of the state operation (thus *inside*), while their membership is deliberately left suspended as "undocumented" individuals who have no official resort to participate politically in the state as citizens (thus *outside*)."[21] It is difficult to declare that migrant workers exist or should exist outside the American support system because they are such a vital part of the economy. Migrant labor is not only necessary but is welcomed in an attempt to fuel the capitalist way of life. While the narrative about their lack of economic production continues to be effective in certain circles, scholars and businessmen alike also frequently challenge this myth.[22] The exclusion of migrant workers in society is not a natural and logical result of their unproductiveness. It is not the case that they provide nothing and, therefore, deserve nothing. Exclusion from society is a result of political efforts to ensure that their voices do not carry any weight in the governance of the state. The barring of immigrant participation is that promise made good.

Their exclusion is a product of a concerted effort to deny rights and privileges that are supposedly given to those who contribute to a neoliberal society. That they have a seemingly dual existence—both inside and outside society—is not inherently offensive to "true" Americans and citizens of modern states. Quite to the contrary, it seems that there would be much less resistance to migrant workers if they allowed themselves to be compliant laborers and asked for nothing in return.[23] The inside/outside relationship that cannot be tolerated is the one where individuals are given access to services, despite not falling within the political parameters of society (not having citizenship or official papers that represent the gateway to regulation and political participation). Migrant workers are ". . . an affront to conventional notions of citizenship, which equate political, social, and civil rights with the criterion of legal residence."[24] Because migrant workers are courted for their labor, those living in neoliberal society should recognize their contribution to the capitalist system. The fight to block their inclusion into modern, neoliberal society could be explained through the terms of conventional racism. Indeed, if the marginalization of migrant workers were justified by their difference in skin color, nationality, or culture, it might work to conceal the workings of modern, biopolitical racism. The denial of the most basic of health services and care is a symbol of political exclusion. Migrant workers represent a population that is supposed to be different from Americans. The proof is that they are disposable while real Americans are, allegedly, protected.

THE CASE OF COASTAL IMMIGRANTS

The victims of Hurricane Katrina, as Giroux explains, show that U.S. citizenship does not guarantee protection either. The similarities between migrant laborers and Katrina evacuees was made more obvious when "[c]ries of desperation and help [by the victims of Hurricane Katrina] were quickly redefined as the pleas of 'refugees,' a designation that suggested an alien population had inhabited the Gulf Coast."[25] Intimations of the foreignness of Hurricane Katrina survivors were undoubtedly connected to the fact that most of them were people of color. This is not, though, the only link between the coastal "refugees" and the migrant workers. These groups remain largely unsupported thanks to the neoliberal art of governance. When their precarious life conditions are brought to the fore, they are blamed and/or depicted as a hindrance to economic prosperity. Their invisibility would not only conceal their disposability but would also conceal the disposability of human life that is inherent within neoliberal governments. Neoliberal governments could appear to run more smoothly if they would remain hidden.

Although skin color helped to shape the description of Hurricane Katrina evacuees as alien or immigrant beings, Giroux suggests that their foreignness in a neoliberal context is best expressed through their disposability. Because they are largely non-white populations, they can be more easily cast as those who do not matter or do not deserve the same treatment as "worthy" Americans.[26] This depiction of an unwanted alien population is compounded by the idea that people of color do not pull their weight in society. They are seen as undeserving people who have not appropriately and commensurately contributed. Such portrayals foster the feeling that migrant workers and Hurricane Katrina victims are disposable. They are not useful or productive; they only bleed the system dry. While these groups are simultaneously inside and outside society, the reading of their dual existence is often misrepresented. It is not the case that they contribute nothing to society.[27] They are often the wellspring of cheap labor that is necessary for neoliberal governments. Thus, they are very much a part of the system. They fall outside the system, contrary to popular belief, when they seek assistance and find that none is afforded them. In short, the ways in which these disposable groups function inside and outside the system is reversed. They are not disposable because they offer nothing and take advantage of unearned benefits. They are disposable because they can be used and discarded without much notice or fuss from dominant society.

Unsurprisingly, many of the same narratives used to describe migrant workers are mapped onto these coastal "refugees." As Giroux notes,

> Katrina lays bare what many people in the United States do not want to see: large numbers of poor black and brown people struggling to make ends meet, benefiting very little from a social system that makes it difficult to obtain health insurance, child care, social assistance, cars, savings, and minimum-wage jobs if lucky, and instead offers to black and brown youth inadequate schools, poor public services, and no future, except a possible stint in the penitentiary.[28]

It would be easier to believe in the greatness of American society and neoliberal governance if poor people of color could be blamed for their low standard of living and quality of life. In order for the neoliberal narrative to work, the victims of Katrina would have to be likened to populations similar to migrant laborers. They are transformed into refugees because their lives do not match up with the idealized image of a prosperous U.S. citizen. Instead of confronting how it has become possible that citizens—who should be given political rights and support services—can still exist outside the protection of the state, the dominant narrative paints this poor population of color alone as responsible for the tragedy that has befallen them. There is a familiar refrain. They are poor and fall outside the net of support because they do not contribute to society. If only, the story goes, they would be more productive; they would be fully inside the American system. Then, they would have access to support and protection. Because they are seen as unproductive people and a drain to the economy, they are lumped in with other disposable populations. They are of no use and will only eat up resources unless worthy, productive Americans can dispose of them.

While some Americans may take some comfort by believing that they belong to a different order than migrant laborers and Katrina survivors, they are still stories that Americans largely would rather not confront. As much as Americans would want to believe that they live in the best and most equitable society, these horror stories about the lack of care do reveal an ugly truth. The lives of Katrina victims suggest that "[t]he state no longer protects its own disadvantaged citizens—they are already seen as dead within a transnational economic and political framework."[29] Color discrimination may be part of modern racism but it is misguided to think that neoliberal racism operates according to the exact same rules as conventional racism. Nationality, for instance, does not play as large a part in modern racism as it did in prior formulations of racism.[30] If neoliberal societies discriminate against migrant workers, it is not due to differences in nationality.

Having legal citizenship, as evidenced in the case of Hurricane Katrina survivors, is also no guarantee of federal support. More to the point, it is not only migrant workers and Hurricane Katrina evacuees who fall beyond the scope of protection. A closer look at the lives of migrant workers shows that contributing to the national economy does not elevate one's status or guarantee protection from the state. Neoliberal societies require more than contributions to the economy. Instead, ideal economic subjects are those who can abstain from asking for assistance or, at least, making their needs visible. An analysis of these situations shows that a vast majority of the population—who are struggling to find work and healthcare—are just as disposable as these cultural scapegoats. For this reason, it is beneficial for proponents of neoliberal governance to make invisible disadvantaged populations. Giroux explains:

> The central commitment of the new hyper-neoliberalism is now organized around the best way to remove or make invisible those individuals and groups who are either seen as a drain or stand in the way of market freedoms, free trade, consumerism, and the neoconservative dream of American empire. This is what [Giroux calls] the *new biopolitics of disposability*: the poor, especially people of color, not only have to fend for themselves in the face of life's tragedies but are supposed to do it without being seen by the dominant society. Excommunicated from the sphere of human concern, they have been rendered invisible, utterly disposable, and heir to that army of socially homeless that allegedly no longer existed in color-blind America.[31]

The less the plight of the disadvantaged and poor is seen, the less likely the rest of the population will be to recognize the dangers and disposability of their own lives. When tragedies strike or when health services are needed, these cracks in national protection and neoliberal governance are exposed. Because growth in capitalist margins can only be sustained with lower wages and fewer benefits, cheap labor is needed to fuel the economy. There is, then, no way to provide greater services or support for the growing number of the nation's poor. Neoliberal ideology is contingent upon making invisible the storylines that point to the failing support system within this art of governance.

This means, among other things, that a discourse of self-reliance needs to be integrated into what it means to be "American" and modern. Since natural disasters and health problems are unavoidable, they cannot be erased from the course of anyone's life. Neoliberal philosophy, however, proposes that productive members of society would not drain the state of further resources. In other words, true Americans would not seek help. They would be able to resolve their problems without making those problems known to the world. The only way to do this is to fend for oneself and provide for one's family without asking for governmental assistance. Those who cannot make their hardships invisible are categorized as a drag to the economy, outside the purview of the American empire, and disposable.

Still, it is better to keep this version of America in the forefront of everyone's mind—even if it means that there is more than a hint of traditional racism that is attached to this narrative. After all, American culture has never been able to rid itself fully of the ugly currents of racism that haunt its history. Yet as Levinson notes, "[t]he death of all is the dirty secret of racism."[32] If, conversely, Americans could peel back racist stereotypes of lazy and opportunistic non-whites, they would see another form of racism is being cultivated in neoliberal communities. The modern form of racism is concealed within neoliberal ideology and, to a certain extent, is hidden under debates about conventional conceptions of racism. Modern racism does not only target people of color, although they do continue to be populations at great risk. Racism in neoliberal societies shows the vulnerability of the greater population in the interest of the survival of the state. It is not just the people of color who can be sacrificed in the name of national interests.

The more this fact is hidden, the better modern society can function without resistance from dominant culture. Of course, the exploitation of people of color should not be tolerated but it has so far not created an outcry for changes to capitalist society. If, however, there was a sense that those other than people of color or those within dominant society too would be affected, there might be greater opposition to the status quo. This modern form of racism, rather than the conventional form of racism that turns on somatic qualities, is the dirty secret of neoliberalism.

THE DIVERSION OF CONVENTIONAL RACIAL DISCOURSE

Neoliberal governments flourish if biopolitical racism remains covered over by various concerns. While immigration debates can reveal neoliberal racism, old racist tropes can be injected into these debates to help conceal this modern form of racism. Even though those who propose and support draconian immigration policies insist that they want to move away from the discourse of race, the conversation often leads back to just that topic. Much of the scrutiny and volatility revolves around whether or not immigration regulations are racist. While proponents of Arizona's immigration reform (Arizona Bill 1070), e-verify programs, and the recall of the *jus solis* (just to name a few) largely deny that these policies are motivated by racism, even backers of these regulations recognize that they do open themselves up to abuse and can lead to legalized racism. Considering how readily sympathizers of anti-immigration policies recognize and concede to the existence of these racist undertones, perhaps they have no intention of hiding the strands of racism that support their positions. If present attempts at immigration reform are, like Joseph Heathcott and other critics charge,[33] responses to the fear that the white political majority has lost some of its privileges, it may be beneficial for supporters to allow these programs to be associated with racism.

One of the most contentious regulations in the past years centers on Arizona's law that allows police officers to ask for and check the documents of anyone whom they suspect to be an illegal immigrant. Defenders of the program quickly point out that this policy only comes into effect if the suspected party has already been stopped for another offense. Still, it does not take much to connect such a law to racial profiling. As Ross Douthat, conservative columnist of *The New York Times*, notes: "For an overzealous minority, it opens obvious opportunities for harassment and abuse."[34] This often means that brown people are subject to a higher level of suspicion than whites. Sharper critiques by writers and clergy liken the policy to the racial profiling and race discrimination under Nazi Germany. "Basically this law forces all people of color to have to carry identification papers similar to Nazi Germany under Hitler. If the person fails to carry identification which segragates [sic] whites from people of color this is racism in the highest form."[35] Arizona's law is seen as more than an official platform to harass the non-white population—legal or illegal. It is a policy that cannot be divorced from the legalized privileging of the white community. Since whites do not fit the profile of the problematic "Mexican immigrant," they can rest assured that they will not have to provide proof of their legal status—even if they are cited for other infractions. Arizona's law can, therefore, help maintain at least one codified privilege for whites.

The maintenance of white privilege seems like a more logical motive for such a law than greater control over immigrants, especially in light of the police opposition. "Arizona's police chiefs association opposed the new law. Local enforcement agencies don't want responsibility for enforcing national immigration laws because they say it makes them less effective at their day jobs. When people in immigrant communities see the local police as deportation agents, they become less likely to report crimes and help in investigations. Conditions worsen."[36] Because the police within these communities do not want to enforce such laws, communities are not made safer by Arizona's strict immigration laws. Instead, these laws ensure that those who may be subject to deportation will live in the shadows. Even if they have valuable information to offer, they would likely not come forward and risk deportation. The Arizona law cannot be effective in driving out unwanted immigrants without causing dire side effects.[37] "'It is literally designed to make life so unbearable for undocumented immigrants that they leave the state,' said Frank Sharry, founder and director of America's Voice, which pushes for comprehensive immigration reform. 'And in doing so it puts a target on the back of every Latino-looking person in the state.'"[38] But the policy does more than alienate Latino-looking individuals on an abstract level.

Questions about the effectiveness of the law lead Eugene Robinson, 2009 Pulitzer Prize winner, and others who report on the Arizona law to conclude that it is nothing short of an assault on the Latino community—retribution for those who are seen as responsible for the shrinking of white privilege. Robinson notes, "Arizona is dealing with a real problem and is right to demand that Washington provide a solution. But the new immigration law isn't a solution at all. It's more like an act of vengeance. The law makes Latino citizens and legal residents vulnerable to arbitrary harassment—relegating them to second-class status—and it is an utter disgrace."[39] Even for those like Robinson who sympathize with the frustrations of those living in Arizona and other border states, the social cost of the law seems too high of a price to pay. The cost of driving out unwanted migrants is not worth demeaning entire communities who have positively contributed to society.

However, if the goal were to draw attention away from how immigration problems are linked to the workings of neoliberal society, then the volatilities of racial discourse would be a feasible remedy. Casting immigrants as a distinct group of brown people who do not deserve the protections and privileges of dominant, white society could hide the fact that protections accorded to the relatively privileged classes are now being stripped away by the globalized economic system rather than migrants from south of the border. Of course, politicians recognize that racial tensions over immigration should not be allowed to escalate too far. Robert Draper recorded, "On the hourlong drive back to his house in Seneca, . . . [that Senator Lindsey] Graham brooded restlessly. The clashing passions on immigration particularly worried him. He feared riots were imminent. 'I've got to find some way to let some steam out,' [Graham] said. 'Find a safety valve. You know what I mean? I've been thinking about that all morning.'"[40] There must be a delicate balancing act. The need to fuel the neoliberal economy with cheap, disposable labor guarantees that America will continue to court immigrants. This also means that anxiety over immigration will not abate any time soon. But why do tensions need to be relieved? The answer, perhaps, is so neoliberal society, which is dependent upon the influx of immigrants, can survive.

Discourse about racism, similar to Foucault's analysis about sexuality, could be used to regulate populations. ". . . [One has] to speak of it as a things to be not simply condemned or tolerated but managed, inserted into systems of utility, regulated for the greater good of all, made to function according to an optimum."[41] Racism, not unlike sexuality, is not completely disavowed. Politicians may state over and over again that they abhor racism but they, nevertheless, make use of racism. The not so hidden racism within Arizona 1070 could, indeed, function like Graham's desired safety valve. Racism within immigration laws can work optimally if they seem to be targeting the Latino community but be ineffective in actually limiting the number of migrants. Arizona's law and those like it need to work in such a way as to give whites a sense of privilege, and thus relieving some tension within dominant society, while not actually providing them with a greater social safety net than migrant laborers. As a bonus, the discourse about racial privilege might even create enough controversy to divert attention away from the economic forces that make more and more people disposable. Because it draws attention to traditional forms of racism, it also works to divert attention away from neoliberal racism.

CONCLUSION: NEOLIBERAL RACISM AND DEATH OF THE SPECIES

The death of the other, foreigners, or citizens of color is not seen as detrimental to proponents of neoliberal ideology as the death of the nation and, ultimately, the species. Their deaths are tolerated and seemingly preferred. Part of managing the life and resources of the nation means stewards of the state must let some die as a result of lack of care. "Racism surfaces, [Foucault] contends, precisely when the State 'fails' to manage the life of the nation. After all, bound to the legal edicts and financial interests, the state cannot but permit 'bodies of death' (for example 'foreigners' as cheap labor) into the midst of the population."[42] This is not to say that policies that aim to withhold medical attention from immigrants and the poor do not cause a stir. Concerns about racist attitudes and treatment, however, could be seen as a result of government mismanagement rather than actual concern for the lives of the disadvantaged. ". . . [R]egulation's power rests not in the murder of the enemy but in the murder of a dying that some 'other' embodies."[43] If the nation were flush with resources, then the need to determine who should be protected or rendered disposable would not be so pressing. And if the nation could properly regulate its populations, the public would not have to be confronted with issues of death and dying. Death, in general, would not be as visible in society. Race and racism, in turn, enter into the public forum when the nation is seen as unable to properly support its constituents while maintaining its own growth and prosperity. When the life of the nation is in jeopardy, the public, by and large, come to accept that certain parts of the population are disposable. The disadvantaged must die so that the nation of entrepreneurs can live on and thrive.

Despite causing some heated exchanges about racism, it is not the deaths of the disposable people of color that must be banished from political debate. "The excluded within *real existing racism* . . . is not the Other life or identity but the *Other of life* (death), the biological incarnation . . . of the physical corruption of the entire species. . . ."[44] What needs to be hidden from public view is the logic internal to neoliberalism that must cast a wider and wider net of disposability over the population. Neoliberal rhetoric works to divide the population into groups that are either dependent or self-reliant. The key to this modern racist split is the idea that those in the latter category represent the best of humanity and are the lifeline for the nation and the species.[45] It is a foregone conclusion that those groups that depend upon the government for their survival will die. Regarded as lacking the spirit of enterprise, they represent the past of humanity and are, in a sense, already dead. Those of the entrepreneurial class, in contrast, will continue to live on even if resources are diverted. Despite belonging to a part of society that is seen as deserving protection, this race of people would not need it to survive. Their breed is depicted through neoliberal myth as indestructible. The greatest blow to neoliberal ideology would be if this historically privileged group believed that this species of entrepreneurs—which is suppose to encapsulate them—is also susceptible to death. Neoliberal philosophy dictates that such a superior species of human beings would survive and thrive, especially with the passing away of the weaker race. If these superior, self-reliant populations are also vulnerable to death, then that would mean that there is a defect in neoliberal society and logic.

Questions concerning why more and more people—not just people of color—have a declining standard of living and quality of life suggest that Americans are beginning to sense that they have been lead astray by the neoliberal dream. Those who once thought themselves to be distinct from the disadvantaged now recognize that they are treated as if they are disposable. They are coming to realize that they, too, have decreased access to health services.[46] Perhaps a greater portion of the population is coming to understand that they are falling into the category of inferior race. Luckily for neoliberal governments, this is not an easy realization with which to come to terms. Perhaps Westerners would rather try to reenforce and re-inscribe traditional forms of racism in the efforts to avoid grappling with a modern from of racism that would render the privileged in-groups disposable. It is easier to search for scapegoats than to look for flaws within neoliberalism. "Nicholas Mirzoeff has observed that

all over the world there is a growing resentment of immigrants and refugees, matched by the emergence of detain-and-deport strategies and coupled with the rise of the camp as the key institution and social model of
the new millennium."[47] Modern racism is covered over again and again
as those seemingly privileged sections of the population maintain an
allegiance to the neoliberal agenda that is simultaneously leaving them
behind, unsupported. Instead of calling for neoliberalism to be rethought,
a vast number of people seem to be in favor of re-instituting separate and
distinct treatment of the population. This is, of course, part of the neoliberal philosophy, which relays the idea that the unproductive and needy
should be quarantined from those who would carry the banner for future
humanity. Old prejudices can be used to reinforce the idea that it is the
poor people of color who are the problem. And if only they could be
contained, detained, or deported, the country would continue to grow
and reach empire status. In order to do so, the state must ensure that
immigrants who do enter the country can contribute to the nation's economic health.

NOTES

1. The moniker "Mexican" is often used to refer to anyone from Central or Latin
America.

2. Ron Paul, Republican presidential candidate, and Representative Joseph Wilson
have described migrant workers as threats to the economic welfare of the country on
their official websites. Ron Paul states that, "After decades of misguided policies
America has now become a free-for-all. Our leaders betrayed the middle class which is
forced to compete with welfare-receiving illegal immigrants who will work for almost
anything, just because the standards in their home countries are even lower." See "On
the Issues of Border Security," last modified July 20, 2011. http://www.ronpaul.com/
on-the-issues/border-security/.

3. Joe Wilson echoes this sentiment on his official website by stating, "After
decades of misguided policies America has now become a free-for-all. Our leaders
betrayed the middle class which is forced to compete with welfare-receiving illegal
immigrants who will work for almost anything, just because the standards in their
home countries are even lower." See "Immigration: Protecting America's Borders,"
last modified June 12, 2013, http://joewilson.house.gov/Issues/Issue/?IssueID=27226.

4. That biopolitics and neoliberalism are inextricably intertwined, for Foucault, is
evident in his 1978-1979 lectures at the Collège de France. While Foucault often promises to address biopolitics in greater detail in "The Birth of Biopolitics," the history and
workings of neoliberalism take center stage. What this seems to suggest, then, is that
biopolitics should be understood within the context of neoliberalism—which has come
to dominate modern society. Neoliberalism is a form of governmentality that allows
biopolitics to thrive.

5. John McCain was widely criticized for his assertion that illegal, Mexican immigrants are behind the fires raging in Arizona. Many journalists, however, have reported that there is no evidence to support McCain's claims. His words are, instead,
traced back to the idea that immigrants are to be blamed for everything that is wrong
in America. See Ujahla Seghal, "John McCain Blames Immigrants for Arizona Fires,"
The Atlantic Wire, June 19, 2011, accessed July 22, 2011, http://
www.theatlanticwire.com/national/2011/06/john-mccain-blames-arizona-fires-illegal-

immigrants/38984. Because McCain is nationally recognized, he must somewhat conceal racist undertones in his stance towards immigrants. Bob Kellar who has served as Santa Clarita councilman for ten years, however, does not have to hide his sentiments. When questioned about his position on immigrants, he claimed to be a "proud racist." Although his statement was given as a defense of his conservative values in an exchange with a hostile interlocutor, it is nonetheless telling that he did not back away from being described as a racist. This suggests that racism, particularly against immigrants, is not a negative quality in a politician. Politicians, on all levels of government, can insist that they despise racism. Yet the willingness to be labeled a racist is an indication that racism towards immigrants does not hurt, and might even help, officials get elected in certain parts of the country. See Susan Abram, "Heated Emotions at Santa Clarita City Hall: Kellar Denies Being a Bigot but Stands by 'Proud Racist' Remark," *The Daily News of Los Angeles*, January 27, 2010, A1.

6. José Luis Villacañas Berlanga, "The Liberal Roots of Populism: a Critique of Laclau," trans. Jorge Ledo, *CR: The New Centennial Review* 10 (2010): 165.

7. There is an increasing amount of governmental programs that aim to make the population healthier. Examples include increased taxes on cigarettes and soft drinks. See Janet Adamy, "Soda Tax Weighed to Pay for Health Care," *The Wall Street Journal*, May 12, 2009, accessed June 12, 2013, http://online.wsj.com/article/ SB124208505896608647.html. While these programs are controversial, the justification for such regulations can be traced back to the future cost for the state.

8. Brett Levinson, "Biopolitics and Duopolies," *Diacritics* 35 (2010): 249.

9. Levinson, "Biopolitics and Duopolies," 249–50.

10. Phillip Kretsedemas, "Immigration Enforcement and the Complication of National Sovereignty: Understanding Local Enforcement as an Exercise in Neoliberal Governance," *American Quarterly* 60 (2008): 560–61.

11. Foucault, himself, believed that state racism was a hallmark of modern society. He believed that this modern manifestation of racism was different from past versions of racism. Only state racism was modern racism. See Michel Foucault, *The History of Sexuality: An Introduction*, trans. Robert Hurley (New York: Vintage Books 1990), 149–50.

12. Wilson is also (in)famous for his "You lie" outburst which was couched, by him, as a defense of America's medical resources against the influx of undeserving migrant use. See "Joe Wilson Says Outburst to Obama Spech 'Spontaneous,'" CNN, September 10, 2009, accessed June 10, 2013, http://www.cnn.com/2009/POLITICS/09/10/obama.heckled.speech/. See also Kristina Wong, "Sarah Palin Takes a Stand on Immigration," ABC News, May 21, 2010, accessed July 23, 2011, http://abcnews.go.com/Politics/sarah-palin-takes-stand-immigration-controversial-arizona-law/story?id=10707136 Sarah Palin, former vice presidential candidate, goes one step further than Wilson when she explicitly links the entrance of immigrants with the death of the country. "If these policies are not reversed, the future is grim. A poor, dependent and divided population is much easier to rule than a nation of self-confident individuals who can make a living on their own and who share the traditions and values that this country was founded upon." For Palin, the immigrant does not share the values of Americans because they are, evidently, unable to support themselves. In other words, they only serve to drain the system.

13. Proponents of Mexican immigration, coincidentally, often use another strand of state racism to make their case. The most popular rationale for Mexican immigration is that Mexican immigrants will help the nation's fiscal health by providing much needed, affordable, low-skilled labor. These sometimes interwoven, sometimes conflicting, interpretations of health show how valuable the philosophy of state racism is in determining the worth of individuals or groups.

14. Ross Douthat, conservative pundit, echoes the sentiments of Ron Paul, Joe Wilson, and Sarah Palin in his article, "The Borders We Deserve," *The New York Times*, May 3, accessed July 23, 2011, http://www.dallasnews.com/opinion/latest-columns/ 20110531-ross-douthat-finally-an-immigration-reform-worth-duplicating.ece.   He

states, "But instead of shrugging as low-skilled workers jump the border to compete with the struggling American working class, our immigration policy should focus on recruiting well-educated migrants, opening the door to greater legal immigration from Asia, Africa and Europe." The insinuation is that the Mexican migrants are of a low quality. They have little to offer but much to take from America.

15. Mike Hill, "Whiteness as War by Other Means: Racial Complexity in an Age of Failed States," *Small Axe* 13 (2009): 73.

16. Kretsedemas, "Immigration Enforcement," 555.

17. Catherine Chaput, "Rhetorical Circulation in Late Capitalism, Neoliberalism, and the Overdetermination of Affective Energy," *Philosophy and Rhetoric* 43 (2010): 16.

18. This sentiment can often be found in the way that politicians and public figures gesture to America's history as a nation of immigrants. Yet as much as they say they appreciate immigrants who enter the country legally, they, at other times, do not distinguish between the legal and illegal labor force.

19. As a radical right-wing activist and practical strategist, Norquist has been enormously instrumental and successful in shaping tax policies designed to "starve the beast," a metaphor for policies designed to drive up deficits by cutting taxes, especially for the rich, in order to paralyze government and dry up funds for many federal programs that offer protection for children, the elderly, and the poor. See Henry Giroux, "Reading Hurricane Katrina: Race, Class, and the Biopolitics of Disposability," *College Literature*, 33 (2006): 182–83.

20. Charles T. Lee, "Bare Life, Interstices, and Third Space of Citizenship," *WSQ: Women's Studies Quarterly* 38 (2010): 69.

21. Lee, "Bare Life," 62. Emphases are in the original.

22. Silence on the part of the business community, which tends to side with conservatives, is often interpreted as a sign that they do not agree with the anti-immigrant view that seems to pervade popular conservative rhetoric. John Whitaker, "Mexican Deaths in the Arizona Desert: The Culpability of Migrants, Humanitarian Workers, Governments, and Business." *Journal of Business Ethics* 88 (2009): 372–73.

23. Kretsedemas cites a story about a boy, Edgar, who dies as a result of medical neglect to illustrate this point. "So long as Edgar's undocumented parents avoided the use of all publicly funded services, it is unlikely that these sorts of screening practices would never have revealed their legal status." See Kretsedemas, "Immigration Enforcement," 568. Edgar's undocumented status is of no real importance until he is in need of support services.

24. Kretsedemas, "Immigration Enforcement," 553.

25. Giroux, "Reading Hurricane Katrina," 177.

26. Barbara Bush defends the failings of the government and her son, President George W. Bush, by stating, "So many of the people here, you know, were underprivileged anyway, so this is working well for them." (Quoted in Giroux, "Reading Hurricane Katrina," 176) She seems to recognize that the conditions at Houston's Astrodome were sub-par. Still, she insists that those conditions were perfectly acceptable for this population. The insinuation is that the conditions would not, however, been adequate for those of a more socially privileged class.

27. While journalists and academics do call attention to the contributions by the poor and underclass of America, it is also all too clear that politicians and government officials do not address their plight. Their needs and lives are not, as Charles Blow notes, not glamorous enough to catch the attention of those who are supposed to represent them. See Charles Blow, "They, Too, Sing America," *The New York Times*, July 15, 2011, accessed July 23, 2011, http://www.nytimes.com/2011/07/16/opinion/16blow.html?_r=3.

28. Giroux, "Reading Hurricane Katrina," 177-178.

29. Giroux, "Reading Hurricane Katrina," 182.

30. Seyla Benhabib, for one, argued that the Spanish Inquisition was an attempt to protect and solidify Spanish national identity against the infiltration of Jews. See Seyla

Benhabib, "Sexual Difference and Collective Identities: The New Global Constellation," *Signs* 24 (1999): 350–51.

31. Giroux, "Reading Hurricane Katrina," 175. Emphases are in the original.

32. Levinson, "Biopolitcs and Duopolies," 73.

33. Heathcott believes that perceived encroachment on the privileges of dominant American society cause the greatest panic in Americans. Although the economy does play a role in the backlash against immigrants, Heathcott does not believe that the economic downturn alone accounts for the wave of anti-immigration movements. He believes that the most troubling element of the poor economic landscape is the loss of white privilege that seemingly accompanies it. See Joseph Heathcott, "Moral Panic in a Plural Culture," *Crosscurrents* 61 (2011): 39–44.

34. Ross Douthat, "The Borders We Deserve," *The New York Times*, May 3, 2010, accessed July 23, 2011, http://www.nytimes.com/2010/05/03/opinion/03douthat.html.

35. See "Arizona Illegal Immigrant Law," Politico.com, April 23, accessed July 22, 2011, http://www.politicolnews.com/arizona-illegal-immigrant-law/. Giorgio Agamben, as is well-known, also believes that the Holocaust is now a template for the marginalization and criminalization of stateless people. See Giorgio Agamben, "The Camp as the 'Nomos' of the Modern" in *Homo Sacer: Sovereign Power and Bare Life*, trans. Daniel Heller-Roazen (Stanford: Stanford University Press,1998), 166–80. When the idea that America is turning into a police state makes its way into the mainstream media, it shows that this danger is not relegated to the sphere of academia.

36. Eugene Robinson, "Arizona's Immigration Frustration," *The Wall Street Journal*, April 27, 2010, accessed July 22, 2011, http://online.wsj.com/article/SB10001424052748703465204575208382473306238.html.

37. Kristina Wong notes changes in Palin's position towards immigration. While running for the office of vice president, Palin spoke to Spanish-language television network Univision (October 26, 2008) and stated, "There is no way that in the U.S. we would roundup every illegal immigrant . . . there are about 12 million of the illegal immigrants. . . . Not only economically is that just an impossibility but that's not a humane way anyway to deal with the issue." See Kristina Wong, "Sarah Palin Takes a Stand on Immigration," ABC News, May 21, 2010, accessed July 23, 2011, http://abcnews.go.com/Politics/sarah-palin-takes-stand-%09immigration-controversial-arizona-law/story?id=10707136#.UbiYtZWE7ww. Wong, however, goes on to chronicle how Palin, like other conservatives, have had a change of heart in regards to immigration regulation. What was deemed impractical and inhumane before is now acceptable. This is evidenced by the growing support for the Arizona law by conservative leaders.

38. Quoted in Huma Kahn, "Legalizing Racial Profiling?," ABC News, April 22, 2010, accessed July 23, 2011, http://abcnews.go.com/Politics/arizona-immigration-bill-draws-fire-nationally-gov-brewer/story?id=10438889.

39. Eugene Robinson, "Arizona's new immigration law is an act of vengeance," *The Washington Post*, April 26, 2010, accessed July 22, 2011, http://www.washingtonpost.com/wp-dyn/content/article/2010/04/26/AR2010042602595.html.

40. Robert Draper, "Lindsey Graham, this Year's Maverick," *The New York Times*, April 7, 2010, accessed July 22, 2011, http://www.nytimes.com/2010/07/04/magazine/04graham-t.html?pagewanted=2.

41. Michel Foucault, *The History of Sexuality: An Introduction*, trans. Robert Hurley (New York: Vintage Books, 1990), 24.

42. Levinson, "Biopolitcs and Duopolies," 73.

43. Levinson, "Biopolitcs and Duopolies," 72.

44. Levinson, "Biopolitics and Duopolies," 73. Emphasis is in the original. See also Michel Foucault, *Society Must Be Defended: Lectures at the Collège de France 1975–1976*, trans. David Macey (New York: Picador, 2003), 247.

45. Ladelle McWhorter, *Racism and Sexual Oppression in Anglo-America: A Genealogy* (Bloomington: Indiana University Press, 2009), 140.

46. Many researchers and journalists have used a study and paper called "Barely Hanging On: Middle-Class and Uninsured," by the Robert Wood Johnson Foundation to draw attention to the rising anxiety of America's middle class over the lack of access to health care. The emphasis on the health care available to the middle class, rather than the poor, works as an indicator of the growing problems and failures with health care in America. See "Barely Hanging On: Middle-Class and Uninsured," The Robert Wood Johnson Foundation, March 2010, last modified August 7, 2011, http://rwjf.org/files/research/58034.pdf.

47. Nicholas Mirzoeff, *Watching Babylon: The War in Iraq and the Global Visual Culture* (New York: Routledge, 2005), 145. Originally quoted in Giroux, "Reading Hurricane Katrina," 180.

FOUR

Biologizing the Race of Terror

While public figures often argue that their opposition to Mexican immigration has more to do with issues of economics than race, race features prominently in their attempts to limit immigrants who may have connections to Islam. Bias against those of a different religion is not a new phenomenon but modern racism, according to Foucault, relies not only on crystallizing otherness but also on creating a hierarchy of human potential. Those who fight to block Muslim immigrants suggest that Muslims have the potential to destroy both the American way of life and undercut the gains of modernity by adhering to a backward religion that has no respect for reason and logic. This present fear of the religious other grows as Westerners come to embrace the notion that biological science can delineate races and explain how religious ideology can be passed down through heredity.

What, then, does this mean for modern conceptions of race? How does the scientific understanding of race fit within the now widely accepted idea, at least in academia, that racial constructions are determined by politics? In this chapter, I will show how biological science and politics combine to biologize race and explore how the war on terror and, by extension, on Muslims are a result of the biopolitics of religion. Westerners seem to believe that the deployment of scientific discourse, no matter how irrational or backward the logic of biologizing religion, marks them as superior beings. By making use of science—a tool that supposedly belongs exclusively to enlightened cultures, Westerners hope to justify discrimination against religious others while still believing themselves to be the best representatives of human progress.

Jacques Rancière proclaims that it is meaningless to define a race by one's religious belief. Making sense, however, is not the ultimate criteria for racing a religion.[1] Conceptions of race, as Michael Omi and Howard

Winant argue, depend on politics rather than on a definitive standard. Yet frequent gestures are made to uncover a seemingly firm foundation of race in natural, scientific, and biological explanations. It is this search for biological rationale to ground political formations of race that have led to the biopolitics of race. Michel Foucault suggests that political and biological discourses combine to plot different races along the curve of human evolution. True to form, Western political rhetoric often divides the modern and rational from the religious—anti-modern and irrational.

Foucault, however, insists that the modern racing of religion is not complete until these differences are biologized. Once a certain religious group is identified as belonging on a lower rung of the ladder of human development, their constitution is seen as different from those who are at the top of the human hierarchy. This assertion of faulty biology is often used to cast aspersion, not coincidentally, on groups that are deemed politically dangerous. Western immigration policies, for instance, include language that espouses the inferior biological make-up of Muslims, which renders them resistant to modernization and reason. Therefore, the biopoliticization of religion in the United States can perhaps most clearly be seen in the case against Islam. While politicians claim that regulations limiting Mexican immigrants have nothing to do with race, they make even less effort to cover over their efforts to connect Islam to race via biology.

RACE AS POLITICAL CONSTRUCT

Attempts to discriminate against religious others through scientific race mark a shift away from the long-held belief that politics defines race. According to Omi and Winant, understanding the political construction of race depends upon recognizing that the sociopolitical climate of the time influences which readings of race are offered, tailored, and contested. Omi and Winant emphasize, through their racial formation theory, that race is not a fixed concept. Categories of race are pliable and flexible. Racial discourse is shaped in relation to the theories and knowledge that are accepted by the public as sound. They attribute the instability and "messiness" of race to a hegemonic political structure. Because modern politics operates through indirect power, concepts of race are a result of "common sense" understandings and challenges against them.[2] Racial discourse is formed through a give and take between unquestioned or, at least, widely accepted definitions and the contestation of them. There is a chance through hegemonic rule, unlike in a dictatorship, for the opposition to have their say and take part in reshaping readings of race or other social constructs, which they find oppressive.

Omi and Winant believe that "[f]ar from ruling principally through exclusion and coercion (though again, these are hardly absent) hegemony operates by including its subjects, incorporating its opposition."[3] Political resistance is not only possible but also key in developing ideas of race. Ideas that run counter to the established rule must be integrated and recognized in order to maintain a certain level of popular support. Omi and Winant believe that the subordinated help shape their own identity and how others see them. Political opposition contributes to changing common sense perceptions of social constructs. Subordinated groups are, in turn, more likely to consent because their ideas have been used to reform what they found problematic.

HAS BIOLOGICAL RACE RETURNED?

The theory that politics determines race seemed to be formed as a way to explain how conceptions of race have transformed throughout history and as a means to challenge the legitimacy of the more pernicious ideas about race. A shift toward a political conception of race was supposed to be a move away from the belief that there were biological differences between races.[4] While it is now widely accepted that race is not determined through biology but rather through politics, Ladelle McWhorter and Omi make the case that biological race remains with us. A political understanding of race does not automatically relegate biological race to the past. Though the racial formation theory provided by Omi and Winant shows that the idea of race is defined through social and political struggle, this does not mean that a past theory about race loses all credibility or culture saliency once a new theory is offered. Political contestations of race do not preclude the possibility that theories about race can be accepted, discarded, re-imagined and/or re-introduced. Just because biological race had been widely denounced by scholars does not mean that this idea cannot once again be embraced—if it ever really disappeared from general culture or popular thinking.

What space, though, does biological race occupy in modern society? Because biology can be used to refer to anything concerning life forms, it hardly seems out of line to equate biological race with morphological race. Indeed, the general public still tends to rely on morphology as an indication of racial difference. Skin color, the shape of one's eyes, and other physical traits are often used in the process of race classification. While people generally may understand biological race in terms of visible physical variances among bodies, thinkers of race argue that the underlying principle of biological race has more to do with invisible rather than visible qualities.

McWhorter, following Foucault, does not believe that somatic differences are the most important factor in biological race. Although biological racial categories did largely match up with morphological divides, biological race was meant to denote the differences in the internal structure and constitution of different bodies.[5] These biological differences were meant to establish not just a race hierarchy but were used to identify the highest qualities of the human race. Biological race reinforced the idea that there were intrinsic differences among races. Intellectual rather than physical variances were chief among them. McWhorter argues that biological race actually shifts away from thinking of race in morphological terms. Under the rubric of morphology, physical features determined race. Because biology, in contrast, allowed humans to be divided along a developmental and evolutionary curve, these somatic differences were no longer the crux of race.

A biological understanding of race made it so the most important indicators of race were those that were not visible to the naked eye. Visual markers, of course, were still used as aids in distinguishing one race from another but they were now only signifiers of the "real," unseen differences between peoples. The biologism of race and the discourse of developmental hierarchy were used to give credence to theories about intellectual superiority and greater capacities for freedom within the Anglo-European population. Since races were, essentially, differentiations along the trajectory of human progress, it stands to reason that certain peoples would be more developed than others. Some races would likewise suffer from retardation and show signs of stunted capacities.[6] These biological differences were further used to justify prejudicial policies.

Although many scholars denounce biological race as discriminatory, Omi argues that the use of and credence given to genetic tests has revived these notions. While McWhorter's analysis of biological race—by her own admission—may seem idiosyncratic[7] because it does not use physical difference as the primary referent for race, Omi's understanding of race helps to support her position. Not only does Omi suggest that biological race continues to operate in the minds of many but he also shows that biological conceptions of race belie this belief in a superior race. Omi, too, warns that scientific race is re-emerging.

> Notions of innate racial differences haunt ongoing debate about the political and social meanings of race. . . . DNA testing is increasingly being utilized for a range of legal and social purposes. The increasing reliance on such testing gives an aura of legitimacy and "scientific" backing to specific notions of race that are then utilized to stratify populations and advance legal claims for inclusion and exclusion.[8]

Although scientific or biological race would not seem to be popular, we need to recognize that a scientific understanding of race, nonetheless, continues to affect politics. Those who align themselves with either conservative or progressive political worldviews have resisted biological race—albeit for different reasons. Conservatives may want to deny any—science or social—basis for race. Progressives may, to the contrary, want to analyze how racial discourses grow from sociopolitical struggles but there is no ignoring that science still plays a hand in our understanding of race. Thinkers of race are, of course, suspicious of the re-emergence of biological race because the science that supports the innate differences between races is also often used to support a race hierarchy. The re-biologizing of race, after all, fuels the idea that there are genetic differences between races that lead to greater and lesser capacities among races.[9]

RELIGION AND RACE

Even though Omi, in "'Slippin' into Darkness': The (Re)Biologization of Race," focuses on the ways science is used to divide anew people along the color line; this does not necessarily go against his explanation of the racial formation theory. Because race is constantly challenged and re-worked, it is neither stable nor a stand-alone category. Race is only one of many socially constructed fields and can extend beyond morphology. This is why race often overlaps, intersects, and fuses with class,[10] gender, and sexuality.[11] While it may seem strange—as McWhorter herself admits—to argue that sexual orientation can constitute a racial category,[12] there are more orthodox examples of racial categories that elucidate the main thrust of her position. Religious affiliation, likewise, blurs the line between traditional and unconventional concepts of race. The Jewish people, for instance, are now generally considered to encompass both a religious and racialized community.

Yet Foucault argues that religion did not always constitute a racial category. There is ample evidence to document the ways Westerners attempted to define religious communities—the Jewish community in particular—sometimes as a separate political entity and sometimes as a distinct biological group. Foucault, however, suggests that Jewishness did not become racialized until the rise of biopolitics. Religion has long created vast differences among peoples but it was only after the Nazi state sought to identify and propagate the highest human qualities, according to Foucault, that Jews became a different race.

Foucault, though, is not the only one who believes that religion was not always racialized. Omi and Winant suggest that religious differences were proto-racial in nature. On the one hand, they do not deny that religious differences created large chasms between peoples. Nevertheless, they insist that the project of race only began in earnest with colonialism and Western imperialism. Religion served as a rehearsal for the coming racial divisions. They argue that the Christian European stance towards the non-Christian other did not produce a clear and structured concept of race. Colonialism marked a new era in dealing with the other. The unsystematic manner in which Europeans thought the other only became consolidated through a social structure of exploitation, appropri-

ation, and domination that followed colonialism. This organized fashion
of thinking and standardized interaction with the other is what separated
the colonial racial formation project from what they understand as proto-
racial projects that were brought on by religious differences. Religion
may have laid the groundwork for thinking about the differences between peoples but the concept of race, they argue, was first crystallized
through colonialism. [13] Omi and Winant further assert, "race is a concept
which signifies and symbolizes social conflicts and interests by referring
to different types of human bodies." [14] This difference in body type as
difference in race, they argue, only came to be after Europeans encoun-
tered those whom they eventually would colonize. While Omi and Winant believe that religion was not an original part of race formation, they
do think that religion has come to be racialized. Omi and Winant, like
many others, recognize anti-Semitism as proof of the racialization of religion. [15]

The process of racing the Jewish community included discourses that
set to define Jews as both a foreign political and biological group. Hannah Arendt's analysis shows that political and biological readings of Judaism converged in revolutionary Europe. As European Jews became
increasingly ostracized, they became more and more associated with a
biological identity. They were not accepted as full members of a European nation and, therefore, did not have a national identity as such. The
Jewish identity was transnational and understood to be tribal in nature.
Jews were described, therefore, as part of a religious family rather than a
politico-national community. Arendt concedes that stereotypes about the
tribal nature of Jews were not altogether incorrect. She, however, fills in
the historical framework that allows us to see that a perfect political
storm surrounded Jews and created anti-Semitism amidst revolutionary
Europe.

It could be argued that Jews empathized more with those who practiced their faith than their countrymen of the same nationality. Arendt
suggests, in contrast, that this was the case because Jews were deliberately kept from fully assimilating with the culture of each European nation.
Jews were always within a special legal zone. They were either over-
privileged or underprivileged. Each European country (France, Germany, Austria, Poland, etc.) had laws that both benefited wealthy Jews and
discriminated against poorer Jews. In response to this "special" treatment
that excluded them from their local national community, they associated
with others of the same faith across Europe rather than their countrymen.
The transnational character of Jewish fellowship fed into the long-standing belief that Jews privileged tribal connections over national ties. This
Jewish tendency, as Arendt argues, is not a function of the Jewish religion
or Jewish people as some anti-Semites would charge. It is an outgrowth
of European laws and culture. The composite sketch of the Jewish race
seems to be built upon the idea that they work to strengthen tribal con-

nections and blood ties. This larger Jewish family was created, in large part, because they were ostracized within their home countries. In other words, the Jewish race—based on tradition and heritage—was not shaped by a particular call to religious loyalties but by European policies that created a nation within nations.

Arendt further argues that anti-Semitism grew even stronger as political tensions that surrounded the constitution of the modern European nation mounted. Questions surrounding the relationship between the people and the state were reflected in the attitude towards the Jewish population. Were the Jews the key to maintaining the status quo as the revolutionists believed or were they the seeds to undoing the nation as the ruling class thought? These contradictory readings of the Jewish community showed that they were caught in the crosshairs of political struggle within European nations. While Jews were hated by opposing factions for disparate reasons, their religion was chosen as a common explanation for their treacherous nature. Jews became the symbol of those who could thwart both the revolutionists and the aristocracy. Because Jews held financial resources and often funded aristocratic projects, they drew hatred from those that fought against the ruling class.

Revolutionaries, on the other hand, believed that Jews wanted to protect their wealth and special status by supporting the ruling class. Those who opposed the aristocracy drew a line between Jewish legal privilege which allowed them to amass large sums of money and the financial support of old sovereign powers. In order to protect this special status given to their religion and, accordingly, their wealth and power, the Jews were—in the minds of the revolutionaries—seen as agents against progress. The aristocrats, likewise, saw their religion as the reason why this collective of people could not be trusted. Their true loyalty belonged not with the nation but solely with those who shared their religion. Jews were alternately credited with the power to destroy past and future Europe. They held, in short, the ability to undo past Western power and foil the burgeoning power of the Western people.[16]

BIOLOGIZING RELIGION

The anti-Semitism that Arendt describes, according to Foucault's theories, is only a lead-up to a new form of anti-Semitism—the form that truly biologizes race and races religion. Certainly, growing concerns over the constitution of the European nation contributed to the biologizing of Judaism but the new version of anti-Semitism did not come to full fruition until the ascendance of science. Political discord surrounding Jews, as Arendt showed, had existed for some time. Anxiety about national cohesion, future prosperity, and continued survival of the community was channeled into racial discourse. Malignant figures of a different race were thought to be the cause of the nation's problems. In order for the nation to remain strong, foreign elements must be found and purged. But it was the mix of scientific knowledge and political unease that cemented the idea that those of different religions belonged to different races.[17] Religion was raced when biology and politics became fused.

For Foucault, Jews became a race through biopolitics. He suggests that biological race, as we know it, came into being when the state powers, institutions, and regulations became mixed with the project of human evolution. The nation did not simply work to maintain the imagined or mythical purity of blood. Pure blood was no longer a matter of myth; it was the key to the future of humanity. The state began to implement disciplinary regulations to ensure racial purity and human excellence. Blood and nation would later be connected to horrific effect in Nazi Germany.

> Racism took shape at this point (racism in its modern, "biologizing," statist form): it was then that a whole politics of settlement (*peuplement*), family, marriage, education, social hierarchization, and property, accompanied by a long series of permanent interventions at the level of the body, conduct, health, and everyday life, received their color and their justification from the mythical concern with protecting the purity of the blood and ensuring the triumph of the race. Nazism was doubtless the most cunning and the most naïve (and the former because of the latter) combination of the fantasies of blood and the paroxysms of a disciplinary power. A eugenic ordering of society, with all that implied in the way of extension and intensification of micropowers, in the guise of an unrestricted state control (*étatisation*), was accompanied by the oneiric exaltation of a superior blood . . . [18]

Biological race, according to Foucault, took shape when bodily functions became the target of the state. The state expanded its powers under the guise of turning the myth of a superior blood into a reality. Nazi Germany used the idea of a pure blood to murder millions and regulate the remaining population. Those of inferior blood must be exterminated in order for a great nation to emerge. Millions of Jews and others of inferior blood and bodies were killed so that, as the logic goes, that the superior race would not be poisoned by them. And it was up to the state to protect and foster the growth of such a people. Since the state was seen as the defender of the supreme race, regulations of all sorts could be put in place. The Nazis garnered increasing control over the individual and social body by suggesting that a nation worthy of a great race would not come into being otherwise.

Seyla Benhabib, however, argues that the biologization of Judaism was not particular to Nazi Germany. She suggests that the goal of the Spanish Inquisition was quite similar. Inquisitors General believed that Jews were tainted not by their religious practices but by their blood. Benhabib argues that the discourse about "natural" and biological difference was used to expel and exterminate Jews during the Spanish Inquisition. Religion, during the Spanish Inquisition, became a matter of biology and not cultural lineage. Without biological discourse, the racing of religion would not have been possible. Benahabib explains that the Spanish Inquisition targeted Spanish Jews not because of their doctrinal beliefs or religious practices but because their religion was seen as a signifier of unclean blood. Religion, in this case Judaism, was not just an indication of a set of practices or beliefs but a stamp of biological identity. Religious lineage was no longer an indication of inherited practices, traditions, and customs. It, instead, became connected to physiology. The Jewish lineage translated into biological heredity. Unclean blood became a symbol for what must be identified and purged. Once the link between religion and biology was made, the hunt could begin. The Inquisition was not only an attempt to determine who had "cleanliness of blood" but also to eradicate any genealogical trace of unclean blood.[19]

These trials were, according to Benhabib, meant to ease the anxiety about the frailty of national identity. Seeing differences in religion as naturalistic differences, Benhabib, allowed the lines between collective identities to become more rigid. There would be less of a danger of melding into the other. One simply was or was not Jewish. Either one had unclean Jewish blood or not.[20] Biological discourse was used in order to create firm identities that could resist dissolving into the other. If one's constitution was determined by nature, it could not be changed so easily on an individual basis. The make-up of the community, however, could transform over time. Allowing the other to intermix and interbreed freely could lead to the weakening of the community. The Inquisition was formed, in part, to prevent the dissolution of the Spanish identity and nation.

Benhabib explains that the anxiety of losing one's self-identity and the unfortunate antidote—making a collective group the carriers of different and threatening naturalistic traits—is an old and recurring fear. One's sense of self is fragile because it is not only an individual identity but also one that is part of a collective identity. Both, however, are shaped through fragments and myths that connect to one's sense of self and others. A sense of self is molded by the differences one sees between herself and the other in an alternate collective and/or the collective other. How one views those who are dissimilar, likewise, helps to shape an identity of the self. Creating rigid boundaries between oneself and the other creates a greater sense of security. If the differences between oneself and the other are natural and immutable, there is a lesser chance that one will dissolve into the other.[21] Many fascist and repressive regimes throughout history have exploited this fear to exterminate or purge a group from the community, nation, or state. History has shown that this move is more successful if the differences between the privileged and outcast collectives are seen in biological terms.

Still, Foucault's theories challenge Benhabib's belief that anti-Semitism during the Spanish Inquisition represents an attempt to biologize race. The traditional differences ascribed to Jews, as Hannah Arendt describes, and the biologizing of Judaism, as Seyla Benhabib describes, are not yet placed in the context of natural human development or evolutionary difference. Judaism is not raced in the modern sense, for Foucault, until they and other groups are plotted along the human evolutionary curve. Arendt shows that Judaism as a collection of practices and beliefs were an outlet for political anxiety. Yet this prejudice against Jews was largely rationalized through myth and politics rather than through natural science. The kind of discrimination against Jews that Arendt describes was indicative of a struggle between cultures and traditions. The biologization of Judaism as explained by Benhabib is, likewise, not dependent upon biological science. Despite using the language of biology and nature, Benhabib—by her own admission—believes that the goal of the Spanish Inquisition was to shore up national identity. The Spanish Inquisition was largely a political project that made use of biological terminology. Yet the biological discourse employed, for Foucault, falls short of biologizing race in the modern sense.

The biologization of race, for Foucault, entails the location of the best qualities along the trajectory of *human* evolution. Racing religion does not become biopolitical until God is largely removed from the equation. Modern biological discourse, as Sylvia Wynter explains, must shift from supernatural causation to natural causation. "The shift, therefore, from the explanatory principle of Divine Providence and/or retribution, as well as from that of witchcraft and sorcery, to that of the new principle of laws of nature, of events happening cursus solitus naturae (in the accustomed ordinary course of nature) [works] as the explanatory model that underlay the scientific revolution."[22] The unclean blood of the Jews was directly connected to their status as heretics. The "natural" and biological distinctions between Spanish Jews and Spanish Christians were still attributed to one's relation with God. Spanish Jews were demonized because they represented a violation of a divine decree. Divine rather than natural law determined their "dirty" and "sinful" constitution.

The religious racism, which Foucault describes as properly biological, must be connected to nature and disconnected from supernatural discourse. Discrimination against Jews in Nazi Germany was not an outgrowth of a suspicion or hostility against their religious beliefs, customs, and practices. Because Hitler attributed the biological inferiority of Jews to nature rather than God, racism—religious or otherwise—in the Third Reich took on a different character. The Jews were a problem for the Nazis because their faulty biological constitution threatened all of humanity. It is for this reason that Foucault saw this as a different form of anti-Semitism. The biological discourse of naturally inferior beings, represented by Jewish identity, was also employed in political propaganda.

Biological racism became a key instrument for governmental powers and regulations. Thus, biological racism and state racism became one.

The state, rather than God, became the overseer of human progress. State policies, instead of divine providence or intervention, were offered as the key to human development. The role of the modern state was not, as it was before, to keep the peace between heterogeneous peoples. Nor was the Nazi state ultimately concerned, unlike their prior Spanish counterparts, with religious identity or purity. The goal for the National Socialists, as Foucault sees it, was to make sure that differentiation of races occurs so that the strongest of humanity survive.[23] Those who lacked these superior qualities or were unable to integrate them must be destroyed. Hitler wanted to eliminate the Jews because they were the symbol and manifestation of all other races.[24] If the pure German lineage—as the most evolved humans—were to thrive, all inferior races must be destroyed. The Nazi state, through the rationale of realizing the greatest of human potential, justified murderous policies and laws. Of course, mythological prejudices against the Jews still existed but it was ultimately the logic of natural human evolution that biologized their religion and justified their execution.

RACING ISLAM

The new anti-Semitism and new racism of Nazi Germany painted Jews as those who possessed generally lowly qualities. It is, however, the specific discourse of irrationality that allows for the racing of religion today. Religious people, by and large, and Muslims, in particular, are cast as those who are incapable of or resistant to reason. The religious are thought to cling to their faith, in no small part, because they cannot grasp or accept a rational ordering of the world. While the myth of bad blood and familial ties has never completely disappeared, modern religious racism tends to be built on the idea that there are certain types of people who are not fully evolved intellectually.

> So that as the earlier Spirit/Flesh master code was being relegated to a secondary and increasingly privatized space, the new rational/irrational master code, which was to be the structuring of the rearranged hierarchies of the now centralized political order of the modern state, was being projected upon another "space of Otherness." This was that of the projected hierarchy of a graduated table, or Chain of all forms of sentient life, from those classified as the lowest to those as the highest. It is, therefore, as the new rational/irrational line [that] . . . comes to be actualized in . . . institutionalized differences . . .[25]

The hierarchy that ranks the rationality of beings would also be used to justify a political order. The modern state would, supposedly, mirror the natural ordering of the world. Those who are irrational or less rational must be kept in check. Otherwise, they could impede or destroy all the advances made in modern society. This is precisely the discourse that dominates the anxiety about the Islamic faith and is used to justify regulations aimed at anyone suspected of having ties to Islam.

As the West came into sharper relief through its self-proclaimed modernity and civility, the East became more and more blurred as all that which lacked Western sensibility and rationality altogether. Non-Westerners were simply backward and barbaric. The most dangerous of all non-Western cultures, at the moment, are those that are connected to Islam. Westerners—the populace and academics alike—regard Muslims as a greater threat than the other Eastern peoples. Although Jacques Rancière may think it absurd that religion be equated with race,[26] it is not only the uneducated or intolerant that believe that religion is a substantial factor in determining who belongs in which racial category.

Famed political scientist Samuel P. Huntington claims that "the clash of civilizations" will be a result of a war between cultures. Although many scholars have criticized Huntington's clash of civilization, his theories connect religion to race and highlight the clash between the Western and Islamic civilizations.[27] Huntington's cultural divisions refer not only to geography (Western, Latin America, and African) but also to religion (Buddhist, Islamic, and Hindu). He asserts that, "Of all the objective elements which define civilizations, . . . the most important usually is religion. . . . To a very large degree, the major civilizations in human history have been closely identified with the world's great religions. . . . Yet civilization and race are not identical."[28] While a civilization is not identical to a race, it is not wholly disconnected from race either. Huntington believes that the world is divided into eight civilizations: Western, Latin American, African (possibly), Islamic, Sinic/Chinese, Hindu/Indian, (Russian) Orthodox, and Japanese.[29] More to the point, he carves out the world and defines "civilizations" not only according to region but also in terms of religion. He seems to suggest, among other things, that his system for understanding the world order is not one based on race, even though some of his categories match Western conceptions of race.[30] Accordingly, his analysis suggests that the Sinic and Islamic civilizations are the main opposing forces to the West. They are viewed as the races that have the most potential to destroy Western civilization.

Sarah Ahmed further explains that the dangers believed to be posed by those from the Middle East, South Asia, or those who simply "look" Arab seem to be directly linked to Islam. "Indeed, Leti Volpp suggests that the responses to September 11 facilitated 'a new identity category that groups together people who appear 'Middle Eastern, Arab or Muslim.'"[31] The Orient has become a bit more diverse in the eyes of the West, while still remaining within harmful and sweeping stereotypes.[32] While the West recognizes some differences between Eastern cultures, there remains a tendency to group many disparate people together in order to strengthen the West's sense of itself. Even if the Orient is not all the same, the West still needs to locate a group of people who will serve as the opposition to Western values and culture. Westerners, who hope to identify that group especially after 9/11, have often been in search of those who might be practitioners of Islam.

Ahmed suggests that the suspicion that Americans feel towards those who "look Muslim" is fortified by the discourse propagated by the "war on terror." The formulation used to describe the struggle for the survival of America and Americans is juxtaposed to the "Islamic terrorist." Despite the rhetoric that the war on terror is not a war against Islam, the phrase "Islamic terrorist" is so commonplace that it is difficult *not* to associate Islam with terrorism. It is as if there is no other type of terrorist besides the Islamic terrorist. The terrorist becomes synonymous, through word association, with the Muslim.[33]

> The work done by metonymy means that it can remake links—it can stick words like *terrorist* and *Islam* together—even when arguments are made that seem to unmake those links. Utterances like "this is not a war against Islam" coexist with descriptions such as "Islamic terrorists," which work to restick the words together and constitute their coincidence as more than simply temporal. The sliding between signs also involves "sticking" signs to bodies: the bodies who "could be terrorists" are the ones who might "look Muslim."[34]

Once the link between "Islam" and "terrorist" is established, the association game can go both ways. The "terrorist" is Islamic and all those who practice Islam are terrorists. It is as if the figure of the terrorist perpetually shadows Islam. One word cannot be thought or uttered without the other. Thus, when the idea of a terrorist is summoned, the image of a Muslim follows close behind. As Ahmed argues, the Muslim and the terrorist have been stuck together. Any fear that a terrorist might rightly generate is unfairly transferred onto anyone who might be Muslim. Muslims are, then, the embodiment of that which Americans should fear. Islam is made to seem as that which directly opposes Western civilization and all that it stands for—progress and reason. One of the prevailing Western discourses about Muslims is that they languish in a pre-modern society because they do not have the capacity to participate in the civilized world.[35] "Muslim terrorists" can only tear down that which they do not understand and they do not understand the ways of the world because they are irrational.[36]

THE IRRATIONAL WEST

The irony is that for all the talk of rational and irrational beings, the way Islamic identity is construed in the West is also without logic. Many of the violent acts and policies against Muslims are not only harmful but also nonsensical. This helps to prove McWhorter's point that modern racism is no more than scientific racism that is now stripped of any claims to factual evidence. "The racism we now know as 'race prejudice' and 'bigotry' was scientific racism minus its scientific warrant, clinging to the political and social world like the shells that locusts have left behind."[37] This form of racism, unlike in times past, cannot claim to have the backing of the scientific community. Yet biological language and themes remain. There are those who have evolved to be fully rational and there are those who have not. "This line separates the world of Western reason on the march towards a future of common rational prosperity and an 'oriental' world doomed, for an indefinite period, to languish in irrational classifications and the obscure identity of laws, religion and poverty."[38] The goal of modern politics is to make sure that the irrational people occupy a different space from the rational. The preoccupation with the highest representatives of humanity, which is at the center of Foucauldian biopolitics, allows the West to carve out spaces that will contain the irrational and pre-modern.

Policies aimed at localizing threats to the modern West from religious others can be seen in both the horrific aggression towards Muslim Bosnian women and in a U.S. policy of "special registration," which has received little negative attention. What is noteworthy in these two cases is that they both make use of biological themes but are lacking in cogent reason. That is to say, there is biological language but the underlying theory behind each policy is illogical. This is a marker of biologized religion within biopolitics. As McWhorter and Rancière suggest, fact and reason are not crucial to the biologizing of otherness. It is, instead, the narrative of protecting the future of humanity that is crucial in both the biologizing of religion and biopolitics.

Benhabib argues that the rape of Muslim Bosnian women is sanctioned through a twisted logic of biological cleansing. The torture and sexual assault of women is a common tactic used in war but the rationale behind the rape of Muslim Bosnian women shows that there is a biopolitical strategy at play. The goal is not just to humiliate and torment women—although that is certainly also part of the game plan. The larger objective was to create more Bosnian Serbs. By raping and impregnating Muslim Bosnian women with Serbian seed, there would be more Serbian offspring. Benhabib, however, points out that this reasoning is faulty because the children born from these acts of sexual aggression would not be "purely" Serbian. They would, because of their mothers, also be carriers of Muslim Bosnian identity.[39] Benhabib's point is that the path of sexual coupling—forced, in this case—will never be able to fully rid the population of the unwanted seed of Islam. This plan is not only horrifying; it is also illogical.

"Special registration," as Moustafa Bouyami explains, was a law that targeted, in contrast, any man suspected of having ties to Islam. And it sought to do so by creating and tracing an Islamic biological lineage. This law does not simply work to restrict travel into the United States from nations that are predominantly Muslim. Special registration is required of any man who travels from and/or those who have ancestors from a list of suspicious countries. For instance, a man born in Sweden to Iranian parents would require special registration. Islam is so engulfed with suspicion that it needs to be traced back to one's ancestors. In other words, the law treats Islamic religion like a race. Islam or the destructive parts of the religion seems to be inheritable. Despite not living in a principally Islamic culture, a male is suspect if he has any family members who belong to or lived in a state where Islam was the dominant religion.[40] Not only does this law employ shaky logic but also the efficacy of the law is tenuous at best. Bouyami asserts, ". . . the dull thud of this blunt program was its own stupidity since it was unlikely to result in the capture of a terrorist, who, if he or she were in the country already, would logically not bother to register before carrying out any nefarious activity."[41] The law, perhaps, presupposes that Muslim terrorists are irrational or stupid enough to register for a program that would undermine their plots.

While special registration is not a well-known example of biologizing religion, Barack Obama's 2008 presidential bid put American suspicions that Islam can be inherited on full display. Questions about Obama's faith showed that many Americans believed that Islam could be transmitted like other hereditary traits (eye color, height, skin pigmentation, etc.). Part of the political attack on Obama depended upon circulating the idea that he was a Muslim. His proclamations of being a Christian were not enough to dispel the myth that he was a Muslim. Obama was born into Islam because his father, as the story goes, was a Muslim.

Franklin Graham, the son of famed evangelical leader Billy Graham, stated that he took Obama at his word when he said he was a Christian. However, Graham also explained that Islam is transmitted from father to son much the same way that Judaism is passed through the mother. The implication is that Islam can be treated like a race; it is inherited from the father. Graham's genealogical trace of Islam is also an ingenious way to get around the fact that Christianity is a faith to be freely chosen by the practitioner. Even if his father was a self-proclaimed atheist, the seed of Islam exists within him and can still be passed along to his son. This pronouncement by Graham only furthered the idea that Obama was not American and/or Christian enough to be the president of the United States. Because his father was a Muslim, it would be difficult for Obama to distance himself from the Islamic faith—especially in the minds of the people who were already suspicious of him. Neither Barack Obama Sr. nor Jr. claimed to follow Islam but this still left Graham with concerns. He begrudgingly admitted that he believed the presidential candidate when he said that he accepted Christ. But why should the son's disavowal of Islam be taken any more seriously than that of his father? Graham's message, whether he intended it or not, seemed to be that Obama was born into Islam and is a Muslim. In any case, this idea that Obama was a Muslim—by fact of his birth—spread and worked to deepen the feeling that Obama was a foreigner and un-American.[42]

CONCLUSION

Because the rationality behind the targeting of Muslims, ironically, lacks any kind of sense—scientific or otherwise, a more logical explanation of racism towards religious others, as Étienne Balibar points out, is the consolidation of Western culture and power. This narrative relies more on biologized race, à la Foucault, than on scientific experimentation and evidence. As Rancière asserts, the absolute rationalization of social behavior, at the heart of Western society, leads to the emergence of racism on a geopolitical level.[43] On the one hand, there are certain people—rational Westerners—who represent the best of the human race who must govern over the world to ensure progress. On the other, there are those who are incapable of governing themselves. Through biopolitics, the West has proposed the idea that they are the future of humanity. And if the evolution of humanity is to continue, Westerners must consolidate their power and ensure that those who are anti-West are kept within particular territories. Seen in this light, the racing of religion is similar to the colonial origins of racism identified by Omi and Winant. All that does not belong to "white" culture is deemed a problem and racist policies and programs are subsequently put in place to create unequal status between whites and non-whites. Christianity, as part of white culture, seems impervious to racing—just as whites were historically considered the group without a race. The normalizing of whiteness and Christianity makes it so that the faith of the white, Western civilization is not marked as a backward religion. It is a religion that can go unseen and would not disrupt modern society. The more Christianity can pass as a secular religion, the more converts it can attract.

The racing of religion in the West has had, to be sure, very specific targets—Judaism and Islam. Benhabib, nonetheless, believes that the greater problem for modern society is religion in general. Anxiety about Islam is also anxiety about the friction between modern civilization—and all that it is suppose to represent—and religion. Can there be space for religion in modern society? She proclaims that:

> . . . the most significant development in politics today concerns the unsettling of the identity of the democratic people, the *demos*, as a result of the rise of deterritorialized religious movements, including but not restricted to political Islam. This development calls into question the relation of the *demos* to the nation, when understood as an *ethnos*, and places on the agenda the transformation of repressive understandings

of both ethnicity and religion so as to allow for a larger, more inclusive democracy.[44]

The question of how religion and democracy coexist is one that cuts to the heart of modern politics. There is no question that there is greater freedom of movement now than at any time before. The principles of democracy, however, seem to be most challenged not by the movement of people but by the movement of religion. Encounters with different religions have called the people of a particular nation to reflect on their cultural ties and unity. The interaction with different religions poses special problems for modern democracies. Deterritorialized religion presents both political and ideological problems for modern states. Democracies, because they operate under the idea that difference is to be tolerated and included, are now confronted with the challenge of including those who are shaped by a different ethic. And Western democracies, which claim to separate state from religion, must now also deal with how to understand how religion, itself, can be reconciled with politics. Indeed, it is a common Western idea that there is no room for religion in governmental decisions. Western politics is forced to consider how inclusive it is when there is an influx of others who believe not only in a different religion but have a different conception of the place of religion.

Westerners need to rethink the claim that religion only makes tensions between civilizations and races worse and, therefore, has no place in the modern world. Balibar urges Westerners to consider how the purported backwardness of religion is understood as playing a part in the publicized clash of civilizations. The assumption that religion is not compatible with modernity is another way of degrading and barbarizing the non-Western other. Many self-fashioned religious cultures strive to balance religion with modernity. These cultures may reject Western life, as Huntington points out, but that does not mean that they reject modern life. Balibar, who is critical of Huntington, agrees that one need not belong to a secular community to be tolerant of other religions or participate in "civil society." He further explains that the move towards secularism is a mechanism to defend Christianity.

> Many European historians and theologians even believe that it is Christianity that has separated the sacred and the secular realms in general. As a consequence secularism can be brandished as a shield against other forms of religious universalism (above all Islam), antagonistic with Christianity, and becomes an instrument to protect "domestic" cults. . . . The dominant form of European "secularism" (this is particularly the case with French laïcité) is also a form of resistance to real multiculturalism, since many cultures are deemed to be too "religious" to become acceptable in the picture. This is not far from transforming Western culture into a secular form of religion indeed.[45]

The privileging of secularism and the problematizing of religion are, in Balibar's view, extensions of Western racism. Not only does the move to push religion out of the public and political realm help Christians to maintain a monopoly on their community but it also works to mark other religions and peoples as inferior. Those who practice other religions are incapable of understanding the place of religion in modern society.

The insinuation is that only Christians know how to maintain a balance between one's private religion and public life. Adopting secularism, however, does not mean that Christians are forced to give up their religion or beliefs. What it does is keep other religions from sharing the cultural stage. There is less room for other faiths to reach those who are not already in their community. Christianity will, thus, remain the dominant religion because Western Christians will have less exposure to other religious beliefs. Non-Christians do not necessarily have to be converted to Christianity to be converted to Western ideology. If non-Christians choose not to convert, they can instead lead or—appear to lead—a secular life. Adhering to secular practices is an acceptable way for non-Christians to prove that they can act and behave rationally. Thus, the push towards secularism can be seen as an outgrowth of the biologization of religion. Muslims are seen as a threat to modern civilization and the future of humanity because they resist Western ideals and are, thus, impervious to reason. For the greater good of humanity, they must be relegated to particular geopolitical spaces where they cannot debilitate or harm modern peoples.

NOTES

1. Rancière uses the words *ethnicity* and *species* rather than *race* here but the thrust of his argument is that the Western categorization of peoples is suspect. Because he is ultimately commenting on how divisions among people are created, I believe his sentiments also apply to race. See Jacques Rancière, *Chronicles of Consensual Times*, trans. Steven Corcoran (New York: Continuum, 2010), 5. See also Linda Martin Alcoff, *Visible Identities: Race, Gender, and the Self* (Oxford: Oxford University Press, 2006), 235–37.

2. Michael Omi and Howard Winant, *Racial Formation in the United States: from 1960s to the 1990s* (New York: Routledge, 1994), 66–67.

3. Omi and Winant, *Racial Formation*, 68.

4. Omi and Winant's section "From Science to Politics" indicates that the transition to a political and social conception of race follows a scientific understanding of race. Omi and Winant, *Racial Formation*, 64–65.

5. See Ladelle McWhorter, "A Genealogy of Modern Racism, Part 1: The White Man Cometh" in *Race and Sexual Oppression in Anglo-America* (Bloomington: Indiana University Press, 2009), 63–96. In this chapter, she traces the movement towards the idea that race was structured around the body.

6. McWhorter, *Race and Sexual Oppression*, 101.

7. She states that Foucault's conception of race can be seen as idiosyncratic but she ultimately follows his lead. (McWhorter, *Racism and Sexual Oppression*, 35)

8. Michael Omi, "'Slippin' into Darkness': The (Re)Biologization of Race," *Journal of Asian American Studies* 13 (2010): 349.

9. Omi notes that present efforts to biologize race still work to reinforce a race hierarchy but those at the top have changed. Asians, instead of "whites," occupy the top rung of the racial ladder. See Michael Omi, "'Slippin' into Darkness,'" 348.

10. See also Howard Winant, "Race and Race Theory," *Annual Review of Sociology* 26 (2000): 179.

11. Omi and Winant, *Racial Formation*, 68.

12. McWhorter argues that race and sexuality must be thought together (McWhorter, *Racism and Sexual Oppression*). See also Howard Winant, "Race and Race Theory," *Annual Review of Sociology* 26 (2000): 179–80. He explains how theorizing race continues to be challenging because it can be oriented around ethnicity, class, and nation.

13. Omi and Winant, *Race Formation*, 61–62.

14. Omi and Winant, *Race Formation*, 55. McWhorter, to the contrary, suggests that the inception of race did not depend upon different types of bodies. "Regardless of how they looked, individuals belonged to a race if they grew up in its traditions, spoke its language, and practiced its religion" (McWhorter, *Racism and Sexual Oppression*, 63). McWhorter believes that the first understanding of race referred to heritage, lineage, and tradition. Before Western conceptions of race became oriented around morphological and somatic markers, races were identified and distinguished from one another through a collection of practices. Religion was part of the package of traits that determined who belonged to which race. Along with languages and customs, religion was an indication of one's heritage. McWhorter may have a different reading from Omi and Winant on the role of religion in racial discourse but they all draw a similar conclusion about the present state of religion and race. Namely, religion—particularly Judaism—constitutes a race.

15. Omi and Winant (*Race Formation*, 182) point to George L. Mosse's *Toward the Final Solution: A History of European Racism* as an analysis of how anti-Semitism began to be racialized. See George L. Mosse, *Toward the Final Solution: A History of European Racism* (New York: Howard Fertig, 1978).

16. See Hannah Arendt, "The Nation-State; The Birth of Anti-Semitism," in *The Origins of Totalitarianism* (New York: Harcourt Brace Jovanovich, 1973), 11–53.

17. Omi and Winant, too, allude to the fact that the development of religious race coincided with the rise of scientific knowledge in the 18th century (Omi and Winant, *Race Formation*, 61–63).

18. Michel Foucault, *The History of Sexuality: An Introduction*, trans. Robert Hurley (New York: Vintage, 1990), 149–50.

19. Seyla Benhabib, "Sexual Difference and Collective Identities: The New Global Constellation," *Signs* 24 (1999): 351.

20. Benhabib, "Sexual Difference," 351.

21. Benhabib, "Sexual Differece," 350–51.

22. Sylvia Wynter, "Unsettling the Coloniality of Being/Power/Truth/Freedom: Towards the Human, after Man, Its Over-Representation—an Argument," *CR: The New Centennial Review* 3 (2003): 305-306.

23. Michel Foucault, *Il faut défendre la société: Cours au Collège de France 1975 – 1976* (Paris: Gallimard, 1997), 70–71.

24. Foucault, *Il faut*, 232.

25. Wynter, "Unsettling the Coloniality," 307.

26. Rancière, *Chronicles*, 4.

27. That David Brooks, a *New York Times* op-ed columnist, would criticize Huntington shows that the clash of civilization does have a certain amount of cultural currency. Huntington's theories do not belong strictly in the realm of academia. See David Brooks, "Huntington's Clash Revisited," *The New York Times*, March 3, 2011, accessed June 11, 2013, http://www.nytimes.com/2011/03/04/opinion/04brooks.html.

28. Samuel P. Huntington, *The Clash of Civilizations and the Remaking of the World Order* (New York: Simon & Schuster, 1996), 42.

29. Huntington, *Clash of Civilizations*, 45.

30. In an effort to break with the Western tendency towards "Orientalism," he tries to emphasize the distinctions that exist in the East and that happens largely through religion. He distances himself while not completely breaking from a racially divided world by incorporating religion into his system. This can only be the case if religion plays a substantial role in determining who belongs to which civilization but religion is not the primary determinant of race. Western is code for Protestant, Latin Americans represent the Catholics, Africans are pantheists, and Huntington himself concedes that Sinic largely refers to the adherence to Confucian ideals. (Huntington, *Clash of Civilizations*, 45)

31. Sarah Ahmed, "Affective Economies," *Social Text* 22 (2004): 131. See also Leti Volpp, "The Citizen and the Terrorist," *ULA Law Review* 49 (2002): 1575)

32. Not all Eastern cultures are equally suspect and suspect for the same reason. Islam stands alone as the religious civilization that most threatens the West. Japanese culture, although a source of anxiety before, does not trigger the same type of fear as those who might be from the Middle East or South Asia (Rancière, *Chronicles*, 6). It seems that very particular figures are associated with dangerous religions. While the Chinese are represented as a threat to the United States, their treachery was not a by-product of their religion. It is often attributed to their adherence to communism or their economic policies (Robert J. Samuelson, "The Real China Threat," *The Washington Post*, August 20, 2008, accessed on April 18, 2012, http://www.washingtonpost.com/wp-).

33. Although Steven Salaita argues that anti-Arab racism rather than Islamophobia is more accurate in describing the racist discourse that has intensified since 9/11, he comes to the same conclusion as Ahmed. Anti-Arab racism, Salaita seems to suggest, is a racism that targets those who are suspected of having any connection to a problematic part of the world (see Steven G. Salaita, "Beyond Orientalism and Islamophobia: 9/11, Anti-Arab Racism, and the Mythos of National Pride," *CR: The New Centennial Review* 6 (2006): 245–66). Ahmed claims that "Muslim" sticks to certain people—no matter if they have any connection to Islam or not—and also works to explain how Islamophobia has grown beyond just religious bounds. In other words, she explains that prejudice against "Muslims" is not just a bias against those who ascribe to the Islamic faith.

34. Ahmed, "Affective Economies," 132.

35. Rancière, *Chronicles*, 6.

36. While the trope about the irrational, poor Muslim terrorist continues to have cultural cache, the stereotype is largely unfounded. See Austan Goolsbee, "Even for Shoe Bombers, Education and Success Are Linked," *The New York Times*, September 14, 2006, accessed June 11, 2013, http://www.nytimes.com/2006/09/14/business/14scene.html.

37. McWhorter, *Racism and Sexual Oppression*, 142.

38. Rancière, *Chronicles*, 12.

39. Benhabib, "Sexual Difference," 351.

40. See Moustafa Bouyami, "Racing Religion," *CR: The New Centennial Review* 6 (2006): 267–93.

41. Bouyami, "Racing Religion," 273.

42. See Andy Barr, "Rev. Franklin Graham: President Obama 'born a Muslim,'" *Politico*, August 20, 2010, accessed November 13, 2011, http://www.politico.com/news/stories/0810/41292.html.

43. Rancière, *Chronicles*, 12.

44. Benhabib, "Turkey's Constitutional Zigzags," *Dissent* 56 (2009): 28.

45. Étienne Balibar, *We, the People of Europe?: Reflections on Transnational Citizenship*, trans. James Swenson (Princeton: Princeton University Press 2004), 224–25.

FIVE

The Race of Sexual Degenerates

Aside from concerns about invading Mexican and Muslim populations who will harm national economy and national security, respectively, there is a more overtly racist fear that the influx of immigrants will lead to the browning of America. Controllers, therefore, must inspect sexuality in order to ensure that the demography does not undergo such a change. Questions about sexuality, however, are meant to do more than root out lascivious behavior that is often attributed to people of color and will be, it is feared, the downfall of the United States. Foucault's work on sexuality also highlights why those with abnormal sexuality are seen as a race unto themselves.

Immigration policies, as many contemporary scholars point out, elucidate how abnormal sexuality is a key element to be weeded out. It has become more palatable to reject an immigrant for her sexual abnormalities than for her race. Still, this does not signal that conventional concepts of race are no longer a valid means for turning an immigrant away. Instead, the split between normal and abnormal sexuality shows another iteration of race that stems from the Western tendency to think in binary terms and the central role of heteronormativity in regulating modern populations. To understand how the world has been divided between the good and the bad sexuality, it is important first to disentangle sexuality from sex. Only after understanding how heterosexual practices have become naturalized and idealized can we understand how the sexually abnormal have become a race of sexual degenerates. Establishing heterosexual norms was not simply a means of ensuring human procreation; they were also used to aid in the reproduction of a particular kind of culture. Foucault's study of sexuality has further spurred a wave of thinkers, both complimentary and critical, to investigate the ways in which heteronormativity has been created within a larger system, which aims to control and regulate the population through immigration laws.

If the generation of people and culture are central to the modern bio-political state, then immigration policies can help elucidate prevailing ideas about who is and is not desired. Since the propagation of the population and tradition is not wholly dependent upon some original and pure group of citizens, immigration policies reveal more than just a path to legal membership. Immigration regulations, as a means to control the reproduction of the nation and society, work to codify social norms—including conventions about sexuality. Yet it would be a mistake to think that immigration policies are aimed only at molding those who hope to enter the country. These regulations do not simply work to make immigrants inculcate norms and, thereby, become accepted within their adopted nation. They also work to normalize the existing population. Immigration policies even call into question the belonging of those who have not had to cross physical borders to enter the country. In other words, immigration regulations are just as much for "insiders" as "outsiders."[1]

While the immigrant's sexuality is often linked to the protection of race—in the conventional sense of the term, the heightened inspection of the citizen's sexuality shows how biopolitics gives rise to a racism that separates those with normal sexual appetites from those with abnormal sexuality. Anxieties about the sexuality of immigrants do more than just point to suspicions about their purported lack of restraint. Immigration policies also call into question the membership of those citizens who do not subscribe to social norms. Citizens and immigrants, alike, can be members of a different race if they follow abnormal sexual practices.

In what follows, I will explore the ways in which sexuality has been linked with race. The conflation of sex and sexuality, while covering over the distinction between the two, makes clearer the link between sexuality and race. Establishing heteronormativity ensures the reproduction of the people and culture. When sex and sexuality began to be separated, the idea that heteronormativity was necessary to preserve the race remained. However, this was not the only link between sexuality and race. The growing importance of sexuality within modern biopolitics also showed that race was not simply seen in terms of skin color and somatic differences. The problematization of sexuality exposes the ways standards of sexuality are used to reproduce a certain culture and anchor a particular kind of society. Race, therefore, can be divided in terms of those who conform to sexual norms and those who transgress them.

THE CONFLATION OF SEX AND SEXUALITY

Because of the legacy of Western dualism, issues of sex and sexuality have often been conflated so the male and female sex can be joined together through heterosexual union. On one side, there is the mind, the male, and the active. On the other, there is the body, the female, and the passive. While the split between the sexually normal and abnormal has not always received attention from scholars, attempts to identify heterosexuals as normal and all others as abnormal is very much a part of the Western philosophical tradition. Heteronormativity, some argue, is one of the leading reasons it is difficult to separate sexuality from sex. Despite cultural shifts that blur such distinctions as the mind and the body, the belief that heterosexuality is normal and good remain strong.

In order to challenge sexual dualism, it is necessary to recognize sexual plurality. Sexuality cannot be divided simply into heterosexual (read "normal") and homosexual (read "abnormal"). The nonheterosexual category, of course, spans a broad range of individual practices and identities (bisexual, transgender, intersex, asexual, etc.). Growing studies in sexuality also show that race and ethnicity add to sexual multiplicity. While thinking sex and sexuality together often has the effect of glossing over sexual difference, many leading scholars believe, in contrast, that thinking sexuality and race together has the potential to challenge heteronormativity. Because Westerners are accustomed to thinking of race as a multi-leveled ladder, equating sexuality with race could help to bring out the complexities of sexuality as well. This, of course, does not mean that what is privileged in the West (the "white" race and heterosexuality) will automatically disappear. Still, the complication of sexuality in this manner could help to challenge the heterosexual and homosexual divide that seems to be at the center of sexual dualism.

Since heterosexuality has become the norm, there has been a tendency to divide sex and sexuality into two asymmetrical categories. Heteronormativity dictates that there are two sexes: the male sex and the female sex. Proper behavior, appetites, and desires that support heterosexual norms are ascribed to each sex. The script was set so that an individual should only engage in sexual activity with those from the opposite sex. Thus, the male sex is frequently given positive attributes of activity and strength. He takes the lead by pursuing the female and initiating sexual contact. In short, he possesses a healthy sexual appetite. The female sex is supposed to be the passive, weaker, inferior sex. She is pursued, submits to sexual activity, and has an unhealthy attitude towards sexual intercourse. These corresponding dichotomies between men and women have been so engrained in Western thinking that the distinction between sex and sexuality can be difficult to discern.

Growing studies in the field of sexuality, however, show that there is no "natural" correlation between sex and sexuality. Scholars work to prove that the binary systems of both sex and sexuality are created to reinforce heterosexual norms. By de-centering heterosexuality, thinkers from myriad disciplines began to expose the gaps between sex and sexuality. The emergence of queer theory and transgender studies, for instance, brought with it questions about the natural connection between the sex and sexuality of an individual as well as questions about the role of heteronormativity in the reproduction of culture.

This dichotomy between men and women has been further imprinted into the social consciousness by both scientific and philosophical discourse. Scientists and philosophers alike have proposed that "nature" has neatly assigned each sex discrete organs and somatic qualities that must be used in conjunction solely with each other. Philosophers have also supported this position by carving out particular attributes for each sex. The male sex, of course, came to represent the good, healthy, normal sexuality. And while the depiction of the female sex and sexuality did vary, the female sex has historically been seen as the bad, unhealthy, and abnormal sexuality. Sex and sexuality became conflated because there is recognition of only two sexes. This, in turn, gave rise to oppositional dispositions towards the sex act. In other words, one's anatomical parts determined good and bad sexuality.

The goodness of the male sex is, in part, related to the perception that men are equipped with the active body part—the penis. Males are the active agents who are entrusted by nature to propel the human species forward. Without the male sex, humans would cease to exist. In addition, they are supposed to be the initiators of sexual intercourse. His penis is what allows him to provide the seed for his own progeny. It is also thanks to the male sex, the story goes, that future generations arise. Women may not desire sexual intercourse or the sexual advances of men. But luckily, as philosophical and scientific discourse relay, it is the male who is instilled with a healthy sexual appetite that can ensure the human species lives on. The male biological constitution is such that it can and should dominate the female sex in order to ensure a robust human population.

While women's sexuality has been described both as unwilling and insatiable, philosophers have often portrayed female sexuality as unhealthy and abnormal.[2] There is no dearth of literature depicting women as apathetic or resistant to sexual intercourse. Furthermore, thinkers from various disciplines have sought to show that women do not and should not gain any pleasure through the sex act. Because men are the active agents, women should necessarily be passive in the sex act. The female sex organ, in contrast to the active male penis, is a receptacle. She is equipped with a womb, which is seen as an apt metaphor for her passive sexual nature. Her anatomy allows her to carry progeny to term and deliver them but it does not allow for pleasure during sexual intercourse. Women are described as naturally averse to the sex act. Since women are designed by nature not to feel sexual pleasure, men must overcome their problematic sexuality in order to prolong the human species. Female sex and sexuality have long been conflated because women's passive sexual organs were thought to be the origin of her resistance or apathy towards the process necessary for propagation

Yet women's resistance to the sex act is not the only sign of her unhealthy sexuality. When there is acknowledgment of female sexual pleasure, this is also seen as a sign of her abnormal sexuality because she is believed to be acting against her nature. Women who are not sexually averse would be considered sexual inverts.[3] She is assuming the inverse, male role if she enjoys sexual acts.

NECESSARY DISTINCTIONS BETWEEN SEX AND SEXUALITY

The distinction between sex and sexuality cannot be fully understood unless these rigid dichotomies between the male sex and his idealized sexuality and the female sex and her problematic sexuality are untied. In response, contemporary scholars have focused more on sexuality than sex. To break the mold that conflates sex with sexuality, thinkers have placed the two into different spheres. Sex is a natural phenomenon. Sexuality, in contrast, is seen as a social construct. One's sex is seen, generally, as a biological or physiological given.[4] It is sexuality that is culturally created and, therefore, sexuality that offers a larger forum for contestation. Although there are certainly those who are identified as having abnormal genitals (intersex, for instance), it seems that society is more troubled by what people do with their sexual parts. Abnormal sexuality deals with the meaning attached to sexual organs and their proper functioning. The project to separate sex from sexuality, therefore, must also address sexual standards and norms.

Yet many feminist scholars warn that challenges to heteronormativity should not be so centered on men. They have noted that homosexual men have too often come to represent the resistance of heteronormativity. This might be the case because women's sexuality has always been problematized. There is a long history of depicting women's sexuality as somehow missing the mark. When women exhibit behavior that does not conform to sexual norms, this is—in a sense—par for the course. When men break from the heterosexual norm, in contrast, this is seen as a real break from how the idealized sexuality should function.

Despite the focus on male sexuality, texts such as Simone de Beauvoir's *The Second Sex* drew attention to how sexuality was imbued with social meaning. She argued that the creation of Woman went hand-in-hand with the oppression of women. Her assertion that "one is not born a woman, but rather becomes, a woman"[5] worked to dislodge the idea that one's biological make-up determined, among other things, one's disposition—sexual or otherwise. She sought to show that becoming a woman was a result of social rather than biological engineering. Women were not necessarily and naturally troublesome, resistant, or passive. The interpretation of women's sexuality, instead, was a reflection of society's stance towards them. The discourse concerning women's sexuality was part of a larger reading of women. If women were seen as predisposed by God or nature to problematic behavior, then it would be easier to make the case for patriarchal values. It would be the job of the better, male sex to control those belonging to the female sex. Because women are created in relation to men, it is not surprising that women are given problematic attributes. Male characteristics, in juxtaposition, are made to seem ever more ideal in comparison.

If women are, in part, oppressed because they are believed to be an amalgamation of an inferior sex and problematic sexuality, then this discourse must be challenged in order to bring women out of man's shadow. One path to fighting the social oppression of women, therefore, is to question the discourse that joins sex and sexuality. Feminists exposed the social norms surrounding sexuality by arguing that one's sex does not prescribe a particular sexual disposition or orientation. It is not biology or physiology but rather cultural readings and standards that create, on one hand, the superior sex with normal sexual appetites and, on the other hand, the inferior sex with abnormal sexual appetites. If nature does not predetermine behavior and dispositions, as Freud concedes; then change is possible.[6] Unlike Freud, however, feminists believed that it was social norms that needed to be changed. It was the norms—rather than the women—which were problematic. They argued that neither natural nor psychological defects were the cause of women's abnormal sexuality. Instead of searching for other (psychological) paths to remedy problems that afflict women, feminists argued that it was the norms and standards of sexuality themselves that needed to be rethought. By questioning norms, feminists hope that the familial and political order, which work to oppress women, will also begin to be questioned.

On the one hand, challenging sexual norms does not only benefit women. If the link between sex and sexuality is not supported by nature but by culturally created norms, then it is not just the conceptions of female sexuality or Woman that are changed. On the other hand, challenging sexual norms seemed to have put a greater spotlight on problematic male sexuality. Some argue that male sexuality, more often than not, comes to represent the challenge to sexual standards. The attention paid to abnormal male sexuality still contributes to a privileging of the male. Men, again, become the focus of sexuality to the detriment of women. It is as if the abnormal sexual behavior is the real problem for society because female abnormal sexual behavior is already known and accepted.

Too much emphasis and concern over abnormal sexual practices of men also helps to cover over the fact that women sometimes face discrimination on account of both their sex and their sexuality. The focus on male sexual norms works again to conflate female sex and female sexuality. Society is perhaps beginning to see that there is a difference between the male sex and socially acceptable male sexuality. Men can have either normal or abnormal sexuality. Women, however, still seem to occupy a zone of abnormality. There is no conceptual space between the female sex and female sexuality. They both fall back into the realm of the abnormal and inferior.

While concern over abnormal or pathological sexuality is not anything new, Foucault's analysis aims to trace how these categories are established in order to regulate the population as a whole. One of his goals is to show that sexual norms work to control and regulate everyone. Whether or not this project was realized is still up in the air. There is plenty of evidence to suggest that male sexuality, even in Foucault's own work, continues to take center stage. His work on normalization could be construed as another way in which the male is privileged. Through his theories of normalization, he shows that the so-called "normal" (men, heterosexuals, heterosexual men) among us are also affected and shaped by sexual regulations. He points out that those who follow normal or acceptable sexual practices are just as aware of sexual norms as sexual deviants.

Normal individuals are constantly reminded of what counts as ideal and standard sexual practices. Sexual norms must weigh on the mind of the normal just as much as the abnormal. The normal must take care to follow the script of normal sexuality and are, therefore, controlled by sexual norms too. If they do not properly regulate their sexuality, there could be no guarantee that the normal would not become abnormal.

Yet his work has been helpful to many scholars who want to de-center male sexuality. His analysis was meant to highlight the ways in which sexual controls continue to expand and pervade all corners of modern life. By framing sexuality within the context of political, national, and community survival, he provided a foundation for those who wanted to understand why the sexuality of women and particular races were seen as more problematic than others. Because Foucault acknowledged and wrote about how sexual mores function to identify female sexuality as a problem, his linking of race and sexuality has also been helpful for those who believe that the non-white male is not the only subject worth studying.[7]

SEXUAL AND RACE DISCRIMINATION IN IMMIGRATION LAWS

That sexual perversion and psychopathology are hallmarks of racial infe-riority may seem to run counter to conventional conceptions of race. However, earlier U.S. immigration policies provide a record of how sexu-al health and perversion was intimately connected with race discourse. Although lawmakers tried to downplay the racism within previous im-migration laws by highlighting the sexual deviousness of other races, they argued, however unconvincingly, that their objections to particular immigrant populations had more to do with their sexual inclinations and habits than their race. Even critics of their own time could see, though, that sexual pathology could not be separated from race. Sexual perver-sion has long been a distinguishing factor of different races. The differ-ence between the immigration policies of the past and today is that the racism within the policies was more closely linked to conventional delin-eations of race. It is easier to see how sexual pathology was used to support explicit racist language because it matched up with traditional racial designations.

When scholars analyze how Asians, for example, were targeted for being sexually perverse, they also saw that these discourses of sexual abnormality and race inferiority could not be separated. The sexual devi-ancy of the Asian was emphasized to prove that their race was proble-matic. Highlighting the problem of sexuality was an attempt to mask race discrimination, even if it was not ultimately successful. Although immi-grant women of color are regulated because they are seen as potential sources of sexual and biological corruption,[8] Asian women were among the first targets of laws that equated sexual deviance with race. The Page Act is often held as an exemplar case of racializing sexuality. Even though the legislation was to be aimed generally at all immoral women, its purpose was clearly to bar Asian women from entering the country. U.S. consuls, under the Page Act, were required to ensure that any Asian immigrant was not under contract for "lewd and immoral purposes."[9] The heightened scrutiny of Asian women, in general, and Chinese wom-en, in particular, through the Page Act reveals why abnormal sexuality was racialized. Anna Marie Smith also argues that Chinese women were denied entrance into the country because the Page Act officially equated Chinese women with prostitution.[10] Thanks to the Page Act, Chinese women were synonymous with sexual depravity. The Page Act made it difficult to separate the Chinese race from sexual abnormality.

Siobhan Somerville's analysis of immigration laws points further to the connection between the assumed immorality of Asian sexuality and the restriction of immigrants from China, Japan, and other Asian nations. It is not a coincidence that the Chinese Exclusion Act followed only seven years behind the Page Act.[11] In other words, the Chinese Exclusion Act was structured to close any loopholes in the Page Act. The Page Act could be used effectively to bar Asian women from entering the United States on the grounds of sexual immorality. The Chinese Exclusion Act, in contrast, does not emphasize the suspect nature of Asian sexuality. Instead, it charges that Chinese laborers are dangers to the "good order of certain localities. . ."[12] Perhaps, the legislators of the Chinese Exclusion Act steered clear from language that impugned Asian sexuality because it was already established to be problematic through the Page Act. There was no need to restate the case.

Deirdre Moloney suggests, however, another reason why the Chinese Exclusion Act did not make mention of sexual immorality. She believes that the state was still suspicious of immigrant female sexuality. It was easier, though, for the government to argue that immigrant women were a danger to society because they were likely to become a burden to the community and the nation. That the Chinese Exclusion Act and the Likely to Become Public Charge (LPC) law were both passed in 1882 points to a restructuring of means to restrict immigration women.

> [W]omen who were suspected of prostitution or who lived with their partners or children outside of a formal marriage were often excluded on the basis of the LPC provision rather than on grounds of prostitution or moral turpitude. Indeed, LPC and other provisions related to economic dependency were the most common reason for exclusion, in large part because they were easier charges to substantiate.[13]

The movement away from language that explicitly notes the sexual immorality of Asian women does not mean that their sexuality was no longer a concern for the state. Asian women were still equated with the sexual deviant. The case was just made in a more circuitous fashion. The Chinese Exclusion Act was directed at maintaining the good order of localities. Wording of the LPC law, on the other hand, revealed how immigrant women were supposed to be dangers to the community because they resisted heteronormativity. Asian women could threaten the community because they engaged in prostitution or because they operated outside the typical framework of marriage. In other words, engagement in prostitution no longer needed to be proven. What needed to be proven was what was already assumed; Asian women were sources of communal corruption. The Page Act coupled with the Chinese Exclusion Act served as a virtual ban for the immigration of Asian women because Asian women were synonymous with prostitution. Thus, their sexual immorality was a threat to the public. Reading the Chinese Exclusion Act together with the Likely to Become Public Charge law produced the same result but through a different logic. Immigrant women were identified as contrary to good order because they were believed to be incapable of supporting themselves outside the confines of official marriage or prostitution. These immigration laws passed in 1882, therefore, worked to further restrict the immigration of Asian women into the country through a subtext of sexual abnormality.

THE BIOPOLITICS OF SEXUALITY

On the one hand, it is easy to see why sexuality has been thought together with race. After all, immigration laws such as the Page Act show how problematic sexuality has been attributed to non-white races. On the other hand, there are some reasons to resist thinking sexuality as a category of race. McWhorter, who ultimately argues that sexual oppression is a form of racism, had her own reservations about thinking race and sexuality together. The potential dilution of race discrimination was among her concerns. Luibheid seems to have the opposite concern. Tying together sexual oppression and racism, she argues, detracts from how sexual norms work to oppress those who are believed to fall outside such categories. Luibheid believes that sexuality should be divorced from racial categories because the conflation of sexuality with race makes it difficult to analyze the particular way sexual norms are used to determine who is a fit or unfit candidate.[14] Foucault's analysis of sexuality, which heavily influenced both McWhorter and Luibheid, may offer a solution. By emphasizing how modern racism operates by dividing the population between the normal and the abnormal, Foucault—McWhorter argues—draws on a key principle of race formation. If Foucault's analysis of race is seen through the lens of establishing norms, then race and racism are not restricted to discussions about the ranking of those with particular somatic qualities and the discrimination against them. Because norms take center stage in Foucault's modern conception of race, there would be a better chance that sexuality is not overshadowed—as Luibheid fears—by concerns over racism. Indeed, discussions about whether or not people with particular skin color or who come from certain backgrounds are or are not discriminated against often generate a toxic atmosphere that leaves little room for anything else to be unpacked. Since sexual norms and heterosexism play a central role in Foucault's analysis of modern racism, it might not be as problematic to discuss sexuality and race together. Many scholars, to the contrary, believe that there are philosophical and political benefits to thinking sexuality and race together.

McWhorter, following Foucault, argues that there is precedence for thinking about how race is used to describe other differences besides skin color among people. She draws on Foucault's examination of seventeenth-century England. Despite the differences between the seventeenth-century race war that Foucault describes and race discrimination as it is typically understood today, these discrepancies in past and present race formations can help elucidate how Foucault's concept of modern racism works in contemporary immigration policies—especially in regard to the banning of the sexually abnormal. In the earlier era of race war, morphology was not the primary distinguishing factor between races. Nor did one race believe that they were of superior moral or intellectual stock. Similarities include the desire to defend the community against invaders and the division of the population in two. Foucault shows, therefore, that race formation need not revolve around skin color or any of the other hallmarks of conventional race.

As an example of a case that does not follow the somatic model of race conflict, Foucault pointed to what he believed was the first case of race war: the Saxon revolt against the Norman government led by James I.[15] The self-proclaimed Saxon underclass fashioned themselves as an indigenous race that was conquered by a race of alien invaders. In order to make this claim, the splitting of the population into two camps needs to be made. "In early race war discourse, there is no presumption of an essential morphological manifestation of racial difference—Normans look pretty much like Saxons."[16] Different physical qualities, therefore, were not the crux of race distinction. McWhorter further adds, ". . . the bad thing about Normans is not that they are essentially intellectually or morally inferior to Saxons, but that they are here among us, planting their fiefs upon Saxon land. . . ."[17]

Similarly, McWhorter points to how differences of religion, tradition, and language—none of which necessarily were expressed through morphology—were used as divisions between races. Homosexuals, therefore, do not need to look physically different from the dominant population to be considered a separate race. They need only be labeled and depicted as a threat to society. And, of course, this campaign against homosexuals was quite successful. McWhorter states, "It is hardly necessary to assert that the most pervasive image of the homosexual in our culture is that of the sexual predator—the lurking, child-molesting, virgin-corrupting, disease-spreading pervert."[18] While the deformity of the homosexual cannot necessarily be seen on the physical body, the creation of the homosexual cannot be separated from biological discourse. The biological claims made to support homophobia, in turn, help show why sexual deviancy is connected to biopolitics.

McWhorter suggests that present-day attitudes towards homosexuals are informed by scientific discourse.[19] Abnormal sexuality need not present itself through somatic qualities. Pathological sexuality, instead, is the expression of some type of biological failing. What we see, then, is that biological science does not only deal with morphological traits. Sexual deviants are suspect because they represent a lesser stage of human evolution. Their proclivities make it so either they are unable or unwilling to conform to the rules of society—including heteronormativity. If, perhaps, they were more developed beings, they would not have these urges to break with heterosexual standards or could rein in their abnormal sexual appetites. Because they are seen as belonging to a lower order of humanity, homosexuals are for all intents and purposes a different race of people.

> These creatures are, either continually or episodically, outside the governance of reason. Their affliction in every case is a matter of development—either faulty, arrested, or retrograde. They cannot be assimilated to society both because they cannot manage their own behavior well enough to function within its civil constraints and because they pose a biological threat to it in the form of contagion and corruption of germ plasm.[20]

McWhorter believes that modern racism depends upon the idea of human evolution, which makes use of scientific rhetoric to divide the community.

Eduardo Mendieta suggests that the key in understanding how race operates in Foucault's work is to see that race is "a mechanism of power that proceeds or is guided by a logic that is executed in twos. The logic of race is a logic of a bifurcated social body."[21] Because the scientific discourse surrounding sexuality helped to split—however unevenly—the population into the normal and the abnormal, Foucault believed sexuality was a useful mechanism for regulating and controlling the population. Sexuality became ever more laden with meaning through biopolitics because it linked the life of the individual with the life of the community and the human species. Everything was at stake with sexuality.

The culture, the community, and the human race hung in the balance of good sexual practices. If good and normal sexuality prevailed, then all would be well. If, on the other hand, the population allowed bad sexual practices to creep into their lives and community, all could be lost. Foucault showed that the issue of sexuality was a useful mechanism for controlling and regulating the population because it worked on small and large scales. By reinforcing and proliferating sexual norms, individuals would be made ever more aware of and cautious about their own sexual proclivities. Self-regulation was encouraged. Each sexual act, thought, or impulse could and should be scrutinized by the individual so as to ensure that they fit with sexual norms.

Since sexual discourse was linked to the survival of the human species, it also became tied to racist ideology. Part of protecting the human species was making sure that the best of them would prosper. This meant that sexual discourse was entangled with race discourse because sexual practices were key for producing the best human beings. Through themes of normal and abnormal sexuality, traditional conceptions of race were folded into the biopolitical distinctions between the races. On one side were those who had healthy sexuality and carried the hopes for the future of humanity. In early U.S. immigration policies, the healthy race was constituted primarily of Northern Europeans. All non-white and non-Northern Europeans were considered to have pathological sexuality.

They could not be entrusted to carry the mantle for future generations because they lacked the finer qualities. Immigration regulations help to codify the belief that inferior races shared at least one common character-istic—a pathological sexuality. Because of their less than ideal sexuality, they would create further problems (moral, economic, cultural, etc.) and burdens for the Americans who stylize themselves as the most developed of nations.

Because normal sexuality was already in a precarious state, those who had abnormal sexual practices should not be allowed to infiltrate the community. Asking those who followed normal sexual practices to main-tain vigilance against themselves and their unhealthy sexual desires was already a tall order. The task of promoting and sustaining a healthy com-munity would be made even more difficult if others with different cul-tures and values were allowed to enter the country. It was not just the borders of the individual psyche that needed to be defended. Political and national borders also reflected the heightened concern over the intru-sion of pathological sexuality. "If they [homosexuals] were outside our national boundaries, we had to close our borders to them."[22] Those be-longing to the unhealthy and abnormal race of sexual deviants must not be allowed to intermingle with the healthy race. This is why the cam-paign to defend community borders from a pathological sexuality can be seen so clearly in immigration policies.

That a state would seek to limit the number of homosexuals coming into the community is not surprising considering the importance hetero-normativity plays in modern society. In order to produce the "right" type of individuals who will allow the human race to reach its destiny, indi-viduals must reproduce. Heterosexuality, therefore, is privileged over homosexuality or other sexual practices, which do not have procreation as its ultimate and only goal. Heteronormativity becomes paramount for the preservation of the species. Those who do not adhere to these norms are seen as counterproductive or a hindrance to the trajectory of the human species. Resistance to heteronormativity is seen as a hindrance or obstacle to the survival of human species. Interpreted in this manner, those who stray from heterosexual practices must be deeply flawed and disturbed. Who would willfully contribute to the end of the human spe-cies? The answer: only those who differ radically in kind from normal people. Thus, heterosexuality becomes a baseline for the normal and good race. All who do not conform to heteronormativity are automatical-ly determined to belong to a different, bad race that can only infect the good race with their pathologies.

Just because somatic qualities are no longer at the center of discrimi-nation, however, does not mean that racism no longer exists. Modern racism or the racism of biopolitics has become embedded and recoded in psychological and intellectual language. This way of thinking racism is, in fact, not new. This type of discrimination borrows ideology from a past form of racism. Expanding colonial empires depended upon the idea that natives represented an intellectually and spiritually stunted human form. Homosexuals and sexual deviants become raced in much the same way as Africans, Asians, Italians, etc. via their inferior psychological qualities. While the attribution of psychological defects to raced bodies might have been more obvious in early U.S. immigration policies, the theme that psychopathological individuals represent a different race still carries some currency in present-day immigration policies. This time, though, it is the homosexual race—rather than the oversexed races—that needs to be blocked from entering the community. Homosexuals and sexual perverts, with the help of the Immigration Act of 1917, were classified as constitutional psychopathic inferiors. [23] Such a move made it easier to deny anyone who broke from sexual standards entrance into the country. Psychological defect is the old standby excuse when policy makers want to deny entrance to an undesirable population. Yet those like Somerville, Luibheid, and Judith Butler who analyze current immigration laws recognize this familiar racist pattern. The foundation for identifying the homosexual race has been set. They have already been identified as psychologically inferior and physically dangerous.

IMMIGRATION AND SEXUAL RACISM

It is, however, important to recognize that race discrimination and sexual discrimination can be used separately to block the entrance of immigrants. An immigrant's sexuality or race, alone, can be used to deny entry. It is also necessary to be sensitive to how different segments of the population are targets of multiple forms of discrimination. Scholars such as Mary Eaton and David Carbado suggest that there is a need to separate race discrimination from sexual discrimination. There are those who suffer from both. And if they begin to become the same, they believe that there will be no way to acknowledge "compound discrimination." [24] Luibheid further argues that it is more difficult, however, to understand discrimination of sexuality—especially in the case of women—in immigration policies. "In the instances when sexuality is addressed in immigration scholarship, it is generally conflated with gender, which in turn is often conflated with women—a triple erasure meaning that only women have sexuality, sexuality is gender, and gender or sexuality is normatively heterosexual." [25] Theories that work toward combining sexual discrimination with race discrimination would, therefore, further obfuscate the ways in which immigration regulations discriminate against those who are suspect due to their race, gender, and sexuality.

But, as Siobhan Somerville notes, immigration regulations are particularly helpful in understanding the conflation of sexuality and race. Even though other laws treated race and sexuality as different entities, immigration policies help make clear how sexual discrimination has been combined with race discrimination. Earlier immigration policies like the Page Act may have attracted the negative attention of scholars because of their obvious race discrimination but the sexuality of the immigrant was also part of the equation. Immigration rulings and regulations of the not so distant past show that sexual discrimination seemed to be more prominent than race discrimination. Or, at least, sexual discrimination seems to be a more and more acceptable path for blocking entrance into the country. This could be the case because there is a greater tolerance for sexual discrimination than for race discrimination—even if they are ultimately connected or if the immigrant is suspect on both grounds. It could also be the case that the bifurcation of people into the normal and abnormal categories allows for the assumption that race is already a part of sexuality. For these reasons, immigration policies can give us into the Foucauldian concept of modern race and racism.

Although there are historical and political grounds for keeping race and sexuality separate, immigration regulations serve as a historical trace of how sexuality and race have been conflated. Somerville suggests that U.S. immigration regulations are helpful for understanding how sexuality and race comingle in the eyes of the law. Building on the work of Kimberlé Crenshaw and Eaton, Somerville's studies show that sexuality and race have been thought separately in other areas of the law. These leading scholars in intersecting identities recognize that ". . . in practice, [race and sexuality] tend to be seen as mutually exclusive; indeed, they are rarely discussed together in the same case."[26] Somerville further notes that laws concerning sexuality, unlike laws pertaining to race, are relatively new phenomena.[27] While past immigration regulations show a clear connection between race and sexuality, this intersection—while still present—is not quite so obvious in current immigration code.

Recent immigration cases show an attempt to obfuscate the link between race and sexuality by emphasizing the dangers of sexual deviancy. Still, Somerville suggests that attention paid to sexuality does not displace the concern over race. She believes that a greater emphasis on sexual dangers is an indication that overtly racist legal language is no longer effective and acceptable. "The INA's [Immigration and Nationality Act] removal of racial categories of exclusion, then, indicated not the end of racialized and racist immigration and naturalization policies but the recognition that the explicit *language* of race was losing legitimacy in official constructions of American citizenship."[28] The shift from the racially suspect to the sexually suspect, however, works to strengthen the intersection between race and sexuality. Somerville insists that, although race and sexuality are not as apparently connected as they were in previous eras of immigration law, they are nonetheless inextricably linked. Cases like *Boutilier vs. INS* (Immigration and Naturalization Service) seem to be focused on sexual miscreants but they cannot be separated from race.

According to the ruling, Boutilier was denied entrance into the United States because of his sexual orientation rather than his race.

The judgment against him connected his sexual practices with a pathological mindset, not an inferior race. In this ruling, ". . . the Court had to lay bare that Congress was not concerned with the facts about homosexuality as such; that antipathy toward homosexuals as a group rather than a more general concern for the mental health of the nation was the motivating factor for the exclusion. . . ."[29] The state's greater focus on abnormal sexual identities, however, does not mean that the state is no longer concerned with regulating and controlling problematic races. Sexuality has not replaced race. Somerville believes, instead, that the *Boutilier* ruling shows that sexuality and race are inseparable. Earlier immigration laws made it clear that certain races should be prohibited from entering the United States because they could poison the rest of the population. Their devious sexuality was depicted as a threat to monogamous heterosexual marriage, which served as the foundation of sexual norms.[30] To see how race is implicated even in the *Boutilier* verdict, it is necessary to understand that past immigration regulations, which did not seem concerned with concealing racial discrimination, worked to draw a line between racially inferior people and their suspect mental and sexual constitution. While there are attempts to downplay legal bias towards heterosexuality, Somerville argues that the *Boutilier* case shows that the power of the state is turning its attention towards sexual identities that challenge monogamous heterosexual marriage. Thinking sexuality and race together is not just an abstract exercise. It is a legal reality.

Even though some key laws which emphasized abnormal sexuality as a means to deny immigrants entrance into the country have been repealed, this does not mean that immigration regulations are no longer concerned with immigrants' sexuality. Nor does it mean that sexuality is no longer racialized. The Chinese Exclusion Act, which conflated problematic sexuality with an inferior race, was repealed in 1943. Congressional legislation in 1990 also removed "persons of psychopathic personality" (code for homosexuals) from the list of people who could not enter the country. But, as Somerville notes, this piece of legislation had more to do with the Public Health Service's refusal to identify homosexuals as persons of psychopathic personality than lawmakers' enlightened stance towards homosexuality. Although Congress could no longer justify banning homosexuals on the grounds of psychopathology, legislators used the fear surrounding AIDS to ban gay men and immigrants of color from entry into the United States. They argued that the homosexual was "the etiologic agent for acquired immune deficiency syndrome [AIDS]" and should, therefore, not be allowed to enter and possibly infect the American population.[31] In other words, homosexuals were banned on the basis of physical health rather than mental health. The trope of a (homo)sexual sickness nevertheless remains.

As Freud and McWhorter further show, there is a history for equating sexual abnormality with psychological pathology. It seems that the steps taken to remove the appearance of racial discrimination from present immigration regulations instead point to how racial discourse has shifted. Racial discrimination is no longer acceptable if it is entangled with somatic qualities. It is more acceptable and effective if racial discrimination was expressed through the language of mental failings. Sexual normalcy and racial supremacy, however, have always been tied to both physical and mental qualities. Put otherwise, the description of the inferior human has relied heavily on either bodily or psychological failings.

CONCLUSION: DISMANTLING DUALITIES

Laws restricting immigration have made good use of the many dualities embedded within Western thought. These bifurcations can often be simplified into "good" and "bad." Men, heterosexuals, and the intellect/psyche serve as positive counterparts respectively to women, homosexuals, and the body. Growing attention to the question of sexuality, however, has managed to disrupt these dualities. The emergence of homosexuality and the resistance to heterosexual norms has caused scientists, psychoanalysts, and philosophers to suggest that the split between men and women is not so firm. Issues of sexuality have also cast a shadow over the preeminence of the mind over the body. While the privilege of the mind over the body may not really be in jeopardy, it is worth noting that the claim that unfit immigrants are mentally deficient no longer carries the same weight. Or at the very least, it is not always the case that deficient mental qualities are given as the reason for blocking entry. Westerners have claimed and continue to claim that those with defective psyches should not be admitted into the country.

Yet the more recent narrative that seeks to deny entrance to those with HIV/AIDS—which is often code for homosexuals—depends on a narrative of physical rather than mental fitness and superiority. This is not to say that those who are suspected of being carriers of HIV/AIDS are not also thought to be mentally defective. The concern over the spread of HIV/AIDS is considered by many to be another front in the attempt to reinforce heterosexism. While the main argument against allowing homosexuals to enter the country once rested on their mental inferiority, tactics had to be changed when the Public Health Service would no longer back the claim that homosexuals were mentally defective. The attempt to use a physical, rather than mental, characteristic as a means to block entry shows that the mind/body split has undergone a change. It is telling, though, that policy makers were at least forced to use another rationale to justify their prejudice against homosexuals. Yet women and

homosexuals are still in disadvantaged position when immigrating because of the dualistic, patriarchal, and heterosexual ideals engrained
within Western society.

"And HIV, as Katie King observes, is both altering the terrain of what
counts as the gay/lesbian community and producing new collectivities
that cannot be captured within a gay/straight model."[32] Concerns over
sexually transmitted diseases have worked to disrupt the heterosexual/
homosexual bifurcation. While policy makers try to equate transmitters
of AIDS with homosexuals, this line of thinking does not always work
because social understandings of race influence the way the community
sees those who live with AIDS. Those with HIV/AIDS are not always
automatically thought to contract the disease through homosexual acts.
Attempts to exclude those with AIDS from entering the country cannot
be neatly encompassed in the heterosexual/homosexual divide, even if
lawmakers would like to link the disease explicitly to homosexuals. More
to the point, it is the issue of race that creates problems for those who
would like to use the "AIDS threat" as shorthand for "homosexual." King
suggests that certain races or ethnicities are thought to contract AIDS in
different manners than others. She argues that "Hispanics" are depicted
in a more positive light than "blacks." Thus the explanation about members of each group is filtered through race narratives. Hispanics, according to EuroAmerican discourse, are primarily infected through drug use.
Blacks, in contrast, become infected through homosexual acts such as
anal penetration.[33] When addressing concerns over AIDS/HIV, it is clear
that race is already a factor.

Recognizing the social tendency to view AIDS infection differently in
ethnic communities pushes us to think about race and sexuality together.
But there are also theoretical reasons to do so. Thinking sexuality and
race together could actually help break the many dualities that are a
hindrance to society (normal/abnormal, heterosexual/homosexual, man/
woman, psychological/physical, etc). Crenshaw and Eaton, among others, believe that it would be beneficial to see how sexuality has become
racialized. They believe that the racialization of sexuality would help to
dismantle the sexual binary. Instead of dividing people into either the
heterosexual or homosexual camp, the racialization of sexuality would
show how sexuality does, indeed, come in a multitude of forms. Sexuality seems to be so strictly compartmentalized but this dichotomy would
not be so easy to maintain if sexuality could not only be divided into
two—namely, between the good heterosexual and the bad homosexual.
Eaton insists that racializing homosexuality is a necessary step in destabi-
lizing this binary, which sustains homophobic laws.[34] Once the logic behind the bifurcation of sexuality is unhinged, perhaps the legal code built
upon that logic could also be more readily challenged.

While immigration law seems more focused on male homosexuality
than other abnormal sexual practices, it is not the case that immigration

agents only turn away men with abnormal sexuality or that homosexuality alone is the problem.[35] Goldman details how immigration agents also scrutinize the sexuality of women. These officers are given the responsibility of differentiating between acceptable and unacceptable female immigrants. A large part of that decision is made upon the assessment of the woman's sexuality. Will she be able to (re)produce appropriate citizens or will she "infect" the community through her abnormal sexuality? If immigration officials do not properly weed out the deviants, they could admit women who either challenge the heterosexual norm or those who, while in keeping with heterosexual norms, could produce too many children because they possess a hypersexual nature.[36]

Luibheid reinforces this point when she states:

> Thus unwelcome migrants are often characterized as engaging in "unrestrained" childbearing, which is seen to reflect their deviation from or imperfect mastery over mainstream heterosexual norms, resulting in the birth of "undesirable" children. Or they are portrayed as the bearers of aberrant sexual practices, questionable sexual morals, and sexually transmitted diseases, including AIDS, that threaten to "contaminate" the citizenry.[37]

This seems to suggest that abnormal sexuality is a diverse category but, nevertheless, a category that affects immigrants regardless of their sex. Both sexes can have either healthy or unhealthy sexuality. Greater analysis of how sexual norms work in immigration regulations could help to wrest sex from sexuality.

Today, it seems that immigration legislation is following a similar pattern. Sexual deviants are again being identified but their race does not fall within traditional conceptions of race. It is easier to see that sexual pathology is a racist trope when it is applied to Asians. Asians occupy a place in the traditional field of races. Yet we must remember that the Irish and Italians were also attacked for their sexual perversions. They may not be considered a distinct race from Northern European culture anymore but their inclusion into Anglo-America only shows how racial discourse is prone to shifts. If certain groups can become un-raced, then it seems that new races could be formed too. And one of the keys for locating different understandings of race is to look for the label of sexual pervert. This group, now, includes not only homosexuals but also sexual deviants. While the language of immigration laws may try to conceal the bias against and the racing of homosexuals, the rhetoric within present-day immigration policies show that sexual deviants have an inferior biological and psychological constitution. In other words, immigration policies help to establish the racing of homosexuals and other sexual miscreants.

NOTES

1. This is not to say that there are no differences between the ways citizens and immigrants are regulated.

2. Christine Battersby shows that women have also been depicted as over-sexed, which is in keeping with the theory that they are more closely linked with the body than men. See Christine Battersby, "Stages on Kant's Way: Aesthetics, Morality, and the Gendered Sublime," in *Race, Class, Gender, and Sexuality: The Big Questions*, eds. Naomi Zack, Laurie Shrage, and Crispin Sartwell (New York: Blackwell, 1998), 227–44.

3. Ladelle McWhorter, *Racism and Sexual Oppression in Anglo-America: A Genealogy* (Bloomington: Indiana University Press, 2009), 183.

4. See also Linda Martin Alcoff, "The Metaphysics of Gender and Sexual Difference" in *Visible Identities: Race, Gender, and the Self* (New York: Oxford, 2006), 151–78.

5. de Beauvoir, Simone, *The Second Sex*, trans. and ed. H. M. Parshley (New York: Vintage Books, 1989), 267.

6. If female sexuality were due to physical rather than psychological problems, then psychoanalysis could be of little use. See Sigmund Freud, "Femininity" in *The Complete Edition of the Complete Psychological Works of Sigmund Freud, Vol. XXII*, trans. James Strachey (London: The Hogarth Press, 1964), 139–67.

7. He argued that regulating sexuality was central for developing state racism as developed by the Nazi regime. See Michel Foucault, *The History of Sexuality: An Introduction*, trans. Robert Hurley (New York: Vintage Books, 1990), 149.

8. Dara E. Goldman, "Border Patrol and the Immigrant Body: *Entry Denied: Policing Sexuality at the Border*," *Discourse* 26 (2004): 192.

9. Siobhan Somerville, "Notes toward a Queer History of Naturalization," *American Quarterly* 57 (2005): 666.

10. Anna Marie Smith, "Missing Poststructuralism, Missing Foucault: Butler and Fraser on Capitalism and the Regulation of Sexuality," *Social Text* 19 (2001): 110.

11. Somerville, "Queer History," 666.

12. 1875 Page Act, Chapter 141, Forty-Third Congress, Second Sess., (March 3, 1875) U.S. Immigration Legislation Online.

13. Deirdre M. Moloney, "Women, Sexual Morality, and Economic Dependency in Early U.S. Deportation Policy," *Journal of Women's History* 18 (2006): 98.

14. Eithne Luibheid, *Entry Denied* (Minneapolis: University of Minnesota Press, 2002), xii.

15. Michel Foucault, *Society Must Be Defended*, trans. David Macey (New York: Picador, 2003), 60.

16. McWhorter, *Racism and Sexual Oppression*, 59.

17. McWhorter, *Racism and Sexual Oppression*, 59.

18. McWhorter, *Racism and Sexual Oppression*, 193.

19. McWhorter, *Racism and Sexual Oppression*, 168.

20. McWhorter, *Racism and Sexual Oppression*, 194

21. Eduardo Mendieta, "The Race of Modernity and the Modernity of Race: On Foucault's Genealogy of Racism," Unpublished paper delivered at the meetings of the Society for Phenomenology and Existential Philosophy at Penn State University, State College, Pennsylvania, October 5–7, 2000, 12. Originally quoted by Ladelle McWhorter (McWhorter, *Racism and Sexual Oppression*, 60).

22. McWhorter, *Racism and Sexual Oppression*, 194.

23. Siobhan Somerville, "Queer Loving," *GLQ: A Journal of Gay and Lesbian Studies* 11 (2005): 350.

24. Somerville, "Queer Loving," 346.

25. Eithne Luibheid, "Heteronormativity and Immigration Scholarship: A Call for Change," *GLQ: A Journal of Gay and Lesbian Studies* 10 (2004): 227.

26. Somerville, "Queer Loving," 345.

27. Somerville, "Queer Loving," 339.

28. Somerville, "Queer Loving," 353.

29. Somerville, "Queer Loving," 348.

30. Somerville, "Queer Loving," 349.

31. Somerville, "Queer Loving," 355.

32. Eithne Luibheid, *Entry Denied: Controlling Sexuality at the Border* (Minneapolis: University of Minnesota Press, 2002), 99.

33. Katie King, "Local and Global: AIDS Activism and Feminist Theory," *Camera Obscura* 10 (1992): 88.

34. Somerville, "Queer Loving," 347.

35. Connie Oxford discusses how male homosexuality can also help immigrant men obtain asylum. See Connie G. Oxford, "Protectors and Victims in the Gender Regime of Asylum," *Feminist Formations* 17 (2005): 25.

36. Goldman, "Border Patrol," 193.

37. Eithne Luibheid, "Queer/Migration: An Unruly Body of Scholarship," *GLQ: A Journal of Gay and Lesbian Studies* 14 (2008): 174.

SIX

Racing Gender

While there is some awareness that immigration controls scrutinize the sexuality of immigrants, there is still little attention paid to the ways in which controllers target women. This is perhaps not surprising because the issue of sex and sexuality often become conflated, as I discussed in the last chapter. Suspicion of women, in part, can be traced back to the idea that they are vehicles for dangerous sexuality. However, an examination of immigration policies shows that female immigrants are suspect—even apart from issues of sexuality. The method for supporting and defining the parameters for this group of people are distinct from determining the race of sexual degenerates. While scientific discourse is often used to identify sexual abnormalities, the racing of sex goes as far back as Greek mythology. Echoes of these ancient myths join together with present economic fears to cast foreign women as threats to civilization. Because Greek mythology and economic discourse—rather than science and physical disease—contribute to the racing of women in Western culture, I hope to use these narratives to show the distinct place of sex within the logic of state racism.

Although there is some disagreement about which women were the first foreigners, scholars agree that women often represent the primal other in Greek mythology. Wm. Blake Tyrell believes that the Amazons were the first while Julia Kristeva suggests that the Danaides claim that title.[1] The existence and cultural significance of Amazonian myths, however, only reinforce the greater point that women represented the first foreigners in Greek thought. Since the Amazons and the Danaides were seen as women who were refractory to Greek marriage customs,[2] they were not only depicted as foreigners but as a different race of people. Greek civilization depended upon a patriarchal order, which necessitated that women recognize and surrender to male authority. The Amazons

125

and the Danaides, who refuse to submit to men, disrupt the patriarchal order and, along with it, civilization. Hence, they were cast as un-Greek and lumped together with the other barbarian races.

While the Amazons and the Danaides do not occupy the same cultural space as they once did in Ancient Greek life, I suggest that the legacy of these myths can still be found in present-day thought. If the misogynistic mythology surrounding the Danaides and the Amazons remains, it could help explain why women who want to enter the United States face longer odds than men. Women have more difficulties obtaining permission to enter the country legally and immigration policies continue to make the female body the site of social problems. The mythology of dangerous, foreign women could also help make sense of why female immigrants. Despite their various ethnic backgrounds, women are grouped together and believed to bring a particular set of concerns with them.

Anxiety over "terror" and "anchor" babies is, to be sure, connected to the "browning" of America. I suggest, however, that themes of ancient race and racism that cleave along gender lines also play a part in the opposition to immigration. We are accustomed to seeing that anti-immigration sentiments are linked to a racism that discriminates against those who differ in terms of skin color or religious belief. I intend to show that Western culture relies, too, on a long-held distinction between the male and female races. Since the Danaides and the Amazons represented such a subversion of Greek culture, the Greeks began to see them as a different category of being. This legacy continues and foreign women are still considered a most problematic race.

Female immigrants of today, like the Danaides and the Amazons, are seen as a danger to society because they are believed to be a threat to the standard-bearer of Western civilization in three major ways. 1) They buck the customs of cultured nations. Their presence could destabilize and eventually destroy civilization, if they continue to follow—or worse, impose—their traditions. This is what patriarchy and myth mean to relay. 2) They fall in between categories. The inappropriate aggression on behalf of the Danaides and Amazons make them difficult to place. Their responses to sexual encounters, in particular, prove them to be a monstrous hybrid of male and female. 3) They are also often accused of jeopardizing the economic stability of the state. Instead of supporting and contributing to the prosperity of the civilization, foreign women—past and present— are seen as a drain on precious resources. These themes, of course, are not separate but interrelated and build upon each other.

Aeschylus' *The Suppliants* and Amazon mythology are widely read as attempts to reinforce marriage customs of Ancient Greece, which cannot be separated from patriarchy. Their refusal to marry together with their violence towards men represents a challenge to the twin pillars of civilization. If women do not respect male domination, all is lost. This is the overwhelming message of Greek myths. A similar ethos runs through the

American response to current immigration patterns. There are many that fear the death or weakening of American culture and values through the onslaught of Spanish-speaking immigrants and an influx of those who practice Islam. Those who warn about the dangers that accompany anchor and terror babies seek to emphasize how these others will threaten America.

Little attention, however, is paid to how these debates make foreign women the center of the problem. It is women who make it possible for anchor and terror babies to destroy America from the inside out. Theories about anchor and terror babies do more than convey a prejudice against Hispanics and those of the Islamic faith. They also relay a bias against women. This negative view of women may largely go unnoticed because Westerners take it for granted that foreign females are a problem. Such an attitude is further reinforced by myths of all sorts.

Ancient Greek mythology tells us that the Male is equated with the civilized race and the Female stands for the barbaric race. The danger associated with both the Danaides and the Amazons is attributed to how they fall in-between or occupy two categories. These ancient women were monstrous because they could not be placed neatly in the female category and even took on male characteristics. Aeschylus' suppliants represent an in between race because they allow for a merging between Greek and non-Greek races. Amazons, similarly, conjure up an image of a male/female blend. If the Danaides or the Amazons do not submit or are not beaten back, the fear remains that this third, mixed-up race will prevail. In order to protect against an androgynous invasion and the feminization of civilization, Americans—like their Ancient Greek counterparts—perhaps feel the need to close their borders to foreign women who have the capacity to muddle the distinctions between male and female.

In strength or weakness, women were trouble. The Danaides are, as Aeschylus' title suggests, suppliants and "needy strangers." The Amazons, on the other hand, are infamous for stripping power from men and banishing, maiming, or even killing their male offspring. Amazons privilege girls and women, which the Greeks saw as a drain on society.[3] Today, immigration opponents often turn to neoliberal ideology to characterize female immigrants, likewise, as those who take up valuable and scarce resources. Either they, themselves, need services or they give birth (literally) to those who would devour the wealth of the nation. The feminized immigrant who threatens to bring barbarism to the West is always a suspicious figure. Foreign women have been and continue to symbolize the dangers that impose themselves on the economy of civilization. While myths about the Danaides and the Amazons are meant to highlight the threat women pose to patriarchy, present immigration regulations can most readily target foreign women by using the language of neoliberalism. Yet present discourse concerning outsiders emphasizes these same themes of resource and productivity that appeared in Greek myth.

MYTH AND PATRIARCHY

As is well-known, the Greek household was not considered a space of equals. Men ruled over women. The woman was expected to tend to her husband's needs and submit to his authority. These myths, however, also relay the tension that surrounded Greek marriage. While the Greek patriarchal order eventually prevails over the unruliness of the Danaides and the Amazons, these stories, nonetheless, give voice to fears that the Greeks must have had about their world. Myths about the Amazons, especially, would not have continued to be retold and reworked[4] if there was not a need to reiterate the superiority of Greek life over all others. They are responses to perceived threats against Greek society, from foreign cultures, and a weakening of the Greek race.

When *The Suppliants* begins, the Danaides have already committed the terrible deed against the male order and are now without country. Aeschylus' chorus of maidens explains that they are, in effect, in exile because they have challenged the patriarchal system. The Danaides are the fifty daughters of Danaus, son of Io and an Egyptian king. These fifty daughters were supposed to marry the fifty sons of Aegyptus, their uncle. But the defiant women refuse to bond with their cousins in marriage.[5] Exiled from Egypt for their insubordination, they seek refuge in Greece—where they must become suppliants to be accepted.

The Greeks, however, are wary of outsiders. The Danaides face great difficulties in being accepted because they are doubly foreign. Not only are they born outside of Greece but they also come to Greece because of their disobedience of traditional marriage customs.[6] While Greek women accepted the fact that their husbands would be chosen for them, the Danaides killed those to whom they were betrothed. These daughters of Danaus further challenge the Greek system by taking on the role of the aggressor, which is normally reserved for the male. Instead of submitting to the desires of their male cousins, they deny the sexual advances of the Aegyptiads. Although the Danaides recognize the current of violence that is inherent within the marriage bond, they do not accept their role. Greek custom dictates that women must submit to this marital violence but the Danaides did not.[7] Although they eventually fled from Egypt, they did not simply flee from the Aegyptiads. Through their actions, they committed an act of violence not only against their husbands-to-be but also against society. This is not to say, however, that violence is not tolerated within marriage or society. As Kristeva explains, violence is acceptable if husbands use it to cement the pact of marriage. The Danaides' actions are doubly subversive. Their use of violence, in itself, works to undo marriage and tradition. They did not submit to the sexual aggression of their cousins but became aggressors themselves. These women took up swords[8] and wielded them against men and patriarchy.

Committing a singular act of antagonism against men, as the Danaides did, is bad enough. The Amazons, in contrast, assault men and manhood as a way of life. These warrior women present a culture that is even further from Greek society and, therefore, civilized life. Amazons derive their name from the custom of cauterizing one breast.[9] Tyrrell argues that this act has less to do with a compromised femininity of one-breasted women and more to do with the challenge to patriarchy that comes from the mobility of women. They move in ways that are supposed to be reserved for men. Amazons hunt, fight, and engage in licentious behavior.[10] Thus Amazons represent the polar extreme of Greek society, where women are the ones who are fixed in the home. Because women are the ones who move in Amazon society, they take on male roles and behavior. Unlike Greek culture, Amazonian society assigns housework to men. The men who are not either banished or killed by Amazons are forced to take on the traditional female roles. Thus, Amazonian women represent the overthrowing of male power and the overturning of patriarchy. The proliferation of Amazon society would translate into a society (over)run by women. By restricting the movement of men, Amazons would ensure that men could not take their rightful position in the *polis*.

Tyrrell points out that their movement in the form of sexual promiscuity would also have negative consequences for Greek life. "For society the outcome is no future hoplites because by using her reproductivity for herself the Amazon denies it to society."[11] Amazonian women do not make proper use of their sexuality. Similar to the Danaides, Amazon women do not submit to male aggression that is accepted as underlying the sex act. The Danaides refuse to take part in the proper sexual initiation into society, which is marriage. The Amazons, who also object to marriage, go a step farther. Amazonians represent the exact opposite of the Greek ideal, for they have created a society that does not rely upon men. Tyrrell argues that Greek mythmaking, in general, ". . . must be appreciated as an apparatus for escaping birth from women."[12] In boasting about their autochthonous nature, the Greeks point not only towards their desire to be free from foreign influences but also to be independent of woman. Instead of using their sex and sexuality to produce male progeny and future defenders of civilization, Amazons value sex for the pleasure it gives them (the women) and for its potential to reproduce more female offspring. They are particularly dangerous because they seem to need men less than men need women. Amazons only need men for the sex act, after which they can be discarded or killed. To fight against this philosophy and to enforce the idea that patriarchy is natural, a conglomeration of myths needs to be created to warn about the ill effects that flow from insubordination of the male code. As Posi Loman notes, "Being everything that the Greek women were not supposed to be, the Amazons, who were beaten by Greek men, acted as 'negative role models'. So, among other things, the Amazon myth helped to reinforce the ideology that in a civilized Greek society women were expected to marry and let their man do the politics and the fighting."[13] The exile of the Danaides and the vanquishing of the Amazons, particularly, are a part of these efforts to justify patriarchy and create obedient women.

But something else is made clear through these myths. Greek myths perpetuate the idea that women, in general, are barbaric and need to be tamed. The problem is not that particular women, from Egyptian or Amazonian culture, are adverse to patriarchy. The problem is that all women possess this ability to undo civilization. Tyrrell's reading of Aeschylus' *The Suppliants* details the dangers that Greeks must have felt pressing on their culture. If women were to refuse marriage, their animal nature would rise to the surface. "Marriage is the institution that tames and civilizes female bestiality. Once it is broken down, women outside its control revert to their bestial nature. They become the animals they once were."[14] The unmarried woman is not only uncivilized but also inhuman. This theme is underscored as the Danaides are cast out into the wild and are estranged from those around them. The Greeks saw it as their duty to stamp out the female antipathy towards male rule. This can only happen if the female race is subdued or vanquished. The Danaides and the Amazons provide examples of each. Their dress, skin color, and gender are all indications that they are not civilized people. They are, at best, equal to any other race of barbarians. At worse, they are animals and of a different species. The Danaides are eventually integrated into Greek culture when they conform to the traditional and submissive roles allocated for women. Greek mythology, on the other hand, must relay the annihilation of Amazon culture.

As suppliants, the Danaides become part of the civilized race because they perform acts that reinforce traditional ideas of femininity. They are only accepted after taking on the role of suppliants and casting their aggression aside. Danaus, their father, warns them that they must not in any manner appear bold.[15] Only after heeding their father's advice are the Danaides allowed to speak and make the case for their Greek lineage. Had they taken an aggressive posture or been armed, Pelasgus—the Argive king—would have assumed that they were Amazons.[16] Their appearance marks them as non-Greek women. The Greeks describe them as belonging to the sun-burned race because they have dark skin and Nile burned cheeks.[17] And their mobility (movement from one state to another) makes them all the more similar to Amazons. This last comparison would have proven deadly since Amazons represent a race of nomads that resists and attacks civilized society. It seems that Amazons cannot be integrated or civilized and are the most dangerous race of women. The Greeks must defeat them because they, unlike the Danaides, cannot be pacified or made humble.

The mythology surrounding both the Danaides and the Amazons points to a greater perceived threat to Greek civilization. They are meant to ease the anxiety caused by those who are caught in between barbarism and civilization. As Lloyd Lewellyn-Jones suggests, "The real danger is from the woman who has been integrated, taken into the household. You must marry the Amazon, the woman, but she remains an Amazon, remains a danger."[18] I suggest that integrated women represent a third race—one that is not fully civilized and occupies a space between Greek society and barbarism. In other words, they occupy a space in between male and female. They will never be completely civilized because they will never submit to social rules and patriarchal regulations. Amazons may be similar to Persians because they are both cultures that threaten Greek life.[19] But their sex makes Amazon women quite different from the feminized Persian or barbarian man. Amazonian myth relays the fear that women can never really be conquered or made to obey Greek men. When men (Greek and non-Greek) go to battle, there seems to be an understanding of the consequences. Those taken captive will likely become slaves. In other words, men acknowledge when they have lost and submit to the rules of the game.

Because of their female nature, women teeter on the verge of barbarism and the Amazon—as an exaggerated case—was believed to be incapable of serving the order of Greek men.[20] The Danaides' most troublesome quality, as noted by Lewellyn-Jones and Kristvea, is the fact that they are both inside and outside culture. Tyrrell, in similar fashion, argues that the Amazons' androgynous nature is what has the most potential for disrupting Greek culture. If the Amazons are not defeated in Greek mythology, male and female roles would be subverted permanently and civilization would begin to crumble. Greek myths are a product of a fantasy that would allow ". . . the founding of a pure race of just men."[21] "The house of Athens is self-sufficient, free of taint and problem of the sexed woman, whose nature is foreign in physique, blood, and loyalties."[22] Amazons represent the reverse: a society of all women. They would have the ability to propagate a race of women to counteract a race of *only* men. Women, unlike men, are not thought to have legitimate claims to power. Amazons and their spawn multiply that which the Greeks work to extinguish, the race of women.

FEMALE SEXUALITY: MYTHOLOGY AND PATHOLOGY

These same themes of sexual perversion continue to appear in Western thought as representations of otherness. Kristeva believes that the psychosexual symbolism in Greek mythology has implications for dealings with the immigrant because they, too, represent the foreign. It is no coincidence that Greek myths are as riddled with psychosexual drama as they deal with foreign encounters. She argues that the dramas built into Greek lore have to do with the ". . . fascination and horror that a different being produces in us, such meditations being prerequisite to any legal and political settlement of the immigration problem."[23] The process of grappling with sexual strangeness is not unlike the endeavor to cope with foreign cultures. Each of us has developed tools to understand that which is seemingly outside us. Grappling with our own sexuality makes dealing with foreign cultures possible. Through the former, we collect tools that are necessary for the confrontation with the latter. While Kristeva offers a possible resolution to the problem of strangeness, the history of Western thought is a testament to the struggles between the privileging of the (white) male subject and a more inclusive position. Greek concepts about reproduction and production continue to influence and shape the West. These ancient ideals still work to assign positive qualities to the civilized male and negative characteristics to that which falls outside the male.

The proper use of sexuality that was prominent in the Greek myths about the Danaides and the Amazons are still concerns for more recent thinkers. Though Kristeva holds that psychoanalytic theories about sexuality allow for a positive encounter with the other, psychoanalytic theories as espoused by Sigmund Freud can be seen as supporting the patriarchal hegemony. Freud's reading of femininity, and the sexual pathologies that go along with it, only reinforce the problems of female sexuality that are highlighted in these Ancient Greek myths. Depending upon the pathology that Freud discusses, the label assigned to a woman would change but two things remain constant. Women are expected to deny pleasure and have procreation as the main function of their sex. This, in turn, reproduces the patriarchal order that had taught them how their sex was supposed to function according to nature and culture. Modern society is enmeshed with another slightly different kind of mythology surrounding female sexuality. The stakes, however, are just as high.

Michel Foucault suggests that female sexuality continues to be the site of "problems" because it is thought to have major implications for the future of the society and the future of the human race. Foucault analyzes female sexuality within biopolitics—how the life of the individual connects to the life of the species—but it is not so different from how Greek mythology problematizes the female sex. The techniques to reinforce sexual customs and norms have changed but the meaning is still the same. Psychoanalysis and science take the place of myths but familiar mythological themes remain. The legend of the Danaides and their refusal of sexual advances continue in the problem of the frigid woman. And the sexual perversions of the Amazons are rehashed in Freud's diagnosis of the woman with the masculinity complex. These pathologies carry the same message as Greek mythology. Women need to do their part to obey the patriarchal order of society. Even the "normal" woman, in the context of biopolitics, is not free from this process of hysterization. She, too, must constantly be on the watch for signs that her sex will slip into an abnormal one. How could she be allowed to escape it when the fate of the traditional family and the human species hangs in the balance? She must take care that her bestial nature is under control.

Foucault drew on Freud's description of the frigid woman when he referenced the diagnosis for a woman who feels no pleasure during sexual intercourse but he could have also drawn on the myth of the Danaides. Sexual frigidity corresponds to sex as something that belongs only to men. The frigid wife does not desire sex because it is somehow missing within women. Freud states, "the aim of biology has been entrusted to the aggressiveness of men and has been made to some extent independent of women's consent."[24] Foucault revisits this theme when he analyzes how modern society attributes sex to men and lacking within women.[25] Women are seen as without sex, in this case, because biology has ensured procreation through the male, not the female. Even if the woman is deficient in regards to sex, nature has sufficiently enabled the continuation of the species by planting sex within man. Freud further argues that sexual frigidity of women, although not fully understood, may be a psychological problem and therefore, could be susceptible to positive influence. But it is also possible that this condition is rooted in anatomical factors. Sexual frigidity may or may not be rooted in her sex but it is clearly not something normal. It is either the pathology of the mind or of the body. Freud seems to suggest that if it is a physical problem, he can offer no aid. But luckily, he does believe that there is possibly another approach. If it is an abnormality of the body, it seems that she may have to accept that the desires of the male are normal and ordered by Nature— whether she likes it or not. She must submit to the procreative act for the good of the species despite not having any wish to do so. If it is a mental pathology, there could be hope of a resolution with the help of psychoanalysis. A mental pathology, on the other hand, leads to a gentler, kinder option.[26]

Yet a woman who does experience sexual pleasure also suffers from a sexual pathology. Foucault uses Freud's diagnosis of the masculinity complex to show how woman's sex is tied not to sexual enjoyment but to the function of reproduction that belongs to the truly female sex—the vagina. This condition is similar to a fault that is attributed to the Amazons. Because the clitoris is merely an atrophied form of the male penis, the pleasure that is derived from it is not a feminine one. The clitoris is a male apparatus that just happens to appear in women's bodies.[27] A woman with a masculinity complex refuses to embrace her womanhood and wrongly clings to the pleasure derived from the clitoris. When a girl refuses to face the fact that she will not receive a penis, Freud explains that she takes refuge in her phallic mother or father and increases in clitoridal activity, which is ordinarily a male characteristic.[28] Freud seems to suggest that a woman must relent from pleasuring herself through the clitoris. She must accept that her sex is attached to the vagina, which does not feel pleasure (or at least Freud does not discuss the pleasure associated with the vagina). Her sexual health is tied to the reproduction of the species. In continuing with clitoridal activity, she denies her womanhood. The masculinity complex describes a woman who rejects that her sex is defined by and through the vagina as a site to conceive, bear, and deliver a (male) child. For Freud, she who does not wholly accept this definition of the female sex also rejects what it means to be a woman. She, like the Amazons, uses her sexuality for herself and denies it for society.

Freud's version of normal femininity can be achieved if too much sexual desire is not lost while repressing clitoridal activity. She, then, accepts the fact that she will never be given a penis from her father and replaces her desire for a penis with the desire for a baby that she will make with her husband.[29] This may constitute normalcy for Freud but Foucault still considers this part of the process of the problematization and hysterization of women. Even though this case allows sex to belong to both men and women, Foucault argues that this proper form of femininity works to link the sex of woman to its reproductive function. Desire for and enjoyment of sex belongs to the man. The woman should desire and enjoy sex only insofar as she seeks to create a child, if she is normal. She should not enjoy the sex act itself because the activity is located in the unfeeling vagina, the true sex of the woman. On the other hand, she can feel excitement about the prospect of producing a baby. In other words, the pleasure is not sexual. A woman is only normal insofar as she accepts that her sex is tied to extending her family and civilization through biological methods.

The frigid wife is not pathological in the sense that she does not enjoy sex; the inability to enjoy sexual intercourse is normal. She is pathological because her lack of desire for sex has turned into an aversion that inhibits or surpasses her desire for a baby. The lesson of Ancient Greek myths continues; the female sex is a constant problem for civilization. Frigid women, like the Danaides, cannot overcome their antipathy towards sexual intercourse and, therefore, cannot reproduce the prized male offspring. Foucault illustrates how any woman who does not conform to standards, which dictate that she must use her sex to procreate, is seen as a problem for society. Because she is not willing to perform the reproductive act, her sexual pathology comes under the category of frigidity. Likewise for the woman with a masculinity complex, she is pathological because the impetus for sexual activity is tied to the enjoyment of it. Her desire for sex is rooted in pleasure rather than in her desire for the baby-penis. She refuses to let the pleasure from the atrophied penis, the clitoris, subside and be replaced by the pleasures derived from the possibility of producing a baby-penis.

One could, however, argue that the diagnosis is attached to the fear that the vagina, which is necessary for reproduction, will be ignored. If a woman revels in the pleasures of the clitoris, she may concentrate on the acts that pleasure it rather than the sexual acts that involve the vagina, which is not recognized to feel pleasure. The pathological woman is any woman who enjoys or desires sex beyond the function of reproduction of male offspring. Therefore, the danger of sexual pathology always surrounds the woman. The normal woman does not gain pleasure from the sex act itself but from the desire to propagate. Every time she derives pleasure from the sex act, there is a question that she suffers from a feminine pathology that afflicted the Amazons. Issues of sexual enjoyment keep her in an agitated state. Any moments of sexual pleasure serve as dangerous gateways to female pathologies. There is always a danger that they will slide back and follow their bestial nature. And these female pathologies could have a domino effect on traditional family structures that could hurt the greater society and even the species as a whole. Maintaining normal sexual desires is as much tied to the issue of reproduction as that of the sexually perverse women such as the Danaides and the Amazons. In Western thought, problems with female sexuality help to cover over the greater problem surrounding the female sex.

THE FOREIGN AND THE ECONOMY OF THE FEMININE

Yet Kristeva returns to Greek mythology to offer us a more optimistic reading of how we can possibly reconcile ourselves with the otherness that plays itself out in psychosexual drama of one kind or another. She provides a less xenophobic reading of *The Suppliants*, while still highlighting the tension that surrounds the foreigner in Greek culture. She recognizes that the Danaides represent a rare instance where foreigners are granted protection in Greek society. But the case of the Danaides, however privileged,[30] shows the Greek attempt to address how to best deal with foreigners who were in their midst. The Greeks understood that interaction with non-Greeks was inevitable and already coming to pass. This comingling, from the Greek standpoint, was not entirely bad. On the one hand, the Greeks benefitted economically from the foreigners who lived among them. On the other hand, the Greeks wanted to make sure that foreigners did not influence the Greek polis.[31] The dynamic that allowed the Greeks to profit from foreigners while denying them citizenship, I suggest, is still at work today in immigration debates. Americans, like the Ancient Greeks, prosper economically from foreigners while trying to ensure that they do not integrate fully into political society—the culmination of which is thought to be citizenship.

In order to block or limit the influx of immigrants, some have argued that immigrants are detrimental rather than beneficial to the U.S. economy. Kristeva, undoubtedly, would have preferred that Westerners draw a different conclusion but this assertion is consistent with the Greek stance towards outsiders, as is vividly shown in various myths. In what follows, I will explore how the Greek legacy of the feminized other merges with economic discourse. Women continue to represent that which is foreign. The addition of an economic component further complicates the parallel distinctions between male/female and insider/outsider. Situating the female immigrant within the economic field makes her all the more strange. Because foreign women have the ability to earn and produce wealth, they cannot be contained within the female category. Foreign women may present challenges to the dichotomy between men and women but the desire to hold on to these categories remains. Female immigrants, especially those who benefit the country fiscally, are designated as neither male nor female. They become ever more foreign because they confound the gendered categories that anchor Western civilization. For this reason, they represent the most dangerous kind of outsiders. The foreignness of gender and the foreignness of race have been compounded into the female outsider of more recent history. Because of her earning potential and wealth production, she becomes the greatest threat yet to Western patriarchy.

Thus, the tale telling of the dangers of invading women must again be woven and fortified. Part of the present mythology surrounding female immigrants is built around the "feminization of immigration." This phrase refers to the purported increase of women who immigrate. Although there is data to suggest that women immigrate in greater numbers than men worldwide, immigration trends for America—the country that hosts the most immigrants—go against the grain.[32] More men immigrate to the United States than women.[33] However, the feminization of immigration does not only refer to the volume of female immigrants but also hints to the type of low-paying positions that immigrants fill,[34] which contributes to their low social status. Its meaning could actually be closer to the feminization of race, which explains how "non-white" (read also noncivilized) men have become emasculated. Naomi Zack argues that black men are emasculated because they lack the spiritual qualities that exemplify the white, masculine ideal linked to the ability to make money.[35] In terms of immigration, this quality becomes all the more important because the discourse of economic drain drives anti-immigrant movements and singles out female immigrants of color as would-be dangers to the fiscal health of the nation. We see, then, that race and gender can be conflated to describe who has or lacks the capacity to accumulate capital. If ancient myths separated the civilized race—Greek men from all others, modern myths separate them into categories depending on their entrepreneurial skills. Anglo-European men represent one race while all others belong to the feminized other.

Foucault shows how the discourse of race becomes translated into the language of health in modern society. There is, in effect, a healthy and an unhealthy race.[36] And in the context of immigration, those who promote or diminish the health of the nation are those who are believed to have the capacities for financial independence and dependence respectively. Considering that the economic health of the state is used to propel opinions, rules, and regulations regarding immigration and categories of race can be used to ascribe money-making capacities; I will argue that it is more helpful to discuss immigration in terms of racialization. Although thinking about immigration patterns in terms of race is not particularly novel, it allows us to see, as Stuart Elden puts it, how "[t]he recoding of old problems is made possible through new techniques."[37] Not only does the discourse of health reveal traditional forms of racism that operate insidiously through the discourse of economics but it also connects to ancient racism which holds that women are a race that threatens the male economy. This could explain why women have more difficulty than men when attempting to apply for immigration on economic and humanitarian grounds. Suppliants (needy women) and Amazons (subversive, aggressive women) need to be kept out if the state is to remain healthy and strong.

Reports that women edge out men in numbers contribute to the purported "feminization of immigration" but these numbers do not tell the whole story. These statistics refer to legal immigration channels. When factoring in illegal immigration, the total flow of males immigrating to the United States outweighs the combined number of legal and illegal female immigrants. And even if we were to operate within the confines of legal immigration, a closer look at the data shows that there is not a preference or advantage for female immigrants to enter America.[38] The higher percentage of women immigrating to America is a product of the admissions of wives, daughters, and childcare providers for men who immigrate to this country. Further analysis of the statistics shows that the number of women who are accepted on the basis of humanitarian and economic reasons is lower than that of men.[39] In other words, women are more successful in the immigration process when they are attached to men in some way but they are less successful when they apply on their own merits.

The feminization of immigration may not, then, refer to the sexed body but rather to the Western penchant for equating foreignness with the feminine. This is nothing new. As previously mentioned, the Ancient Greeks often viewed Persians as the feminine other. Even though women often hold positions such as au pair and housekeeper, this is not the only reason why these occupations are considered feminine. Immigrants are feminized because they represent laborers who fill low-skill jobs and, therefore, have little social prestige. It is this lack of prestige that adds more to the feminization of immigration than the raw data that shows a higher number of women than men entering the country. Even though skilled and unattached men have the advantage for entering the United States legally, they often take low-paying jobs far below the skill level they acquired in their home countries. The president of the Organization of Colombian Professionals notes that many professionals feel completely isolated and find it difficult to become acclimated to a new life in America where they have a much lower social status. This fall in status often accompanies their downward economic mobility. [40] The combination of lesser pay and a less prestigious job contribute to a sense of vulnerability and powerlessness. In other words, they feel emasculated. The foreign and the feminine become virtually synonymous.

RACE AND THE LAND OF ENTERPRISE

Although immigration patterns work to show that economics plays a role in shaping gender identity, Western philosophy and history also provides instances of how money-making capacities are used to assign race. What this demonstrates is that neither gender nor racial categories are static. They are, as Ladelle McWhorter explains, "'fictitious [unities' that serve as linchpins] to hold together a disparate set of theories, institutions, practices, and relationships." [41] Gender and race allow us to give a name to the conjunction of characteristics that are formed in and through power dynamics. They are ways to describe why certain people occupy certain positions within society. It seems, then, that inserting economics into racial discourse connects ancient and modern forms of racism through mythologies of the land. Athenian myths reinforced the idea that their autochthonous nature cultivated men with political virtue and prowess. [42] Immanuel Kant, in similar fashion, sought to explain how geographical conditions shaped the Northern Europeans into a mighty race.

Northern Europeans—like the Ancient Greeks—believed that they were atop the race hierarchy because they alone could ensure that civilization prospers. Greek mythologies about the Amazons were attempts to assert that their race was impermeable to the dangers in the face of those of lesser capacities. Kant, likewise, believed that an engrained level of industriousness separated one race from another. He suggested that those not of Northern European descent lacked entrepreneurial skills and, therefore, represented an inferior form of humanity. Kant was among the first to sketch out a theory of races that could explain why people of different regions could vary so greatly while still belonging to the same larger group called humanity. [43] Through this theory, he created a hierarchy of peoples by assigning them different capacities of enterprise. In "Of the Different Human Races," he explains how he thinks the environment can affect human development and solidify the differences between one race and another. He asserts:

> Human beings were created in such a way that they might live in every climate and endure each and every condition of the land. Consequently, numerous seeds and natural predispositions must lie ready in human beings whether to be developed or held back in such a way that we might become fitted to a particular place in the world. These seeds and natural predispositions appear to be inborn and made for these conditions through the on-going process of reproduction. [44]

Kant's reading of humanity is a part of his cosmopolitan theory but it is not the cosmopolitanism that Kristeva envisions. Kristeva's cosmopolitanism is one that speaks from a position of the integration of the other through the strangeness we all find in ourselves. She believes that this strangeness helps us to cross physical and psychical boundaries. [45] Kant's cosmopolitanism begins with the idea that every race draws from the same pool of potential characteristics. But he ultimately argues that varying characteristics cannot now be overcome because they have been cemented within different races over time. Depending upon the environment, humans will develop discrete traits in relation to their region. Over time and through reproduction within the localized group of humans, certain characteristics become prevalent and eventually come to be inextricably linked to that group.

Kant argues that, through reproduction, particular traits have become solidified and others were bred out as a response to a particular region. So although both Africans and Northern Europeans are the product of the original coupling of Adam and Eve, they were made different by the climates in which they settled. Because of the fertile lands of Africa, Kant argues, Africans could easily live off the fruits of the earth without much work. On the other hand, Northern Europeans had to be much more industrious to survive and cultivate a land that was much less hospitable to husbandry. These environmental variables are what led Northern Europeans to be hard-working and Africans to be feckless. [46] Despite their common lineage, these groups have become separated by large gaps in character. The installation of these traits through procreation has now made it unlikely, if not impossible, for the indolent group to be enterprising. Their entrepreneurial capacity could not be developed because their living spaces did not require them to retain this quality that has been refined in the Northern European race. [47] The lack of industry explains why Africans have such a low level of civilization. Accordingly, it seems that Northern Europeans and their societies would always operate at the highest level because of the good qualities they possess, namely productiveness.

THE MONETARIZATION OF RACE

According to Kant's description of the differences between races, non-Europeans do not have the drive or the capacity to be economically prosperous. This does not, however, preclude them from being used to make money by those who possess an enterprising spirit. As Kristeva pointed out through her analysis of *The Suppliants*, profiting from foreigners while relegating them to second-class status is an ancient project. Naomi Zack extends this same philosophy to show why the nexus of race, sex, and economics resulted in the feminization of black male slaves. They became another foreign group that were used to grow the wealth of society but are accorded no rights. Although many thinkers such as bell hooks and Hortense Spillers have written about the feminization of black males, Zack adds another component to the intersection of race and sexuality—capital. She suggests that the equation of femininity with the black race is connected to the monetarization of race that comes into relief through slavery. Sex, race, and capital overlap and support each other to create the backdrop for the enslavement of others.

For Zack, the connection between sexuality and race can be seen in the way in which slaves were equated with livestock. Their sexuality was seen as a direct gateway to breed more labor and, ultimately, provide more workers for the slave owner. Consequently, their race was tied to their ability to reproduce. She argues that it is as if one race—the black race—was inextricably linked to breeding while the white race was defined in relation to spiritual enlightenment. Zack explains that "[t]he key to releasing the relevant nuances is *breeding*. Slaves were livestock to be bred as other livestock, for eventual monetary profit."[48] What separates the white race from the black race, in the context of capital gain, is that whites have the entrepreneurial abilities to make profit while the black race is the means to make that profit. Whites equated slaves with animals—tools for their masters to use in order to foster economic prosperity. Slave owners, unlike their Greek counterpart, wanted to cultivate the bestial nature that was believed to exist within Women, the ultimate other. Amazons were presented as those who refused to do their duty of producing hoplites for the Greeks. Slave owners made sure that the sexuality of female slaves was directed towards serving society by producing laborers to be exploited.

In short, Zack explains that whites are thought to be at the top of the race hierarchy because they have the mental capacities to propel financial prosperity. This reading of Western racial discourse is consistent with Kant's assertion that the Northern European is industrious and has the capabilities to advance society while the African is deficient in these aspects. Blacks do not have the intelligence to do so; they can only contribute to the economic growth through the breeding of future workers. But there is a difference between the way in which black males and females are seen in the economy of reproduction.

Black male slaves, Zack argues, were squeezed out of the monetary order. When the white slave owners realized that they could increase the amount of slave laborers by breeding the female slaves themselves, adult male slaves became less valuable. Although male slaves were necessary to work the land, they were not necessary in the process of reproducing more slave labor. And because "pure black" slaves were considered less valuable than miscegenated slaves, adult male slaves were seen to be more superfluous than female slaves. Slave owners saw male slaves as more dispensable than female slaves. They were not needed for the propagation of more slaves. Hence, if there was an excess of labor, they were the first to be disposed. Despite the voracious sexuality that was understood as accompanying black skin, measures were put in place to ensure that adult male slaves were emasculated. Sometimes this meant literal castration[49] and other times this expressed itself in a figurative castration. But, just as with any animal, these efforts were undertaken to make sure that the black male was rendered less dangerous. They would be tantamount to an impotent and wounded animal, still able to work but no longer housing the capacity for passion that could manifest itself in rage or in a sexual desire that would produce a less valuable slave.[50] The problem of the black male slave parallels the problem Kristeva saw woven into Aeschylus' *Suppliants*. If the goal is to profit from foreigners while denying them the same recognition and status as citizens, then the emasculation of male slaves worked toward this end. But the problem of the foreign woman remains as troubling as ever. Dealings with female slaves are, arguably, even trickier. Whereas Greek mythology eased anxieties over foreign women by neutralizing their sexuality, slave owners could not afford to negate the sexuality of female slaves.

RACING SEX

Since the breedability of the black race is its most valuable characteristic, we must also take a look at how this affects women of color differently than men of color. In this system that equates race with economics, it seems that the black woman is deemed as the sexual being par excellence. The problem of foreign men has been solved because they have been largely removed from the economic order. Foreign women, just as in ancient times, are the main problem. They are not civilized and cannot be trusted to use their sex to properly serve society. Zack explains that white men are thought to derive a pleasure that is similar to a sexual one from making money. White women, who were thought to have a purity that precluded sexual desire, needed to join forces with white men in the institution of marriage in order to ensure that their financial inheritance would be secure.[51] In other words, the desire of white women, if it manifested sexually, was also connected to monetary gain.

Both white males and females, as the logic goes, are fully human because their desire is connected to monetary gain. Black males, to the contrary, are only distantly thought to be human since the connection to financial profit has been cut off for the most part. The castration of men of color made it so that they could be excluded from both the sexual and economic order. It is only because they originally have the ability to reproduce with women that they are considered to be of the same species. Black females, in contradistinction, occupy an intermediary space. They are between whites and black males. They are intimately connected to the money-making process but are not given the spiritual or intellectual capacities that make whiteness special. Their ability to reproduce was tied to the promotion of the community's fiscal health. But as I will later show, it can also be tied to the draining of it. Therefore, they are much more dangerous to the community than black males are because they are more sexualized.[52] They can, I suggest, be seen as a different race because they occupy an in-between position and a more dangerous race because they possess a sexuality that remains hazardous to the economic health of the nation.

Dario Padovan's reading explains how such a splintering of race can occur in the context of biopolitics and state racism. He states that ". . . biopolitics encouraged the distinctions and hierarchies within different human groups, defined as 'races' (but as we know races do not exist),[53] thus fragmenting the biological field. Racism caused the shift of biopolitical strategies of power, introducing rifts into the biological continuum of the population by identifying, recognizing, hierarchically ordered subgroups."[54] Even though male and female slaves have been traditionally thought to belong to the same race, biopolitics allows for the emergence of new divisions to be made within otherwise unified groups. This is how more traditional forms of race were also formed.

It is likely that whites wanted to think that non-whites belonged to a different species from them. But because they recognized that offspring could be produced between whites and non-whites, they were made to share the same species category. In order to solidify this difference, the subcategory of race was put forth and developed. I argue, however, that the inclusion of an economic strand allows subcategories to be further divided. While this subdivision challenges contemporary racial discourse, it is not altogether foreign to Western thought. It has been embedded for a long time in Greek mythology.

THE RACIALIZATION OF SEX AND FISCAL HEALTH

With the addition of capital into the framework of race identification, I believe more insights can be found about the formation of the black female body or the female body of color in general and their position within society. Moreover, I think that this theory might prove helpful in understanding why women have a more difficult time finding paths to immigration on economic and humanitarian grounds than men. It could allow us to see that immigrant women have been depicted as a different race—one that is unhealthy because of their animal-like capacity to breed. Equating women of color with breeding allows them to be seen as beings, which are unhealthy because they jeopardize the health of the economy. Because the cultivation of non-white offspring is no longer thought to be beneficial to society, they are now seen as a detriment to the continued growth of the community, for they take away financial resources that could be used in more productive ways. If economics enables the blurring of lines between race and gender thus resulting in the feminization of black males, I suggest that there can also be another type of crossover—the racialization of gender.

On the one hand, it may seem like a strange way to distinguish one race from another. On the other hand, we have seen that this concept is not so foreign to Western thought. The Danaides and the Amazons represent precisely this kind of racial delineation. Furthermore, this strand of thought has continued to crop up in the West. Fin de siecle sexologists such as Richard Burton and Havelock Ellis use the term "race" to encompass a wide variety of difference ranging from nationality, species, to gender.[55] And Foucault's description of how race is seen through the lens of neoliberalism and the birth of biopolitics allows for this reading of race. I suggest Zack's monetarization of race and sexuality in conjunction with Foucault's suggestion that race is increasingly being seen as cleaving between the healthy and the unhealthy helps to give a framework for the ways in which women can be seen as a different race. Foucault's theory about contemporary racial discourse breaks with Kant's legend of the land but integrates economics into the fold. The emphasis on national prosperity that underlies state racism is founded on the idea that the health of the public, of a particular race could become degenerate—unless unhealthy people were monitored and controlled.[56] The strength of the modern state and its inhabitants is much more easily diminished and susceptible to the degeneracy of others than presented in Greek mythology. Because Foucault argues that race can be defined in relation to health, the economic health of the nation can be brought into the mix. And if we consider the place immigrant women are given in relation to the national economy, we can see how they are defined as a very different group than immigrant men.

Foucault's general claim is that races are split into the healthy and the unhealthy but this division does not apply solely to one's physical state. I suggest that it can also be interpreted in terms of those who contribute towards or work against fiscal health. This does not, however, change the dynamics of who is and is not healthy in terms of the conventional concept of race. In other words, whites are still healthy and non-whites are still unhealthy because the former can help promote monetary health while the others can only do so in a very marginal way. What it does is extend the meaning of health into the economic field.

CONCLUSION

Although there is a move to separate concerns about immigration from race, I suggest that race remains an integral part of the conversation. It may not be discussed in terms of heredity or skin color but, as I have attempted to show, race is not limited to just those characteristics. Since the construction of race has always had an economic component, we must recognize that a discussion about economics does not operate independently from race. Because money matters have always been a factor in constructing race, economic discourse often covers over racial discourse. Neoliberal ideology—which privileges the entrepreneurial self—works to recode old problems.

The tension surrounding foreign women in Greek mythology continues to be a problem for the West. While the Ancient Greeks used myths about the Danaides and the Amazons to advance the idea that the female race could be civilized through marriage and the submission to the patriarchal order, there is another myth presently at play. Because the annihilation of foreign women is not now a possible solution, the continuation of the mythology surrounding the female other relies on the perpetuation of the notion that female immigrants are necessarily needy strangers. Although I have mentioned the purported threat of women who could breed terror babies, I highlight the discourse that depicts immigrant women as the source of economic burden. This strand of thought pervades anti-immigration rhetoric because it can be connected to the economic health of the nation. In order to limit the number of female immigrants into the country, foreign women must be made to seem as a drain to the economy. It is no longer a matter of ensuring the "proper" use of female sexuality. Female immigrants are, instead, the embodiment of bestial nature that works to destroy the civilized race. Pierrette Hondagneu-Sotelo states that present forms of xenophobia against immigrants focus on reproduction.[57] Female immigrants are identified as a greater risk because they do not promote the economic growth of the nation but they also jeopardize it. Since they have the ability to bear children, they are seen as creating new lives that place a great burden on the financial welfare of the nation. Because the non-white women have never been neutralized, they occupy a treacherous intermediary space between races. To have as little contact as possible with this particular breed of humans means to limit their access as immigrants. This would be one way to protect the health of a race. In order to do so, however, a modern-day myth must be spun. This story must ignore how female immigrants have helped the economy and depict them, instead, as a complete burden to society. Although ancient myths about nefarious races of women seem so far removed from modern society, present immigration debates serve to remind us that these tales of dangerous foreigners remain with us.

NOTES

1. She states that "[t]he first foreigners in Greek mythology are women—the Danaides, whose adventures Aeschylus pieced together in *The Suppliants* (493–490 B.C.). See Julia Kristeva, *Nations without Nationalism*, New York: Columbia University Press, 1993), 17. Seth G. Bernadete, in contrast, notes that *The Suppliants* is considered to be the earliest Greek play to be preserved. See Aeschylus, *The Complete Greek Tragedies: Aeschylus II, Second Edition*. eds. David Grene and Richmond Lattimore, trans. Seth G. Bernadete and David Grene (Chicago: The University of Chicago Press, 1991), 2.

2. See Kristeva as it concerns the Danaides (Kristeva, *Nations*, 17). For further detail on the Amazons, see Wm. Blake Tyrell, *Amazons: A Study in Athenian Mythmaking* (Baltimore: Johns Hopkins University Press, 1986), 128 and Jean-Pierre Vernant, *Myth and Society in Ancient Greece*, trans. Janet Lloyd (New York: The Harvester Press Ltd., 1980), 24.

3. Tyrrell, *Amazons*, 55.

4. Tyrrell discusses variations in Amazon mythology in conjunction with political rhetoric concerning public figures such as Heracles, Theseus, and Lysias. (Tyrell, *Amazons*, 2–18.)

5. Aeschylus, *Complete Greek Tragedies*, 10.

6. Kristeva, *Nations*, 18.

7. Kristeva, *Nations*, 18.

8. A phallic symbol, to be sure.

9. Tyrrell explains the etymology of the name "Amazon." "Amazon" is a combination of *a* (no) and *mazos* (breast). (Tyrrell, *Amazons*, 49.)

10. Tyrrell, *Amazons*, 49.

11. Tyrrell, *Amazons*, 76.

12. Tyrrell, *Amazons*, 118.

13. Posi Loman, "No Women No War: Women's Participation in Ancient Greek Warfare," *Greece and Rome* 51 (2004): 38.

14. Tyrrell, *Amazons*, 102.

15. Aeschylus, *Complete Greek Tragedies*, 200.

16. Aeschylus, *Complete Greek Tragedies*, 200.

17. Lynette G. Mitchell, "Greeks, Barbarians and Aeschylus' Suppliants," *Greece and Rome* 53 (2006): 212. See also Aeschylus, *Complete Greek Tragedies*, 160.

18. See Mitchell, "Greeks, Barbarians, and Aeschylus," 13.

19. Amazons are equated with the same things that Persians represent, both Eastern warriors and feminized males. (Tyrrell, *Amazons*, 11 and 77.)

20. I will not go into detail about the differences between the submission of foreign men and women here but I will flesh out the differences between men and women in relation to American slavery.

21. Tyrrell, *Amazons*, 119.

22. Tyrrell, *Amazons*, 124.

23. Kristeva, *Nations*, 30.

24. Sigmund Freud, "Femininity" in *The Complete Edition of the Complete Psychological Works of Sigmund Freud, Vol. XXII*, trans. James Strachey (London: The Hogarth Press 1964), 163.

25. Michel Foucault, *The History of Sexuality: An Introduction*, trans. Robert Hurley (New York: Vintage Books, 1990), 153.

26. Even Foucault recognized that "psychoanalysis was established in opposition to a certain kind of psychiatry, the psychiatry of degeneracy, eugenics and heredity." See Michel Foucault, "Body/Power" in *Power/Knowledge: Selected Interviews and Other Writings, 1972–1977*, ed. Colin Gordon (New York: Pantheon Books. 1980), 60.

27. (Freud 1964, 141.)

28. (Freud 1964, 161.)

29. Freud, "Femininity," 159.

30. The Danaides may have only been extended this courtesy because their heritage can be traced back to Io and Zeus. Thus, they are both Greek and non-Greek. (Aeschylus, *Complete Greek Tragedies*, 310–20.)

31. Kristeva, *Nations*, 18–19.

32. Richard Fry states that ". . . an increasing flow of mostly-male unauthorized migrants has more than counterbalanced the feminization of legal migration, making the U.S. the only industrialized country where the percentage of female migrants has declined over the past 25 years." See Richard Fry, "Gender and Migration," Pew Hispanic Center, last modified July 5, 2006, http://www.pewhispanic.org/2006/07/05/gender-and-migration/.

33. Nancy V. Yinger notes the United States continues to be the nation that takes in the largest amount of immigrants worldwide. See Nancy V. Yinger, "Feminization of Migration: Limits of the Data," Population Reference Bureau, last modified June 12, 2013, http://www.prb.org/Articles/2007/FeminizationofMigrationLimitsofData.aspx.

34. In a meeting on April 5, 2006, the Economic and Social Council of the United Nations reported that "[t]he 'feminization of migration' had also produced specifically female forms of migration, such as the commercialized migration of domestic workers and caregivers, the migration and trafficking of women for the sex industry, and the organized migration of women for marriage." See "ECOSOC News, VOL. 5, NO. 2," United Nations Economic and Social Council, last modified May 31, 2006, http://www.un.org/en/ecosoc/news/ecosoc.newsletter.v5nr.2.pdf.

35. Naomi Zack, "The American Sexualization of Race," In *Race/Sex: Their Sameness, Difference, and Interplay*, ed. Naomi Zack (New York: Routledge, 1997), 152.

36. The distinction between the healthy and the unhealthy race is, of course, not original to Foucault. Nietzsche, whose influence can be seen in Foucault's work, discussed the difference between the healthy and unhealthy as part of his critique of modern society. See Friedrich Nietzsche, *On the Genealogy of Morals and Ecce Homo*, trans. Walter Kaufmann (New York: Vintage, 1989), 122–25. Foucault shows how states can justify discrimination against certain groups if they are labeled as a danger to public health. (Foucault, *History of Sexuality*, 54.) He also makes mention of how biological themes of health are central to state racism in his 1976 lectures, which were a precursor to *The History of Sexuality: An Introduction*. (Foucault, *History of Sexuality*, 71.)

37. Stuart Elden, "The War of Races and the Constitution of the State: Foucault's *Il faut défendre la societe* and the Politics of Calculation," *boundary 2* 29 (2002): 147.

38. In a report about gender and development for the UN, Monica Boyd and Deanna Pikkov explain that migrant women are more likely to enter as wives and dependents of men, who sponsor them, than they are to gain entrance on humanitarian or economic grounds of their own. See Monica Boyd and Deanna Pikkov, *Gendering Migration, Livelihood, and Entitlements: Migrant Women in Canada and the United States* (Ithaca: Cornell University Press, 2005).

39. See *2005 Yearbook for Immigration Statistics*, Department of Homeland Security, last modified June 10, 2013, http://www.dhs.gov/yearbook-immigration-statistics. The

tables, and Chart 9 in particular, show that men are admitted as refugees, asylum seekers, and for employment based-preferences at a higher rate than women.

40. Michael Jones-Correa, "Different Paths: Gender, Immigratiion and Political Participation," *International Migration Review* 32 (1998): 333.

41. Ladelle McWhorter, "Where Do White People Come From?: A Foucaultian Critique of Whiteness Studies," *Philosophy & Social Criticism* 31 (2005): 47.

42. Tyrrell discusses the mental gymnastics that Greeks underwent to assert that they were born from the land. (Tyrrell, *Amazons*, 117–18.)

43. It was very important for him to be able to explain disparity while maintaining unity because his argument was a defense of a monogenist view of humanity—that everyone is a descendant of Adam and Eve, which would coincide with an orthodox reading of the Bible.

44. Immanuel Kant, "Of the Different Human Races," in *The Idea of Race*, eds. Robert Bernasconi and Tommy Lott (Indianapolis: Hackett, 2000), 14.

45. Kristeva, *Nations*, 16.

46. Kant, "Of the Different Human Races," 17.

47. Although Kant argued that Africans were underdeveloped in terms of entrepreneurial skills, he also suggested that they were overdeveloped in other areas, for instance in skin pigments. It was because the Northern Europeans maintained an adaptive character, not too under- or overdeveloped, that made them superior beings. (Kant, "Of the Different Human Races," 16.) This overdevelopment can also apply to sexuality. Unlike the Northern Europeans who could control their sexuality, common stereotypes about Africans depict them as overly sexual beings—unable to control their lasciviousness.

48. Zack, "American Sexualization," 149.

49. Spillers describes the figurative and literal castration. This contributes to the blurring of lines between black males and females. See Hortense Spillers, "Mama's Baby, Papa's Maybe: An American Grammar Book," *Diacritics* 17 (1987): 64–81.

50. It is often thought that the castration of an animal would make them more docile and compliant.

51. Zack, "American Sexualization," 151.

52. Zack states, ". . . insofar as the sexualization of race is an artifact of American white racism, the sexualization of black male race is diminutive in comparison with the sexualization of black female race" (Zack, "American Sexualization," 153). It is the black female that is hypersexual not the black male.

53. Parenthetical text found in the original.

54. Dario Padovan, "Biopolitics and the Social Control of the Multitude," *Democracy & Nature* 9 (2003): 479.

55. See Diana Fuss, "Interior Colonies: Frantz Fanon and the Politics of Identification," *Diacritics* 24 (1994): 35.

56. In Foucault's explanation of the emergence of biopower, he describes how the issue of public health is used to garner support for mechanisms to monitor and control. The racism propagated by the Nazis was effective because it was aimed at the protection of one race—the Aryan race—from those that would destroy its purity. In other words, the strength and health of the race would be undermined if those who were unhealthy were allowed to infiltrate society. (Foucault, *History of Sexuality*, 149–50.)

57. Pierrette Hondagneu-Sotelo, *Gendered Transitions: Mexican Experiences of Immigration* (Los Angeles: University of California Press, 1994), 86.

Conclusion

Immigrants as Indicators of Race

Because of the connections between sex and immigration and sexuality and immigration, there is little wonder that many in the field of immigration studies take interest in Foucault's work. Many Foucault scholars have also used his works to explore sexuality as it connects to the concept of race. By drawing on these resources, I sought to show the ways in which the immigration process helps to reveal modern forms of racism, as described by Foucault. Immigration policies, in and of themselves, do not define race—just as they do not define sexuality. I argue, however, that they help to indicate shifts in racial discourse, the emergence of new races, and illuminate which races are problematic. In other words, I use Foucault's theories to understand better the interworking of race and immigration. By examining racial discourse in this way, we begin to see how those with abnormal sexuality become identified as an unhealthy race. Even though sexuality clearly does play a role in such a study, it is only one piece of the puzzle for understanding the history of race within the United States. Since race has been entangled with everything from mythology to biology, the concept of race is slippery and difficult to grasp. Immigration regulations, at least for the United States, have been constant indicators of race and become integrated with many of the current discourses surrounding race.

While different lenses have focused and refocused racial discourse, immigration policies have reflected predominant themes and tools that pulse through constructions of race. This is not to say that one racial discourse cancels out all past formations of race. Certainly, there are many factors embedded within race formation: mythology, biology, politics, economics, etc. I suggest that analyzing immigration policies in conjunction with Foucault's theories on biopolitics can shed light on which strands of knowledge are the most important for a particular era and how they are used to define race. I further suggest that these mechanisms of power can oftentimes be found in immigration policies.

FOUCAULT AND RACE

Foucault can aid us in tracing a history of racism in the United States because he provides a novel reading of race. The idea that certain immigrant groups must be more strictly controlled or turned away altogether is sometimes seen as a sign of racism. Yet Foucault's treatise on modern race is not limited to a racism that attacks those who differ in appearance from Anglo-Europeans. Instead, his description of modern racism focuses on the creation of the abnormal and their threat to national security. These disparate peoples, with varying abnormalities, become portrayed as various races that share one thing in common. They all work against the life and prosperity of the nation-state and human development, a key theme in neoliberal governments. Racial discourse, like discourse concerning sexuality, is multiplied and amplified through intersecting pathways of knowledge. The abnormal can be recognized and known with the help of economics, biology, medicine, and even myth. Because the study of immigration can lead to a greater understanding of how race and racist discourse has proliferated, it can also help us to be more aware of how policies target certain vulnerable groups. If immigration policies show how races are formed and conceived, they can, likewise, indicate which group has become the problematic other. Immigration policies can also help us to reflect upon our conceptions and treatment of these groups. An examination of Foucault's concept of biopolitics and race can help us to understand the way Western societies identify and create the other.

On the one hand, Foucault's work on sexuality and biopolitics leads to a nontraditional conception of race. Indeed, many contemporary scholars have built on his work to show how the sexually abnormal become as a race unto themselves. The variety of races is no longer identified primarily through somatic qualities. Foucault shows that biopolitics distinguishes between the healthy and unhealthy race. Sexuality, of course, is just one among many ways in which to make this split. On the other hand, Foucault's conception of race is not so different from other ideas of race. Ladelle McWhorter argues that race has never had a fixed meaning. She suggests that the protection of the "white" race has always been at the center of modern Western notions of race. Foucault's conception of race, in general, follows this principle. It is not mere coincidence that those with abnormal sexuality or unhealthy practices are largely non-white. Thus, biopolitical controls are established in order to ensure that the unhealthy races—of which there are many—do not infect healthy whites. And sexual standards can serve as guides.[1] The healthy may be tempted to stray but norms help them monitor their acts, thoughts, and desires and measure them against what is ideal.

The way in which Foucault connects biopolitics to race shows why modern states are concerned with the comingling of the healthy and unhealthy. His analysis of the Third Reich, the greatest and most naïve of biopolitical states, elucidates the inner workings of modern states in their efforts to purify the state. The Nazis developed a eugenics program in order to destroy all of the unhealthy germs that could plague the German race, which was supposed to represent the zenith and destiny of humanity. The highest stakes of biopolitics seemed to be invoked through sexuality. If sexual norms were not abided, the repercussions could be fatal not just to the state but also to the human race. Those who broke with sexual norms not only acted against the health of the state but also the health of the human race. For these reasons, the management of the population became interwoven with racial discourse. Homosexuals and other sexual deviants not only went against the established social norms but they could not contribute the needed offspring that would ensure the continuance of humanity.[2] What, then, could be the reason for their acting against the well-being of the human race? The explanation is simple; sexual deviants could be categorized as a different race. They belong to an unhealthy race of people who have no concern for the future of humanity. Instead of contributing to the development of the human race, they can only inhibit it.

Many scholars have, however, criticized Foucault for not paying attention to state actions that were directed outward. Ann Stoler shows, in *Sex and the Education of Desire*, that Foucault's analysis of biopolitics is incomplete because he does not address the history of colonialism. Neither does Foucault discuss how modern Western states deal with immigration as a means to regulate their population. Recently, Foucault's work on biopolitics has been used to help decipher the logic of American immigration laws. Eithne Luibhéid and Siobhan Somerville argue that immigration policies reveal the standards and codes of "good" citizenship. Immigrants are a particularly useful category of study because they, too, represent a form of reproduction. A nation's immigration regulations help elucidate which characteristics are desired and which are to be rejected. Policy makers use immigration codes to weed out those who would challenge or jeopardize the social norms that they wanted to promote. In other words, immigration policies are crucial for managing the nation's population. The community would be endangered if the wrong immigrants were allowed entrance. Sexual dispositions and identities are, of course, indicators of an immigrant's desirability. Thus, sexuality and immigration directly intersect on the terrain of biopolitics. To this point, Luibhéid and Somerville focus their studies on the ways in which immigration policies target and negatively affect women and those who are thought to break from heterosexual norms.

Because immigration is a form of communal reproduction, race, too, is implicated in such policies. Sexual norms are put in place to ensure that community members properly develop. Only if good citizens are grown and raised can the best traits of humanity be passed. If deviant immigrants were allowed to enter the country, all of this grooming could be undone. The desirable immigrant or the naturalized citizen must not interfere with the cultural and ideological reproduction of the community. This kind of contamination would signal the demise of the white, healthy race and all its goodness.[3] Even though politicians often try to distance themselves from issues of race, race remains part of the discussion. It may be more palatable to proclaim that society must be defended from backwards ideology rather than those who are ethnically different. Yet there is no denying that this line of thinking is also used to target people of color, who are supposedly steeped in stunted cultures.

BIOPOLITICS AND IMMIGRATION

A biopolitical reading of U.S. immigration policies is not needed to see that immigrants have been cast as lesser races both because of their inferior genes or practices. It is no secret that immigration policies discriminate against people of color. However, Foucault's analysis of biopolitics is useful for understanding how disparate discourses join together to diminish attributes of foreign races. He shows that sexual norms are supported by a wide variety of disciplines: science, philosophy, psychoanalysis, etc. Although Foucault spends a great deal of time, in *The Birth of Biopolitics*, explaining the connections between neoliberal economics and biopolitics, there are many other disciplines and fields of knowledge that contribute to the biopolitical philosophy that is interwoven within modern society. It may not be surprising that economic theory is used to paint a negative portrait of certain races. If economics is at the center of modern-day life, as Arendt believes, then economic theory can pervade other, seemingly nonrelated areas.[4] What we see through Foucauldian biopolitics is not only why many discourses support the idea of inferior nonwhite races but also how the categories of races have grown. Differentiation between races is not limited to somatic qualities. Those with suspicious religion, sexuality, and gender are also considered to be of a different race.

Studies of immigration regulations add to his analysis of biopolitics because they focus on the border of society—figuratively and literally. They shine a brighter light on what behavior is acceptable and who can be counted as subjects who are of the community. "Because of a tendency to focus on territorial borders as the site of national exclusion or inclusion, immigration has been a privileged site for scholarship on citizenship in American studies."[5] Immigration controls help to show how even those who belong to the community can be questioned and perhaps even cast out of the community. While it is taken for granted that immigration regulations work to normalize the new members to the culture and customs of the community, applying Foucault's biopolitical analysis to immigration shows how these regulations also work to manage the population already within the national borders.

That sexual discourse would impact immigration policies should not be surprising, even if the intersection is only now beginning to gain attention. It further demonstrates Foucault's point that concerns over sexuality pervade all corners of modern life. Luibheid and Somerville expand on Foucault's analysis and point out that immigration laws are an extension of heteronormativity. Somerville argues that the nonsexual reproduction of community members nonetheless follows heterosexual norms.[6] She argues that laws such as the family reunification act show that immigration policies are ultimately grounded in heterosexual standards. Luibheid, in addition, suggests that heterosexual norms are so entrenched within the immigration process that there are virtually no studies of the treatment of nonheterosexual women.

Highlighting how heteronormativity works within immigration regulations reinforces the idea that sexuality figures prominently within modern society. An examination of immigration laws is helpful for understanding modern society because they are a written record of which sexual norms are in play. While heteronormativity is not always apparent within immigration regulations, they do sometimes provide clear examples of the favoring of heterosexuality. Immigration controls are not only legal code but also work to help to encode heterosexual norms. While general attitudes about sexuality may seem inchoate, they are formalized in immigration laws. When there was less sensitivity to diversity of all sorts, there was little effort to hide biases when crafting immigration laws. Immigration laws still privilege particular forms of sexuality and work to establish certain sexual norms but they are often covered over by psychiatric diagnoses, hygiene regimes, and educational programs. Political correctness may have made it more difficult to find explicit references to heterosexual privilege but they can still be found when read together—as Somerville shows—with other policies that concern health, economics, or population management.

Heteronormativity is so embedded within immigration policies that even the nation's nonsexual reproduction of community members takes its cue from heterosexual reproduction. Naturalized citizens are, of course, those who have obtained citizenship despite not being born to an American parent or on American soil. The eligibility for becoming a "naturalized" citizen, however, depends on an immigrant's sexual identity and perceived status. This leads Somerville to argue that the so-called naturalization process is a reference to the privileged position given to heterosexuality. The heterosexuality of would-be citizens can and must link them to those of their adopted nation. While immigrants may not look the same or share the same culture as the indigenous people, they are recognized as similar beings because they can produce offspring. Immigrants can only be naturalized if they prove to be "natural" beings.

> And sexual reproduction is the mechanism by which this effect is
> achieved: we know that an organism has been fully naturalized—and
> might as well be indigenous—by its successful self-propagation, pre-
> sumably through sexual reproduction. This is another way of saying
> that "naturalization" is a metaphor, one that imagines the political and
> natural worlds as analogous and inextricably linked. This metaphor
> circulated widely in discourses of citizenship in the early republic.[7]

They can only be accepted into the community if they are believed to be
heterosexual. In other words, heterosexuality is a condition for becoming
a naturalized citizen.

   Since heteronormativity plays such a big part in determining who can
and cannot enter into the community, immigration officials on all levels
are given the responsibility for making sure that abnormal and unwanted
individuals do not enter. Women undergo greater scrutiny because there
is such an emphasis on "natural" reproduction. Border guards believe
women warrant additional consideration and inspection because they
have historically been seen as the vessel for offspring. The woman's constitution, therefore, can affect future generations. Her sexual disposition
could affect her progeny and, possibly, the rest of the community.

> The officers charged with carrying out these policies and realizing the
> necessary assessments must differentiate between women's bodies that
> are capable of (re)producing appropriate citizens and those that could
> "infect" the nation with unwanted sexuality and/or genealogy. They
> attempt to guard the nation against inappropriate penetration and—in
> doing so—create a specific code of normative and nonnormative be-
> havior.[8]

Unlike men, the penetration of nonheterosexual women could have an
impact on the future of humanity. While controllers do not view nonheterosexual men as normal or ideal candidates by any means, they are
seen as less of a threat than the abnormal women. A woman can still
reproduce no matter her "true" sexual disposition.

   All the steps taken to enforce heteronormativity lead Judith Butler to
ask whether kinship is always heterosexual. She questions the way in
which policies of family reunification are formed. Here again we see
traces of naturalized sexuality. Only family members who are connected
through heterosexual activity can qualify under the family reunification
act.[9] Or at the very least, those who have no connection that culminates
in heterosexual coupling are excluded from consideration. Homosexual
couples, which cannot produce children "naturally," are largely precluded for using this law to be reunited in an adopted homeland.

   Breaking with heteronormativity is one way to be classified as an
inferior category of people. Western myth and philosophy also show that
the female sex is suspect, and women are abnormal beings. While the
idea that women constitute a race may seem odd, women—as Julia Kris-

teva notes—have been identified as the first foreigners in Greek mythology.[10] The Danaides and the Amazons represent the female race and all of
the dangers associated with womankind. In the case of the Danaides,
they needed to bow to the rule of men before they were allowed to
become part of the community. It goes without saying that these women
were not to have any political power in the Greek city. The Amazons, on
the other hand, could not be accepted into the community. Wm. Blake
Tyrell argues that they were seen as the greatest threat to civilization
because they represented a group of women who were hostile to patriarchy. Amazons could not be integrated into society because their nature
was wild and uncontrollable. In short, these women symbolized the
antithesis of civilization.

IMMIGRATION AND MYTHOLOGY

There is, of course, great continuity between these Greek myths and the
history of Western philosophy. It is well-known that Ancient and Enlightenment philosophers often espoused the shortcomings of women.
Much like Greek legend, these philosophers argued that women needed
to be controlled because they had—among other deficits—lesser intellectual capacities than men. Even though the particular characteristics assigned to women may have changed depending upon the time period,
there has been a great constant idea that has run through Western
thought. Women are considered inferior beings to men and jeopardize
the progress that men have installed in the world.

Immigration policies, unfortunately, mimic these mythological and
philosophical themes about women. While the public has taken notice of
the ways that Mexicans, Muslims, and even homosexuals have been targeted through the immigration process, the treatment and discourse surrounding female immigrants receives less attention. Yet present-day discourse about immigrating women reveals a long-held prejudice against
those of the female sex. They are often cast as one of the most dangerous
kinds of foreigner because they have the ability to bring low quality
people into the world. Anti-immigrant politicians and groups emphasize
the dangers brought about by the immigrant woman and her breeding
abilities. Since the foreign woman is so likely to breed, she is considered
of lesser human stock. She lacks the intellectual capacity to control her
bodily needs. The immigrant woman can also infect the American gene
pool through her unchecked desire to propagate. And because she reproduces so frequently, she is stealing resources from an already burdened
nation. The more that America gives to these undesirable immigrants, the
less it can put towards the betterment of the country. America will not be
able to fulfill its destiny—according to this modern-day myth—if it continues to support the influx of women. In other words, immigrant women

still threaten the foundation of civilized society. Immigration policies are crafted in such a way as to suggest that there was a return of the Amazon.

By focusing on immigration regulations rather than sexuality, the discourse of race emerges as a leading way to manage the population. Concerns over sexuality, of course, do not disappear when immigration becomes a lens for understanding biopolitics. However, immigration policies can be used to show how divergent conceptions of race are created. It could also be said, conversely, that immigration laws reveal the efforts of lawmakers to reinforce the supremacy of the "white" race by emphasizing the inferiority of outsiders. Sexuality remains part of the conversation. There is the perennial fear that the nation will be overrun by a hypersexual race who will give birth to an increasing number of inferior children. Yet a closer analysis of immigration policies reveals other, new ways in which racial hierarchy is invoked. A Foucauldian reading of immigration shows that lawmakers use the need to defend society to establish racial superiority/inferiority. To this end, immigration laws rely on arguments as divergent as religion and economics to make the case that the white race must remain dominant if America is to continue prospering.

A biopolitical analysis that turns on immigration would be similar to one that focuses on sexuality in that they both show that states employ techniques, laws, and norms to manage the population. Greater focus on immigration regulations could also complement Foucault's work on sexuality. Through his examination of sexuality, Foucault shows how the repressive hypothesis actually produced the opposite effect. Sexuality may still be a grand preoccupation for modern people but I suggest that race is another and a study of immigration policies makes this abundantly clear. Race and public safety, after all, are constant themes in immigration debates. While lawmakers often admit that immigration regulations are aimed at managing the health of the population, the intended trajectory of racial discourse remains ambiguous. But like sexual discourse, the insistence that we live in a post-racial society and that race is on longer a problem seems to have resulted in a proliferation of discourse about race.

PROLIFERATION OF DISCOURSE AND LAWS

The idea that sexuality should not be discussed or given much attention gave rise to a greater focus on the matter. Concerns about sexuality were not dampened; they actually multiplied. The supposed call towards the maintenance of sexual prudence and discretion led to a backlash of sorts. It not only resulted in more cultural openness about sexuality but it also led to further study of sexuality. Yet the knowledge produced by these analyses did not necessarily change the way sexuality was viewed in society. Foucault argues, to the contrary, that the information about sexuality largely worked to reinforce sexual norms. The repressive hypothesis, in short, produced greater circulation and awareness of sexual codes and mores.[11] More discussion about sexuality did not, in and of itself, produce challenges to sexual norms. With increased public discourse and knowledge about sexual norms, existing sexual norms were only strengthened as more paths were created to control and regulate the population. Proper sexual attitudes and practices could be dispensed in the name of biological, mental, or cultural education.

I suggest that all the bluster about wanting to get past race works in the same way as the repressive hypothesis. Many scholars question whether or not there is a desire to move beyond race at all. Discussions about race seem to galvanize the American population in interesting ways, especially when dealing with immigrants. Proposals to limit immigration into America have gathered support from across the political spectrum. New nativists and self-proclaimed progressives, albeit for different reasons, ban together to limit immigration. This is an example of how, according to Foucault, forces work together towards a goal despite not having a central head.

We would not be surprised to find that immigration laws were bound up with race in earlier eras. Past lawmakers were quite clear about their desires to welcome only those of particular heritage. Yet the place of race in immigration laws has evolved. For this reason, immigration policies serve as a record for what constitutes the race that is the most suspicious to those in power. At times, medical exams helped policy makers weed out undesirable immigrants. A quick look at American immigration policies shows how everyone from Eastern Europeans, Southern Europeans, Asians, etc. had been targeted as physically suspect at different times. Although science is thought to be detached from prejudice, the medical exams targeting immigrants show, to the contrary, that science can be used to support racial discrimination.

Despite the mythology surrounding America, not all immigrants were welcome or welcomed equally. U.S. immigration laws have long favored Northwestern Europeans. Those from England, France, and Germany had privileged status if they desired to immigrate to America, for they were thought to be the standard-bearers of the superior, "white" race. With the influx of Eastern Europeans to America, lawmakers began to craft policies to block their entrance. Some counted the lack of education and unhealthy physical condition as reasons to limit the number of non-Northwestern European immigrants. The underlying message behind this discourse was clear. They were thought to be of an inferior, non-white race. Indeed, some politicians did not care to hide their motives.

Senators such as Walter F. George, a Democratic senator from Georgia in 1952, also sought to defend the nation by urging Americans to keep control over their immigration policies and, thereby, the community. He hints to the pending dissolution of the nation, if Americans succumb to the pressure of outsiders by consenting to a more lax immigration policy. He defended the merits of the Immigration Act of 1924 by stating that, "The real basic purpose back of the immigration act which we finally enacted in 1924 was to preserve something of homogeneity of the American people. . . . "[12] George's words reinforce the idea that non-Northwestern Europeans are from a different culture and from a diminished gene pool. Medical and scientific inventions made these claims easier to justify.

The Immigration Act of 1924, therefore, elucidates how racial and scientific discourses converged. It is common knowledge that immigrants must undergo a medical examination in order to enter into the country. What is perhaps less well-known is that medical tests were unevenly administered. Much depended upon the immigrant's country of origin. Amy Fairchild notes that Asian immigrants faced the greatest likelihood of being turned back to their home country.[13] The administration of medical exams was part of a concerted political effort to block the entrance of undesirable immigrants into America. While it is certainly plausible that sanitary conditions and health facilities varied widely among countries, concerns over physical fitness seemed to be a convenient justification for blocking the entrance of those deemed to be inferior races.

The political nature of medical exams is underscored when understood within the context of cultural fears. Medical exams were only put in place after concern grew that the American people were shouldering the burden of poor, sick, insane, and criminal immigrants.[14] No laws were passed to limit immigration from Europe before 1882 because there was a great need for labor. The general immigration law passed in 1882 aimed to weed out undesirables. The administering of medical exams was just a part of the filtering process. It seems, then, that medical science was used to cover over concerns about the mixing of "high" American culture with low European culture. At the very least, the path to reducing the number of undesirable Europeans entering the country was made easier through the rationale of physical health. Amidst the realization that the European elite, the most desired immigrants, had not chosen to immigrate to America and the new awareness that World War I created the appearance of America as a much more peaceful and attractive place to live than the slums and ghettoes of Europe, U.S. lawmakers sought to erect stricter immigration regulations. Politicians used medical exams to stave off the wave of diseased and mentally unstable immigrants who most felt the brunt of war-ravaged Europe. Even though one did not have to look very closely to see that it was politically expedient to proclaim that those with subpar health were also of supposedly inferior cultures, there was less political resistance for those who wanted to block immigrants with poor health than those who wanted to deny entrance on cultural or national grounds. The uneven administration of medical tests to incoming immigrants, therefore, was an example of how scientific discourse was effective in passing prejudicial policies.

This method allowed the immigration population to be thinned out without drawing as much ire and criticism as the quota system. However, as Roxana Galusca argues, medical examinations were inextricably connected to American race prejudice.

> By drawing an imaginary borderline between the ablebodied and the disabled, the racially marked bodies and their unmarked counterparts, the immigration regulations on the island reinscribed health and ablebodiedness as national characteristics. Thus, the American nation came to be defined according to medical norms of ability. In its embodiment of the stigma of disease and race, Ellis Island functioned as an indispensable national "laboratory" that reinvented the nation-state as a scientific project, while racializing bodies as metonymic extensions of contamination. Race, pathology, and nationalism intersected and created the backdrop for the Ellis Island processing station. The racialized, disabled, and diseased body functioned as the scapegoat, a political spectacle that helped to consolidate, at the opposite pole, the sanitized, healthy nation-state.[15]

Denying entrance to unhealthy immigrants was seen as a matter of science rather than that of unjustified race prejudice. Concern over the physical health of the individual and the possibility of an infection of the population helps to fortify the notion of the "good" and healthy American and the diseased other. This narrative, of course, helps to support racism while being less obvious than the quota system. A focus on the health and constitution of the immigrant also allowed for greater regulations of those culturally inferior immigrants, like Asians, that were granted entry into the country. The idea that Asians were a hypersexual race was so common that the sexualization of Asian peoples could be clearly seen in early laws to restrict their entrance into the country. And when Asians were granted entrance, they were subject to greater regulations and monitoring so that their sexual appetite and nature would not endanger the nation.

While lawmakers later tried to remove more direct language about the sexualized Asian race, these sentiments did not disappear. Discrimination against Asian races on the basis of sexual perversion remained within laws such as the Page Act and the Chinese Exclusion Act. U.S. consuls, under the Page Act of 1875, were required to ensure that no Asian immigrant entering the country was under contract for "lewd and immoral purposes."[16] The heightened scrutiny of Asian women, in general, and Chinese women, in particular, through the Page Act reveals that abnormal sexuality was racialized. Anna Marie Smith also argues that Chinese women were denied entrance into the country because the Page Act officially equated Chinese women with prostitution.[17] Thanks to the Page Act, Chinese women were synonymous with sexual depravity. The Page

Act made it difficult to separate the Chinese race from sexual abnormality.

Even if there was debate about the infiltration of race discourse into immigration laws at the time of their crafting, scholars of American immigration leave little doubt that these past laws were influenced by ideas of race. Today, the debate about the convergence of immigration laws and race still rages. There are, of course, present-day lawmakers who vehemently deny that any of their proposed immigration policies have anything to do with race. And there are, as before, public and private citizens who believe that race plays a substantial role in forming immigration laws. If past is prologue, the weight of history seems to suggest that the latter group has a more accurate reading of immigration regulations.

RACISM: OLD AND NEW

Traces of racism may not always be evident or obvious in immigration laws because race discourse changes and can take on many different forms. It is now widely acknowledged that Italian and Irish immigrants were, at one time, outside the "white" race. For that reason, they were thought to be problematic immigrants. Now that those of Italian and Irish descent are considered white, they are no longer the suspicious figures they once were. Since immigration regulations could provide insight into contemporary ideas of race, this is all the more reason to pay attention to them. In a day and age where overt racism is less tolerated and, therefore, more likely to be cloaked by other rationales of inferiority, immigration laws could serve as a means to detect emerging racial discourses. Immigration laws continue to help us identify how racial discourse is being formed in society.

Discrimination against certain races, no matter the efforts to obfuscate it with more neutral language, is easier to spot than others. In modern society, we are perhaps more aware of racism against Mexicans but such discrimination can also be covered over with neoliberal rationale. There is little doubt that these groups have historically been seen as inferior races. Politicians seem to fall short when they attempt to explain away racial bias by turning to economic rationale or long-held beliefs about cultural backwardness of certain immigrants. At the very least, a substantial portion of the citizenry recognizes that these are just other iterations of white, Western supremacy. Laws targeting Mexican and Muslim immigrants, in particular, may also help the public connect the dots between the logic of anti-immigration and racism because the logic behind these regulations builds upon long-held prejudices.

Attempts to block the immigration of Mexicans, as a stand-in for all immigrants entering from America's southern border, are often couched in neoliberal language but the stereotype of the unproductive person of color lurks in the background. Through immigration controls, policy makers draw on the idea that Mexicans immigrants will steal the resources of the unwitting host nation, America. Although this narrative contrasts sharply with the use of Mexican workers as a source of cheap and exploitable labor, both contingents believe that Mexican immigrants will destroy America's economy. Yet, as Wanda Vrasti points out, this is not the case. Neoliberal society ". . . functions thanks to the enthusiastic cooperation of white, middle-class individuals, who stand to gain the most from this system of accumulation, but also with the approval of the global poor who desperately seek to access some of the cultural and semiotic goods present in the West."[18] She suggests, to the contrary, that the American economy benefits from immigration and grows in mystique with greater immigration. Because there is no shortage of impoverished people, there will always be a large pool of immigrants hoping to find a better life elsewhere and the West continues to represent the fulfillment of those hopes.

There is, of course, another group of immigrants who receive a great deal of scrutiny. Anyone who might be linked to Islam is subject to special controls. Unlike laws geared towards limiting Mexican immigrants, the legal language concerning Muslim immigrants marks the re-entrance of the use of biological science to support race prejudice. Although science and religion are often thought to exist at opposite ends of the knowledge spectrum, American lawmakers combine them to form the idea of the Muslim race and to block this dangerous species of people.

Although Omi and Winant describe religious difference as a precursor of race construction, immigration policies show that religion now contributes to the racial discourse. This should not be surprising considering that immigration policies relay which people have now become suspicious and who may now constitute a different race. Those from the Middle East have been targets because of their suspect and dangerous religion. Although the identification of race through religion is not altogether new, the use of scientific discourse to support such a claim marks a change in race discourse. Dorothy Roberts insists that present discourse about biological race is significant because this shows a shift away from the widely held view that race was a result of social construction.[19] As Foucault had shown with his analysis of the Nazi regime, this would not be the first time religion and science melded together to produce a threatening race. If we apply Foucualt's theories on biopolitics to contemporary scholarship on immigration, we see that there are other forms of race that emerge through immigration policies.

Because of the divergent discourses and methods used to reinforce race prejudice, an analysis of the history of U.S. immigration laws can be all the more helpful for showing the ways that race has been embedded in policies. Even if race prejudice or favoritism is not immediately clear, past laws suggest that immigration policies are always intertwined with conceptions of race. Such an examination, in turn, can help us to trace how ideas about race are formed and supported. Race prejudice may be difficult to spot or locate at the time because race discourse can take on many different forms and draw support from diverging fields. If race discourse is malleable, immigration laws can help us to recognize who is subject to racism through concrete policies and the debates that surround them. At the very least, a reflection on immigration policies can help us as a society to reflect also on our present conceptions of race. Closer attention to immigration regulations may also help us to understand the unwelcome reality that racism continues to operate in modern society.

Just as those who lived during the time of the first implementation of immigrant medical screenings did not necessarily recognize them to be part of a system of race formation and discrimination, it is possible that we do not yet fully understand how race is shaped in our society. Immigration laws can be helpful in pointing the way towards newly emerging conceptions of race. Because this has been the case in the past, it is likely that immigration laws can do the same in the present. Beyond the instances of Mexican and Muslim immigrants—which are recognized at least by some as being motivated by racism, present-day immigration laws point to other, less discussed concepts of race.

Despite the credo that is attributed to America, it has not always welcomed everyone and everyone equally. Present debates over immigration reveal a tension surrounding immigrants that is veiled by the legend of American generosity towards foreigners. Instead of direct hostility toward immigrants as there was in the past, concerns over economic, cultural, and public health enshroud the issue of racism remains. Even though there is more awareness of what part racism played in American history and immigration laws, there is still a resistance to recognizing the ways in which racism operates within U.S. immigration regulations of today. Americans seem willing to admit, for instance, that certain people (Irish and Italian) were once discriminated against because they were not thought to be part of the white race. Scholars have also done much to raise public consciousness about the ill treatment of various waves of Asian immigrants. When concerns arise about the influence of racism on immigration policies of today, a significant portion of the American population seems to reject this theory out of hand. Or if there is admission that race is a part of the discourse of immigration, groups like the new nativists tend to blame the entrance of race into the debate on the immigrants themselves.[20] In other words, immigrants are the ones who make race an issue. Either theory allows Americans, if they so desire, to believe that current immigration policies are no longer laced with racism—even though past laws have provided ample evidence that immigration regulations and racial discourse often go hand-in-hand.

IMMIGRATION POLICIES: INDICATORS OF RACE

Paying greater attention to the correlation between immigration regulations and attitudes concerning race does not necessarily have to translate into the destruction of all immigration restrictions. It could, however, lead to greater reflection and awareness about our conceptions of race and treatment of the Other. Recognizing the interplay between immigration laws and race discourse could help us to locate ethical trouble spots. For a variety of reasons, it is difficult to identify how race and racism operate in American culture. It does seem, however, that concerns about the formation or existence of race are connected to ethical questions. Whenever race is discussed, concerns about the treatment of others follow. Should those who are different from the in-group be welcomed? Is integration of the foreign group possible or desirable? How are responsibilities shared and divided among those who already belong to the community and those who are new to it? These same ethical questions, of course, are inherent within immigration debates. Denying the connection between race and immigration policies is problematic because it flies in the face of historical evidence. The refusal to see that concerns over race and immigration intersect could also be symptomatic of a more overarching problem that stems from an inability to understand our ethical response to the Other.

If part of the problem is that the Other is difficult to recognize, immigration policies can help us to identify who constitutes the Other. Scholarship on past immigration laws shows that the language of regulations has been a good indicator of which group is considered dangerous and undesirable. Since this pattern seems to be holding, immigration laws do not have to be a tool to be used in hindsight. Immigration policies could also be seen as warning signs. They could help modern society to recognize where more ethical analysis and thought is needed.

Thinkers such as Giorgio Agamben have already spoken out against immigration regulations and declared immigration policy a site of ethical struggle. Agamben sees the legal discrimination against immigrants as part of a greater narrative that has existed since Ancient Greek times and continues in the modern West. He argues, along with Hannah Arendt, that the political outcast foretells the future of humanity.[21] Because modern governments increasingly legalize and sanction prejudice and violence, each of us is in danger. The maltreatment of immigrants is a harbinger of things to come for citizens and those who believe themselves to have claim to political rights. Laws like the Patriot Act show that citizens are not so different from immigrants or foreigners. Such laws work by suspending or repealing civil protections and guarantees in the interest of national security. Concerns about national welfare are not limited to the regulation of the non-white immigrant; efforts to control the population exist beyond and in between the borders of a nation. While the maltreat-

ment of anyone should be a concern for us all, Agamben's theory emphasizes the need for everyone to take note of the policies that target the
outcast, refugee, and immigrant. He suggests that everyone should be
concerned about how immigrants are managed and handled because
these policies will find a way into the lives of the "ordinary" citizen as
well.

An analysis of immigration policies shows the link between ethics as a
relationship between oneself and the Other and ethics as a relationship
one has with oneself. As Foucault states:

> It seems to me that the analysis of governmentality—that is to say: the
> analysis of power as an ensemble of reversible relations—must refer
> itself to an ethic of the subject defined by the relation of the self to itself.
> This means very simply that, in the type of analysis that I have tried to
> propose to you for a certain time, that relations of power—governmen-
> tality, government of the self and others, relations of the self to itself—
> all this constitutes a chain, a weave, and it is there, around these no-
> tions that one ought to be able, I think, to articulate the question of
> politics and the question of ethics. [22]

Because we consent to that which we sanction for others, laws and regulations are means to shape the subject. The art of government is not only
to create an operational society; government also takes part in forming
ethical subjects. Creating ethical subjects, however, requires an intricate
system that reinforces ideas and standards. Citizens may not have to pass
the same types of tests as immigrants but the discourse that surrounds
the immigration process still works to refocus what is acceptable and
unacceptable behavior for the moral subject. Immigration laws help the
citizen understand not only what is required for the immigrant but also
for herself as one who aspires to an upstanding part of the community.
While it is clear that governmental powers affect subjects differently,
laws and regulations help shape ideals of social behavior for all.

Immigration laws are part of a greater worldview that helps to form
the code of conduct that applies to both the immigrant and the citizen.
Luibheid rightly points out that immigrant who is believed to be a lesbian is multiply and more closely scrutinized than the male who seems to
conform to heterosexual norms. Still, Luibheid and Somerville argue that
immigrants are not the only ones subjected to norms and standards when
their sexuality is scrutinized. The regulation process is a continuation of
sexual codes by which everyone is supposed to abide. Foucault's greater
point about biopolitics is that (sexual) norms show that we have been
trained to regulate ourselves. Applying his work on immigration studies
to further prove his case, we see that the process of controlling immigrants for abnormality—sexual or otherwise—may seem to be far removed from the goings-on of the average citizen but such laws only work
to reinforce already established social norms.

Luibheid argues that these perfunctory practices are very much connected to the lives of all who live within the national borders. "Foucault's work particularly contributes to our understanding of how immigration inequalities are institutionally reproduced by drawing attention to supposedly neutral, mundane practices of inspection and regimes of knowledge that actually discipline and subject immigrants in racializing, sexualizing, and other ways."[23] Immigrants are allowed entrance if they are deemed able to follow the codes of the society that have already been sanctioned and reinforced by those living within it. In other words, the regulation of immigrants is not dictated by a different set of standards. The norms that the approved immigrant must follow are the same as the ones for the citizen. Goldman adds, "By policing sexuality, immigration officials construct a corporeal model of desirable subjectivity. Hence, through the articulation and implementation of this model, the border becomes the spatial locus where the national Self regulates . . . bodies in order to maximize its potential to effectively reproduce itself."[24] The self-regulation of the citizen is already underway. The question surrounding the immigrant is whether or not she can operate under the same rules. The conduct that is expected of the immigrant mirrors the conduct that the citizen expects of herself.

These laws, however, can be more than a site of subjugation of immigrants and citizens alike. Judith Butler believes not only that resistance is possible but also that discrimination against others can lead us to rethink ethical action and relationships.

> For, as Butler contends, the subject's own admission of her limitations serves as the condition of her ethical relation to others: "I ascertain that even my process of formation implies the other in me, that my own foreignness toward myself is paradoxically the source of my ethical connections to others" (2003, 95).[25] This marks an important development in Butler's thought, for while previous texts tended to associate dependence with subordination, Butler now acknowledges that the interdependency of subjects can ground a conception of ethics that is not fundamentally oppressive.[26]

Because norms are multiply reinforced, there are also various paths for challenging them. Recognizing the targeting of the other within the immigration process can help to undo social norms that affect us all. By confronting the violence against the immigrant other, we can begin to question the necessity of following certain rules and standards and perhaps think about a different future for society. Such an ethical connection to others can, possibly, lead to the creation of different forms of subjectivity and ideas of belonging.

NOTES

1. Ladelle McWhorter, *Racism and Sexual Oppression in Anglo-America: A Genealogy* (Bloomington: Indiana University Press, 2009), 194.

2. McWhorter, *Racism and Sexual Oppression*, 194.

3. Such debates are still very much a part of the American landscape. While many politicians seem to run away from discussions about race, concerns over race have not been erased from the political forum. There are still some politicians who openly bring up the topic. Pat Buchanan, former Republican presidential candidate, was dismissed from his role as a television personality on MSNBC because of chapters entitled "The End of White America" and "The Death of Christian America." See Patrick J. Buchanan, *Suicide of a Superpower: Will America Survive to 2025?* (New York: Tomas Dune Book, 2011).

4. Hannah Arendt, *The Human Condition* (Chicago: University of Chicago Press, 1998), 38–49.

5. Siobhan Somerville, "Notes toward a Queer History of Naturalization," *American Quarterly* 57 (2005): 659–75.

6. See also Judith Butler, "Is Kinship Always Already Heterosexual?" in *Undoing Gender* (New York: Routledge, 2004), 102–30.

7. Somerville, "Queer History," 669.

8. Dara E. Goldman, "Border Patrol and the Immigrant Body," *Discourse* 26 (2004): 193.

9. Butler, "Kinship," 102–30.

10. Julia Kristeva, *Nations without Nationalism* (New York: Columbia University Press, 1993), 17.

11. Michel Foucault, *History of Sexuality: An Introduction*, trans. Robert Hurley (New York: Vintage Books, 1990), 18.

12. The Immigration Act of 1924 is a law that codifies the national origins quota system. See Walter F. George, "In U.S. Immigration Policy," *Congressional Digest* 35 (1956): 14.

13. Although Fairchild notes that Asian immigrants were the most likely to be affected by medical exams, she argues that few immigrants were denied entrance for health reasons and or medical problems. Economics and the fear that immigrants would likely become public charges (LPC) was the main driving force behind turning immigrants away. See Amy L. Fairchild, *Science at the Borders: Immigrant Medical Inspection and the Shaping of the Modern Industrial Labor Force* (Baltimore: John Hopkins University Press, 2003), 4. Yet Somerville has noted that the claim that someone would become a public charge was very much connected to health issues. Asian women, in particular, were targeted as those who would become public charges because they were seen as having an unhealthy sexual constitution. (Somerville, "Queer History," 666.)

14. Henry Pratt Fairchild, "The Immigration Law of 1924," *The Quarterly Journal of Economics* 38 (1924): 564.

15. Roxana Galusca, "From Fictive Ability to National Identity: Disability, Medical Inspection, and Public Health Regulations on Ellis Island," *Cultural Critique* 72 (2009): 144.

16. Somerville, "Queer History," 666.

17. Anna Marie Smith, "Missing Poststructuralism, Missing Foucault: Butler and Fraser on Capitalism and the Regulation of Sexuality," *Social Text* 19 (2001): 110.

18. Wanda Vrasti, "'Caring' Capitalism and the Duplicity of Critique," *Theory & Event* 14 (2011) http://muse.jhu.edu/ (accessed June 12, 2013).

19. Dorothy E. Roberts, *Fatal Invention: How Science, Politics, and Big Business Recreate Race in the Twenty-First Century* (New York: The New Press, 2011).

20. Robin Dale Jacobson, *The New Nativism: Proposition 187 and the Debate over Immigration* (Minneapolis: University of Minnesota Press, 2008), 40.

21. Giorgio Agamben, "We Refugees," trans. Michael Rocke, *Symposium* 49 (1995): 114–15.

22. Michel Foucault, *L'Herméneutique du sujet: Cours au Collège de France 1981–82*, ed. Frédéric Gros (Paris: Gallimard/Seuil, 2001), 241–42.

23. Eithne Luibheid, *Entry Denied: Controlling Sexuality at the Border* (Minneapolis: University of Minnesota Press, 2002), xxiii.

24. Goldman, "Border Patrol," 194.

25. See Judith Butler, *Kritik der ethischen Gewalt*. Adorno Lectures, 2002 (paper presented at Frankfurt am Main: Institut für Sozialforschung an der Johann Wolfgang Goethe-Universität, October 9, 2003).

26. Kathleen Dow Magnus, "The Unaccountable Subject: Judith Butler and the Social Conditions of Intersubjective Agency," *Hypatia* 21 (2006): 94.

Bibliography

1875 Page Act, Chapter 141, Forty-Third Congress, Second Sess., (March 3, 1875) U.S. Immigration Legislation Online.

2005 Yearbook for Immigration Statistics, Department of Homeland Security, last modified June 10, 2013, http://www.dhs.gov/yearbook-immigration-statistics.

Abram, Susan. "Heated Emotions at Santa Clarita City Hall: Kellar Denies Being a Bigot but Stands by 'Proud Racist' Remark." *The Daily News of Los Angeles*, January 27, 2010.

Adamy, Janet. "Soda Tax Weighed to Pay for Health Care." *The Wall Street Journal*, May 12, 2009.

Aeschylus. *The Complete Greek Tragedies: Aeschylus I, Second Edition*, edited by David Grene and Richmond Lattimore. Translated by Seth G. Bernadete and David Grene. Chicago: The University of Chicago Press, 1991.

Agamben, Giorgio. "Absolute Immanence." In *Potentialities: Collected Essays in Philosophy*, edited by Daniel Heller-Roazen. Stanford: Stanford University Press, 2000.

———. *Homo Sacer: Sovereign Power and Bare Life*. Translated by Daniel Heller-Roazen. Stanford: Stanford University Press, 1998.

———. *State of Exception*. Translated by Kevin Attell. Chicago: Chicago University Press, 2005.

———. "We Refugees." Translated by Michael Rocke. *Symposium* 49 (1994): 114–19.

Ahmed, Sarah. "Affective Economies." *Social Text* 22 (2010): 117–39.

Alcoff, Linda M. *Visible Identities: Race, Gender, and the Self*. New York: Oxford University Press, 2006.

Anderson, Benedict. *Imagined Communities: Reflections on the Origin and Spread of Nationalism* . London: Verso, 1983.

Ante, Spencer. "Keeping Out the Wrong People." *Business Week*, October 4, 2004.

Arendt, Hannah. *The Human Condition*. Chicago: University of Chicago Press, 1998.

———. *The Origins of Totalitarianism*. New York: Harcourt Brace Jovanovich, 1973. "Arizona Illegal Immigrant Law." *Politico*, April 23, 2010. Accessed July 22, 2011. http://www.politicolnews.com/arizona-illegal-immigrant-law/.

Balibar, Étienne. *We, the People of Europe?: Reflections on Transnational Citizenship*. Translated by James Swenson. Princeton: Princeton University Press, 2004.

Barr, Andy. "Rev. Franklin Graham: Obama 'born a Muslim.'" *Politico*, August 20, 2010. Accessed November 13, 2011. http://www.politico.com/news/stories/0810/41292.html.

Battersby, Christine. "Stages on Kant's Way: Aesthetics, Morality, and the Gendered Sublime." In *Race, Class, Gender, and Sexuality: The Big Questions*. Edited by Naomi Zack, Laurie Shrage, and Crispin Sartwell, 2217–244. NY: Blackwell, 1998.

Benhabib, Seyla. "Sexual Difference and Collective Identities: The New Global Constellation." *Signs* 24 (1999): 335–61.

———. "Turkey's Constitutional Zigzags," *Dissent* 56 (2009): 25–28.

Blow, Charles. "They, Too, Sing America." *The New York Times*, July 15, 2011. Accessed July 23, 2011. http://www.nytimes.com/2011/07/16/opinion/16blow.html?_r=3 .

Borjas, George J. "The Economics of Immigration." *Journal of Economic Literature* 32 (1994): 1667–1717.

Bouyami, Moustafa. "Racing Religion," *CR: The New Centennial Review* 6 (2006): 267–93.

Boyd, Monica, and Deanna Pikkov. *Gendering Migration, Livelihood, and Entitlements: Migrant Women in Canada and the United States.* Ithaca: Cornell University Press, 2005.

Brooks, David. "Huntington's Clash Revisited." *The New York Times,* March 3, 2011. Accessed June 11, 2013. http://www.nytimes.com/2011/03/04/opinion/04brooks.html.

Buchanan. Patrick J. *Suicide of a Superpower: Will America Survive to 2025?* New York: Tomas Dune Books, 2011.

Burton, Richard Francis. *The Book of a Thousand Nights and a Night.* London: Burton Club, 1885.

Butler, Judith. "Is Kinship Always Already Heterosexual?" In *Undoing Gender,* 102–30. New York: Routledge, 2004.

———. *Kritik der ethischen Gewalt.* Adorno Lectures, 2002, (paper presented at Frankfurt am Main: Institut für Sozialforschung an der Johann Wolfgang Goethe-Universität, Ocotober 9, 2003).

Carens, Joseph H. "Who Should Get In? The Ethics of Immigration Admissions." *Ethics and International Affairs* 17 (2003): 95–110.

Chaddock, Gail Russell. "US Crackdown on Illegals Irks Business Community." *Christian Science Monitor,* August 14, 2007.

Chaput, Catherine. "Rhetorical Circulation in Late Capitalism, Neoliberalism, and the Overdetermination of Affective Energy." *Philosophy and Rhetoric* 43 (2010): 1–25.

Darwin, Charles. *The Descent of Man and the Selection in Relation to Sex.* New York: D. Appleton and Company, 1871.

Davidson, Arnold. "Ethics as Ascetics: Foucault, the History of Ethics, and Ancient Thought." In *Cambridge Companion to Foucault,* edited by Gary Gutting, 123–48. Cambridge: Cambridge University Press, 1994.

De Beauvoir, Simone. *The Second Sex.* Translated and edited by H. M. Parshley. New York: Vintage Books, 1989.

Dionne, E.J. "Is the GOP Shedding a Birthright?" *The Washington Post,* August 5, 2010.

Draper, Robert. "Lindsey Graham, this Year's Maverick." *The New York Times,* April 7, 2010. Accessed July 22, 2011. http://www.nytimes.com/2010/07/04/magazine/04graham-t.html?pagewanted=2.

Douthat, Ross. "The Borders We Deserve." The New York Times, May 3, 2010. Accessed July 23, 2011. http://www.nytimes.com/2010/05/03/opinion/03douthat.html.

"ECOSOC News, VOL. 5, NO. 2," United Nations Economic and Social Council, last modified May 31, 2006, http://www.un.org/en/ecosoc/news/ecosoc.newsletter.v5nr.2.pdf.

Elden, Stuart. "The War of Races and the Constitution of the State: Foucault's *Il faut defendre la societe* and the Politics of Calculation." *boundary 2* 29 (2002): 125–51.

Ellis, Havelock. *Sexual Inversion.* New York: Arno, 1975.

Fairchild, Amy L. and Eileen A. Tynan. "Policies of Containment: Immigration in the Era of AIDS." *American Journal of Public Health* 84 (1994): 2011–2022.

Fairchild, Amy L. *Science at the Borders: Immigrant Medical Inspection and the Shaping of the Modern Industrial Labor Force.* Baltimore: Johns Hopkins University Press, 2003.

Fairchild, Henry Pratt. "The Immigration Law of 1924." *The Quarterly Journal of Economics* 38 (1924): 653–55.

Foucault, Michel. *The Birth of Biopolitics: Lectures at the Collège de France 1978–1979.* Tanslated by Graham Burchell. New York: Picador, 2008.

———. "Body/Power" in *Power/Knowledge: Selected Interviews and Other Writings, 1972–1977,* edited by Colin Gordon, 55–62. New York: Pantheon Books, 1980.

———. *The Government of Self and Others: Lectures at the Collège de France 1982–1983.* Translated by Graham Burchell. New York: Palgrave Macmillan, 2010.

———. *L'Herméneutique du sujet: Cours au Collège de France 1981–82.* Edited by Frédéric Gros. Paris: Gallimard/Seuil, 2001.

———. *The History of Sexuality: An Introduction.* Translated by Robert Hurley. New York: Vintage Books, 1990.

———. *The History of Sexuality: The Use of Pleasure*. Translated by Robert Hurley. New York: Vintage Books, 1990.

———. *Il faut défendre la société: Cours au Collège de France (1975–1976)*. Paris: Gallimard, 1997.

———. *Introduction to Kant's Anthropology*. Translated by Roberto Nigro and Kate Briggs. Los Angeles: Semiotext(e), 2008.

———. *Society Must Be Defended*. Translated by David Macey. New York: Picador, 2003.

Fox News. "On the Record." Accessed June 12, 2013. http://www.foxnews.com/on-air/ on-the-record/transcript/sen-graham-039i039m-trying-reward-american-citizen- ship-i039m-not-penalizing-children039

Fox, Vincente. "Tough-But-Fair Rules for Tomorrow's Legal Immigrants." *Business-Week* , July 18, 2005.

Freud, Sigmund. "Femininity." In *The Complete Edition of the Complete Psychological Works of Sigmund Freud, Vol. XXII*. Translated by James Strachey, 139–67. London: The Hogarth Press, 1964.

Fry, Richard. "Gender and Migration." Pew Hispanic Center, last modified July 5, 2006. http://www.pewhispanic.org/2006/07/05/gender-and-migration/.

Fuss, Diana. "Interior Colonies: Frantz Fanon and the Politics of Identification." *Diacritics* 24 (1994): 19–42.

Galusca, Roxanna. "From Fictive Ability to National Identity: Disability, Medical Inspection, and Public Health Regulations on Ellis Island." *Cultural Critique* 72 (2009): 137–63.

George, Walter F. "Should Basic Changes Be Made in U.S. Immigration Policy?" *Congressional Digest* 35 (1956): 13–14.

Gillespie, Nick. "Beyond the Family Way." *Reason* 26 (1994): 44–46.

Gilroy, Paul. "From a Colonial Past to a New Multiculturalism." *Chronicle of Higher Education* 51 (2005): B7–B10.

Gines, Katherine T. "Hannah Arendt, Liberalism, and Racism: Controversies Concerning Violence, Segregation, and Education." *The Southern Journal* 47 (2009): 53–76.

Giroux, Henry A. "Reading Hurrican Katrina: Race, Class, and the Biopolitics of Disposability." *College Literature* 33 (2006): 171–96.

Goldman, Dara E. "Border Patrol and the Immigrant Body": *Entry Denied: Policing Sexuality at the Border*. Eithne Luibheid: Minneapolis: University of Minnesota Press, 2002. *Discourse* 26 (2004): 190–96.

Goolsbee, Austan. "Even for Shoe Bombers, Education and Success Are Linked." *The New York Times*, September 14, 2006. Accessed June 11, 2013. http:// www.nytimes.com/2006/09/14/business/14scene.html.

Halperin, David M. *One Hundred Years of Homosexuality: And Other Essays on Greek Love*. New York: Routledge, 1989.

Heathcott, Joseph. "Moral Panic in a Plural Culture." *Crosscurrents* 61 (2011): 39–44.

Hegel, G. W. F. *Philosophy of Mind*. Translated by A.V. Miller. London: Oxford University Press, 1971.

Herszenhorn, David M. "How Illegal Immigrants Fare." *The New York Times*, September 12, 2009.

Higgins, Peter. "Open Borders and the Right to Immigration." *Human Rights Review* 9 (2008): 525–35.

Hill, Mike. "Whiteness as War by Other Means: Racial Complexity in an Age of Failed States." *Small Axe* 13 (2009): 72–89.

Hondagneu-Sotelo, Pierrette. *Gendered Transitions: Mexican Experiences of Immigration*. Los: Angeles: University of California Press, 1994.

Hudson, James. "The Ethics of Immigration Restriction." *Social Theory and Practice* 19 (1984): 201–39.

Hulse, Carl. "In Lawmaker's Outburst, a Rare Breach of Protocol." *The New York Times*, September 9, 2009.

Huntington, Samuel P. *The Clash of Civilizations and the Remaking of the World Order.* New York: Simon & Schuster, 1996.

"In the Media," *Hispanic* 11 (1998):14.

Irigaray, Luce. "This Sex which Is Not One." In *The Second Wave: A Reader in Feminist Theory,* edited by Linda Nicholson, 323–29. New York: Routledge, 1997.

Ivins, Molly. "More Immigrant-Bashing on the Way." *The Buffalo News,* July 7, 2006.

Jacobson, Robin Dale. *New Nativism: Proposition 187 and the Debate over Immigration.* Minneapolis: The University of Minnesota Press, 2008.

Jones-Correa, Michael. "Different Paths: Gender, Immigration and Political Participation." *International Migration Review* 32 (1998): 326–49.

Kahn, Huma. "Legalizing Racial Profiling?" *ABC News,* April 22, 2010. Accessed July 23, 2011. http://abcnews.go.com/Politics/arizona-immigration-bill-draws-fire-nationally-gov-brewer/story?id=10438889.

Kant, Immanuel. "Of the Different Human Races." In *The Idea of Race,* edited by Robert Bernasconi and Tommy L. Lott. New York: Hackett, 2000.

Kershnar, Stephen. "There's No Moral Right to Immigrate to the United States." *Public Affairs Quarterly* 14 (2000): 141–58.

King, D.A. "Should U.S. Deny Citizenship to Children of Illegal Immigrants?" *The Atlanta Journal Constitution,* June 17, 2009.

King, Katie. "Local and Global: AIDS Activism and Feminist Theory." *Camera Obscura* 10 (1992): 78–99.

Klein, Ezra. "When Did Lindsey Graham Change His Mind on Immigration?" *The Washington Post,* July 30, 2010.

Kralev, Nicholas. "Race Hits U.S. 'Birth Defect'; Secretary Sees Legacy of Race in Effect Today." *Newsmakers Interviews,* March 28, 2008.

Kretsedemas, Phillip. "Immigration Enforcement and the Complication of National Sovereignty: Understanding Local Enforcement as an Exercise in Neoliberal Governance," *American Quarterly* 60 (2008): 553–73.

Krikorian, Mark. "Get Tight." *National Review,* March 25, 2002.

Kristeva, Julia. *Nations without Nationalism.* New York: Columbia University Press, 1993.

Kritz, Mary M. "International Migration Policies: Conceptual Problems." *International Migration Review* 21 (1987): 947–64.

"Kyl: Illegals' Kids Shouldn't Be U.S. Citizens," last modified June 11, 2013. http://www.cbsnews.com/8301-3460_162-6733905.html.

Lee, Charles T. "Bare Life, Interstices, and Third Space of Citizenship." *WSQ: Women's Studies Quarterly* 38 (2010): 57–81.

Lehman, Herbert. "Should Basic Changes Be Made?" *Congressional Digest* 35 (1956): 12.

Levinson, Brett. "Biopolitics and Duopolies." *Diacritics* 35 (2005): 65–75.

Locke, John. *Two Treatises of Government.* Cambridge: Cambridge University Press, 1988.

Loman, Posi. "No Women No War: Women's Participation in Ancient Greek Warfare." *Greece and Rome* 51 (2004): 34–54.

Luibheid, Eithne. *Entry Denied: Controlling Sexuality at the Border.* Minneapolis: University of Minnesota Press, 2002.

———. "Heteronormativity and Immigration Scholarship: A Call for Change." *GLQ: A Journal of Gay and Lesbian Studies* 10 (2004): 227–35.

———. "Queer/Migration an Unruly Body of Scholarship." *GLQ: A Journal of Gay and Lesbian Studies* 14 (2008): 169–90.

Macklin, Audrey. "Freeing Migration from the State: Michael Trebilcock on Migration Policy." *The University of Toronto Law Journal* 60 (2010): 315–48.

Magnus, Kathleen Dow. "The Unaccountable Subject: Judith Butler and the Social Conditions of Intersubjective Agency." *Hypatia* 21 (2006): 81–103.

Maillat, Denis. *The Politics of Migration Policies.* New York: Center for Migration Studies, 1979.

McWhorter, Ladelle. *Racism and Sexual Oppression in Anglo-America: A Genealogy.* Bloomington: Indiana University Press, 2009.

———. "Where Do White People Come From?: A Foucaultian Critique of Whiteness Studies," *Philosophy & Social Criticism* 31 (2005): 533–56.

Mendieta, Eduardo. "The Race of Modernity and the Modernity of Race: On Foucault's Genealogy of Racism." Paper presented at the meetings of the Society for Phenomenology and Existential Philosophy at Penn State University, State College, Pennsylvania, October 5–7, 2000.

Milchman, Alan, and Alan Rosenberg. "Michel Foucault: Crises and Problematizations." *The Review of Politics* 67 (2005): 335–36.

Mirzoeff, Nicholas. *Watching Babylon: The War in Iraq and the Global Visual Culture.* New York: Routledge, 2005.

Mitchell, Lynette G. "Greeks, Barbarians and Aeschylus' Suppliants." *Greece and Rome* 53 (2006): 205–23.

Moloney, Deirdre M. "Women, Sexual Morality, and Economic Dependency in Early U.S. Deportation Policy." *Journal of Women's History* 18 (2006): 95–122.

Mosse, George L. *Toward the Final Solution: A History of European Racism.* New York: Howard Fertig, 1978.

Mountz, Alison, et al. "Lives in Limbo: Temporary Protected Status and Immigrant Identities." *Global Networks* 2 (2002): 335–56.

Nancy, Jean-Luc. *The Inoperative Community.* Translated by Christopher Fynsk. Minneapolis: University of Minnesota Press, 1991.

Nietzsche, Friedrich. *On the Genealogy of Morals and Ecce Homo.* Translated by Walter Kaufmann. New York: Vintage, 1989.

Nissen, Jullia. "New Attacks on Birthright Citizenship: 'Anchor Babies' and the 14th Amendment." *States News Service*, August 24, 2010.

O'Sullivan, Noël. "The Concepts of the Public, the Private and the Political in Contemporary Western Political Theory." *Critical Review of International Social and Political Philosophy* 12 (2009): 145–65.

Omi, Michael, and Howard Winant. *Racial Formation in the United States: from 1960s to the 1990s.* New York: Routledge, 1994.

Omi, Michael. "'Slippin' into Darkness': The (Re)Biologization of Race." *Journal of Asian American Studies* 13 (2010): 343–58.

"On the Issues of Border Security," last modified July 20, 2011. http://www.ronpaul.com/on-the-issues/border-security/.

Ortega, Mariana. "Multiplicity, Inbetweeness, and the Question of Assimilation." *The Southern Journal of Philosophy* 46 (2008): 65–80.

Oxford, Connie G. "Protectors and Victims in the Gender Regime of Asylum." *Feminist Formations* 17 (2005): 18–38.

Padovan, Dario. "Biopolitics and the Social Control of the Multitude." *Democracy & Nature* 9 (2003): 473–94.

Page, Clarence. "Let's Keep Our Enemies Straight." *Buffalo News*, September 10, 2010. Accessed July 3, 2012. http://www.highbeam.com/doc/1P2-25820902.html.

Plato. *Gorgias.* Translated by R. Waterfield. New York: Oxford World Classics, 2008.

Pratt, Geraldine. "Inscribing Domestic Work on Filipina Bodies." In *Places through the Body*, edited by Heidi Nast and Steve Pile, 283–304. London: Routledge, 1998.

Prozorov, Sergei. "The Appropriation of Abandonment: Giorgio Agamben on the State of Nature and the Political." *Continental Philosophy Review* 42 (2009): 327–53.

Quiroz-Martinez, Julie. "Immigrants Hit the Road for Civil Rights." *The Nation*, October 9, 2003.

Rancière, Jacques. *Chronicles of Consensual Times.* Translated by Steven Corcoran. New York: Continuum, 2010.

"Rep. Wilson Shouts, 'You Lie' to Obama during Speech." *CNN*, September 9, 2009. Accessed August 9, 2011. http://articles.cnn.com/2009-09-09/politics/joe.wilson_1_rep-wilson-illegal-immigrants-outburst?_s=PM:POLITICS

Reyes, Raul. "Immigration Issue Is a Red Herring." *USA Today*, September 25, 2009.

Riccardi, Nicholas. "Arizona Passes Strict Border Rule; Police Would Gain Broad Powers to Investigate Anyone They Suspect Is an Illegal Immigrant." *Los Angeles Times*, April 13, 2010.

Robert Wood Foundation. "Barely Hanging On: Middle-Class and Uninsured," last modified August 7, 2011. http://rwjf.org/files/research/58034.pdf.

Roberts, Dorothy E. *Fatal Invention: How Science, Politics, and Big Business Re-create Race in the Twenty First Century.* New York: The New Press, 2011.

Robinson, Eugene. "Arizona's New Immigration Law Is an Act of Vengeance." *The Washington Post*, April 26,2010. Accessed July 22, 2011. http://www.washingtonpost.com/wpdyn/content/article/2010/04/26/AR2010042602595.html .

———. "Arizona's Immigration Frustration." *The Wall Street Journal*, April 27, 2010. Accessed July 22, 2011. http://online.wsj.com/article/SB10001424052748703465204575208382473306238.html .

Salaita, Steven G. "Beyond Orientalism and Islamophobia: 9/11, Anti-Arab Racism, and the Mythos of National Pride." *CR: The New Centennial Review* 6 (2006): 245–66.

Samuelson, Robert J. "The Real China Threat." *The Washington Post*, August 20, 2008. Accessed April 18, 2012. http://www.washingtonpost.com/wp-dyn/content/article/2008/08/19/AR2008081902256.html

Seghal, Ujahla. "John McCain blames immigrants for Arizona fires." *The Atlantic Wire*, June 19, 2011. Accessed July 22, 2011. http://www.theatlanticwire.com/national/2011/06/john-mccain-blames-arizona-fires-illegal-immigrants/38984 .

Seifman, David. "McCain Boosts Illegals." *New York Posts*, July 25, 2006.

Smith, Anna Marie. "Missing Poststructuralism, Missing Foucault: Butler and Fraser on Capitalism and the Regulation of Sexuality." *Social Text* 19 (2001): 103–25.

Somerville, Siobahn B. "Notes toward a Queer History of Naturalization." *American Quarterly* 57 (2005): 659–75.

———. "Queer Loving." *GLQ: A Journal of Gay and Lesbian Studies* 11 (2005): 335–70.

Spillers, Hortense. "Mama's Baby, Papa's Maybe: An American Grammar Book." *Diacritics* 17 (1987): 64–81.

Stockwell, Alcott W. "Our Oldest National Problem." *The American Journal of Sociology* 32 (1927): 742–55.

Stoler, Ann Laura. *Race and the Education of Desire: Foucault's History of Sexuality and the Colonial Order of Things.* Durham: Duke University Press, 1995.

Taylor, Charles. "Modern Social Imaginaries." *Public Culture* 14 (2004): 91–123.

Taylor, Chloe. "Race and Racism in the College de France Lectures." *Philosophy Compass* 6 (2011): 746–56.

Tyrrell, Wm. Blake. *Amazons: A Study in Athenian Mythmaking.* Baltimore: Johns Hopkins University Press, 1986.

Veness, Ruth."Investing the Barbarian? The Dress of Amazons in Athenian Art." In *Women's Dress in the Ancient Greek World*, edited by Lloyd Lewellyn-Jones. London: The Classic Press of Wales, 2002.

Vernant, Jean-Pierre. *Myth and Society in Ancient Greece.* Translated by Janet Lloyd. New York: The Harvester Press Ltd, 1980.

Villacañas Berlanga, José Luis. "The Liberal Roots of Populism: a Critique of Laclau." Translated by Jorge Ledo. *CR: The New Centennial Review* 10 (2010): 151–82.

Volpp, Leti. "The Citizen and the Terrorist." *ULA Law Review* 49 (2002): Rev. 1575.

Vrasti, Wanda."'Caring' Capitalism and the Duplicity of Critique." *Theory & Event* 14 (2011) http://muse.jhu.edu/ (accessed June 12, 2013).

Whitaker, John. "Mexican Deaths in the Arizona Desert: The Culpability of Migrants, Humanitarian Workers, Governments, and Business." *Journal of Business Ethics* 88: (2009) 365–76.

Wilson, Joseph. Accessed July 20, 2011. http://joewilson.house.gov/Issues/Issue/?IssueID=27226

Winant, Howard. "Race and Race Theory," *Annual Review of Sociology* 26 (2000): 169–85.

Wong, Kristina. "Sarah Palin Takes a Stand on Immigration." *ABC News*, May 21, 2010, Accessed July 23, 2011. http://abcnews.go.com/Politics/sarah-palin-takes-standimmigration-controversial-arizona-law/story?id=10707136.

Wunthrow, Robert. *Poor Richard's Principle: Recovering the American Dream through the Moral Dimension of Work, Business, and Money*. New Jersey: Princeton University Press, 1996.

Wynter, Sylvia. "Unsettling the Coloniality of Being/Power/Truth/Freedom: Towards the Human, after Man, Its Over-Representation—an Argument," *CR: The New Centennial Review* 3 (2003): 257–337.

Yinger, Nancy V. "Feminization of Migration: Limits of the Data." Population Reference Bureau, last modified June 12, 2013. http://www.prb.org/Articles/2007/FeminizationofMigrationLimitsofData.aspx.

Yuval-Davis, Nira. "The 'Multi-Layered Citizen': Citizenship in the Age of 'Glocalization.'" *International Feminist Journal of Politics* 1 (1999): 119–37.

Zack, Naomi. "The American Sexualization of Race." In *Race/Sex: Their Sameness, Difference, and Interplay*, edited by Naomi Zack, 145–56. New York: Routledge, 1997.

Index

Aeschylus, 126, 127, 130, 141. *See also* Danaides
Agamben, Giorgio, 1, 16, 22–26, 27, 28, 29–30, 33, 38, 163, 164
Ahmed, Sarah, 94–95
AIDS, 14, 118, 119–120, 121. *See also* HIV
Alcoff, Linda Martin, 7, 9
Amazons, 15, 125–128, 129–131, 132–134, 135, 137, 138, 140, 143, 144, 155
Anderson, Benedict, 2
Anti-Semitism, 88–90, 92, 93–94
Arendt, Hannah, 1, 15–16, 22–23, 25, 26, 28, 31–33, 88–89, 89, 92, 152, 163
assimilation, 46
autochthony, 3, 4, 33, 129, 138

Balibar, Etienne, 98, 99–100
Beauvoir, Simone de, 107
Benhabib, Seyla, 90–92, 96, 98
biopolitics, 17, 22, 23, 24, 25, 26, 27, 31, 38, 43, 44, 51, 57, 63, 64, 70, 72, 73, 83–84, 87, 90, 96, 98, 104, 112, 113, 114, 115, 132–133, 142, 143, 149, 150–151, 152, 156, 161, 164
biopower, 17, 48
blood, 88, 90–91, 92, 93, 131
body, 87, 90, 105, 106, 113, 114, 119–120, 126, 133, 137, 143, 159
borders, 6, 44, 68, 75, 104, 115, 127, 152, 163, 165
Bouyami, Mustafa, 96–97
Borjas, George J., 52
Burton, Richard, 143
Butler, Judith, 115–116, 154, 165

capitalism, 26, 35
Carens, Joseph, 50
Chinese Exclusion, 110–112, 118, 159

Christian, 2, 87, 92, 97–98, 99–100
citizenship, 117, 135, 153–154; *Jus soli* (birthright), 5, 28–29, 74; *Jus sanguinis* (right of blood), 5
colonialism, 4, 6, 45, 87–88, 151
community, 2, 87, 88, 89, 91, 99, 100, 109, 111, 114, 115, 120, 142, 143, 151, 152–153, 153, 154, 157–163, 164

Danaides, 125–126, 127–131, 132–133, 134–135, 143, 144
Darwin, Charles, 15
discipline, 152, 165
discourse, 164; biological, 83–84, 86, 88, 89, 90–91, 92, 93, 95, 110, 113, 119, 120, 121, 135–137, 138, 140–141, 143, 144–145, 149, 150, 151, 154, 156, 157, 158, 160, 161, 162, 163; scientific, 9; sexual, 43, 44, 45, 76, 106, 107–108, 113, 114–115, 125, 127, 152, 153, 155
DOMA (Defense of Marriage Act), 118

economics, 1, 10, 17, 21, 22, 27, 28, 31, 36, 37–38, 52–54, 56, 57, 61, 62, 63–65, 66, 67–69, 70, 71, 72, 76, 78, 83, 137, 138, 140, 141, 143, 144, 149, 150, 152, 156
Elden, Stuart, 137
Ellis, Havelock, 143
entrepreneur, 27, 31, 32, 35, 36, 37, 38, 66, 67, 77, 138, 139, 140, 144
Euripides. *See Ion.*
evolution, 77, 84, 85–86, 90, 92–93, 98, 113, 114

Fairchild, Amy, 158, 166
Fairchild, Henry Pratt, 58n5
family reunification, 49–50, 51, 153, 154
femininity, 129, 130, 132, 134, 140

Foucault, Michel, 1, 3, 10, 14, 15, 16, 17, 21–22, 25–28, 30, 31–32, 33–35, 36, 38, 43–44, 48, 51, 57, 61, 62, 63–64, 65, 66, 76, 83–84, 85, 87, 89–90, 92–93, 98, 103, 109, 112–113, 114, 132–134, 137, 143, 144, 149–151, 152–153, 156–157, 161, 164–165
Freud, Sigmund, 108, 119, 132–134

gender, 87, 116, 126, 130, 135, 138, 143, 152; norms, 105
geography, 6, 10, 35, 94
George, Walter, 50, 51, 157
Gilroy, Paul, 7
Giroux, Henry, 67, 70, 71, 72
globalization, 75
God, 92–93, 107–108
governmentality, 26, 27, 62, 63–64, 65, 67, 73, 76, 92, 99, 111, 113, 150, 163, 164
Greeks, ancient, 22, 44; culture, 125–126, 127, 128–130, 131–132, 134, 135, 137, 138, 141, 142, 144–145; politics, 3, 32–34, 125, 129–131, 140, 143, 154–155, 163

health, 16, 28, 105, 107, 115, 119, 121, 134, 145; healthcare, 11, 62, 63, 65, 66, 68, 69, 71, 72, 73, 76; mental, 64, 118; national, 10, 11, 12, 52, 66, 90, 106, 114, 119, 137, 142, 143–144, 150–151, 156, 159; physical, 106, 118, 134, 153, 156, 157, 158, 159; public, 110, 118, 145, 159, 162; state, 43, 114–115, 137, 143–144, 149, 150–151, 159
Heathcott, Joseph, 74
Hegel, G. W. F., 6, 7
heteronormativity, 103–104, 105, 107, 111, 113, 115, 153, 154
heterosexism, 112, 119. *See also* heteronormativity.
HIV, 14, 119–120
homophobia, 44, 113
homosexuality, 10–15, 115, 118, 120
homo sacer, 24, 25, 27, 29
Huntington, Samuel P., 94, 99

immigration: illegal, 1, 11, 31, 47–48, 137; legal, 1, 103–104, 116–117, 118, 120–118, 131, 137, 153, 160–161; from Mexico, 12–15, 61–62, 66, 67, 68, 74, 83, 84, 103, 155, 160–161, 162; from Middle East, 94
immorality, 104, 110–111
insanity, 158. *See also* health, mental
INS (Immigration and Naturalization Service), 117–118
Ion, 3, 31, 32, 33–34
Islam, 83, 84, 93–95, 96–97, 98, 99, 126–127, 161. *See also* Muslim.

Jacobson, Robin Dale, 19n7
Judaism, 90, 92, 97, 98; blood, 90–91; religion, 87; extermination, 90, 91, 93
Jus Sanguinis. See citizenship
Jus Solis. See citizenship

Kant, Immanuel, 6, 7, 16–17, 34, 35, 36, 138–139, 140, 143
Kershnar, Stephen, 49, 50, 52
Kretsedemas, Phillip, 65, 68
Krikorian, Mark, 55
Kristeva, Julia, 3, 125, 128, 131–132, 135, 136, 139, 140, 141, 154–155
Kritz, Mary, 47

Lee, Charles T., 67, 69
Lehman, Herbert, 53
lesbians, 120
Levinson, Brett, 64, 65, 73
life, 83, 93, 100, 109, 114, 128, 129, 131, 137, 150, 152; animal, 23–24; bare, 24, 33; biological, 23, 85; economic, 64; individual, 22, 38, 45, 48, 51, 57, 100, 132, 153; natural, 23, 24, 33, 132; political, 22–23, 27, 32, 38, 99, 100, 126; of the Nation, 54, 55, 56, 57, 62, 65, 77, 114, 126, 150; private, 23, 100, 153
Locke, John, 6, 7, 16
LPC (Likely to become Public Charge), 111
Luibheid, Eithne, 15, 112, 115, 116, 121, 151, 153, 164–165

marriage, 90, 111, 118, 125, 126, 128, 129–130, 141, 144
Marx, 26
McCarran-Walter Act, 59n29
McWhorter, Ladelle, 85–86, 87, 95–96, 112–113, 114, 119, 138, 150
medical examination, 8–9, 157–159
Milchman, Alan, 17, 48
Muslim, 12–15, 21, 83, 84, 93, 94, 95, 96–97, 98, 100, 103, 155, 160, 161, 162
mythology, 90, 91, 92, 93, 150; American, 3–4, 6, 7, 9, 149, 154, 157; Greek, 2, 3, 4–5, 33, 34, 125–127, 128, 129–130, 131, 132–133, 134, 135–136, 138, 141, 142, 143, 144, 154–155

national security, 30, 48, 55, 62, 68, 103, 115, 144, 150, 151, 152, 157, 163
national welfare, 11, 49, 66, 90, 111, 118, 119, 127, 136–137, 144, 145, 153, 154, 155, 156, 163
Nancy, Jena-Luc, 2
Native Americans, 4, 6
Nature, 88, 91, 92, 106–108, 110, 120, 129–130, 131, 132–133, 135, 138, 140, 144, 154, 158, 159
Nazism, 29, 74, 87, 90, 92–93, 150, 161
Neoliberalism, 1, 3, 10, 11, 14, 21, 22, 25, 26–27, 28, 29, 30, 31–32, 34–35, 36, 37–38, 61–65, 66, 67, 68, 69–72, 73, 75–78, 127, 143, 144, 150, 152, 160
New Nativism, 3, 157, 162

Ong, Aihwa, 44
Ordoliberals, 27, 63
Otherness, 2, 10, 12, 30, 83, 93, 96, 131, 135

Page Act (of 1875), 159
parresia (truth-speaking), 33–34
pathology, 110, 118–119, 121, 131, 133, 134–135, 159
patriarchy, 107, 119, 125, 126, 127–128, 129–130, 131, 132, 135, 154
power, 84, 98, 114, 127, 129, 131, 137, 138, 142, 149; sovereign, 21, 22, 25–26, 27, 28, 29, 30, 89; state, 27, 28, 38, 45, 48, 51, 90, 92, 118, 154, 157, 164

problematization, 48, 58, 100, 104, 106, 107–108, 109, 132, 134, 149
prostitution, 110, 111, 159
Public Health Services, 118
purity, 90, 93, 96, 104, 131, 141, 150–151

queer, 105
quotas, 8, 46, 47

race: biological, 2, 33, 85–86, 90, 92, 98, 144; civilized, 5, 6, 88, 99, 113–114, 127, 130–131, 136, 138; and economics, 65, 66, 140, 143; gender, 130–131, 135, 138, 144–145, 155; invisibility of, 7, 9; and land, 5, 34, 110, 125–126, 138–139, 160; physiological, 7, 8, 35, 65, 73; and politics, 22, 31–32, 33, 34, 35, 36, 38, 61, 63, 76, 84, 85, 86–87, 93, 96, 110, 116–117, 150, 151–152, 158, 159, 160, 161, 163; and religion, 83, 88–89, 90, 94, 96–97; scientific, 7–9; and sexuality, 103–104, 109, 112–113, 114–116, 118, 119–120, 121, 125, 141–142, 149–151, 154, 156, 159; and state, 1, 10–15, 16–17, 18, 21, 33, 65, 66, 67, 128, 137, 144, 157, 162, 163
Ranciere, Jacques, 18
refugee, 16, 70, 71, 78, 164
religion, 13, 83–84, 87–89, 90–91, 92, 93, 94, 95–100, 113, 161
Rosenberg, Alan, 17, 48
Roberts, Dorothy, 161
Robinson, Eugene, 75

Said, Edward, 7
September 11, 12, 55, 94, 100
sex, 104–106, 107–109, 118, 125, 126, 129, 131, 132–134, 137, 140, 141, 149, 150–151, 155
sexuality, 87, 105, 144; and the abnormal, 14–15, 103, 104, 105–107, 107–110, 112, 113–115, 116–121, 125, 133–134, 149, 150, 154, 159, 164; deviant, 64, 109–110, 111, 113, 115–117, 119–121, 144, 150–151, 159; and norms, 16, 44, 45, 103–105, 107–109, 112–113, 114, 115, 118, 119, 120–121, 132, 150–152, 153, 156–157,

164–165
sickness: mental, 118–119, 133, 158;
    physical, 158
slavery, 19, 131, 140–141, 142
Somerville, Siobhan, 110, 115–118, 151,
    153, 164
Sotelo-Hondeneu, Pierette, 144
Spanish Inquisition, 90–91, 92
Stoler, Ann Laura, 151
Stockwell, Alcott, 58n10, 58n3, 58n6,
    59n26
Spillers, Hortense, 140

Taylor, Charles, 2
Taylor, Chloe, 39n4
terrorism, 12, 21, 29, 49, 55, 56, 83, 95,
    96, 126, 126–127, 144
transgender, 105
transnational, 88
Tyrell, Wm. Blake, 3, 125, 154

unhealthy, 105, 106, 115, 121, 137,
    143–144, 149, 150–151, 157, 159. *See
    also* sickness.
USA Patriot Act, 163

Vernant, Jean-Pierre, 145
Volpp, Leti, 94

women, 15, 96, 106, 106–108, 109,
    110–111, 119, 120, 125–126, 127,
    128–131, 132–137, 140, 141–142, 143,
    144–145, 151, 153, 154–155, 159
World War I, 46, 158

xenophobia, 12, 17, 135, 144

Yuval-Davis, Nira, 2

Zack, Naomi, 136, 140–141, 143

About the Author

Sokthan Yeng is an assistant professor of philosophy at Adelphi University. She has research interests in the areas of French Contemporary Philosophy, Feminism, Critical Race Theory, and Eastern Philosophy. Her article "Foucault's Critique of the Science of Sexuality: The Function of Science within Bio-power" was published in the *Journal of French and Francophone Philosophy*. She is also working on a book on Western Feminist readings of Buddhism.